D1231571

HOW CHESS GAMES
ARE WON

HOW CHESS GAMES ARE WON

By
SAMUEL RESHEVSKY
International Grandmaster

PITMAN PUBLISHING CORPORATION
New York   Toronto   London

FIRST PAPERBACK EDITION 1973

CONTENTS

Chapter Five THE ART OF DEFENSE

Chapter Six WINNING ATTACKS

Chapter Seven WINNING THE END GAME

HOW CHESS GAMES
ARE WON

1

INFERIOR OPENINGS

A great many players, including a few masters, are inclined to be indifferent to chess openings. Overconfidence leads some to believe that a casual knowledge of opening theory will carry them through successfully. They rely mainly on their tactical ability in the middle game or their prowess in the end game.

To win against inaccurate opening moves it is essential that you have a better knowledge of openings than your opponent. Although the mastery of opening theory and practice, takes a great deal of time, effort, and ability, a thorough knowledge of a few important lines can be gained by almost any player. Books on the subject are available and should be studied.

The main objectives of the opening moves are the development of pieces and control of the central squares. Unless your opponent blunders it is most unusual to seek the gain of material in the opening stage. Against weak opening moves you gain an advantage in time which can be used to obtain better development and control of the center. In turn this positional superiority may result in the winning of material or a direct attack on the King.

Some examples of games won against opening mistakes are given in this chapter.

An Opening Blunder

On his tenth turn in this game my opponent made a questionable move. In itself, this would not have been sufficient to lose the game, but White followed up by making an innocent-looking twelfth move which turned out to be a blunder. Two opening mistakes were too many. After losing a Pawn, my opponent got some temporary counterplay. Accurate defense took care of the threats. Then a lethal attack decided the issue.

KING'S INDIAN DEFENSE

U.S. Championship Tournament
New York, 1951

M. HANAUER   S. RESHEVSKY

1 P–QB4	N–KB3
2 N–QB3	P–KN3
3 P–KN3	B–N2
4 B–N2	O–O
5 P–Q4	P–Q3
6 N–B3	QN–Q2
7 O–O	P–K4
8 P–K4	P×P
9 N×P	R–K1
10 N(4)–K2?	....

More usual here is 10 P–KR3 followed by R–K1 and B–K3.

10	N–B4
11 P–B3	KN–Q2

12 P–B4?   ....

Not only a loss of time but also leads to the loss of a Pawn. A plausible continuation was 12 P–N3, and if 12 ... N–K4; 13 B–K3.

12	N–N3
13 P–N3	N×KP
14 B×N	R×B
15 N×R	B×R
16 P–QB5	....

It only appears as though White has counterplay. I foresaw this possibility and was prepared to meet it.

16 ....   B–B4

16 ... N–Q2; 17 P×P, P×P; 18 N×P would have given White an even position.

17 P×N   ....

Otherwise White loses another Pawn.

17	B×N
18 P×BP	Q×P
19 B–R3	B–N2
20 Q×P	....

If 20 B×P?. Q–N3ch; 21 R–B2, R–Q1.

20 ....   Q–B7

It is true that White has regained a Pawn, but his troubles are just starting.

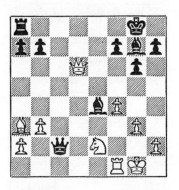

| 21 Q–Q1 | Q×RP |
| 22 B–B5 | B–B7 |

Black's method is simple but effective.

23 Q–Q7	Q×P
24 N–Q4	Q–K6ch
25 R–B2	B–Q6

Threatening to win a piece with ... Q–B8ch.

| 26 N–K2 | Q–Q7 |
| 27 Q×NP | R–K1 |

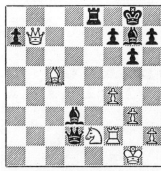

There is no defense. If 28 N–Q4, R–K8ch; 29 K–N2, B–B8ch; 30 K–B3 (30 K–N1, B–R6ch), Q–Q8ch.

28 Q–Q7	Q–Q8ch
29 K–N2	B–K5ch
Resigns	

Defeating the Budapest

Mr. Seidman is one of the American masters who love to inject novelty into the opening. Every time he has faced me he has come up with a new move—good, bad, or indifferent. He must be a firm believer in the element of surprise.

Playing Black in this game, he adopted the inferior Budapest Gambit. On his fifth move he steered away from the book. This innovation turned out to be unsound. It gave me the opportunity to develop my pieces quickly and effectively. I emerged from the opening with a distinct advantage.

Seidman's thirteenth move, P–KB3, further weakened his position. I initiated action on both wings, finally concentrated on the King-side. The attack gained momentum and culminated in a winning sacrifice.

BUDAPEST GAMBIT

U.S. Championship Tournament
New York, 1951

S. RESHEVSKY   H. SEIDMAN

| 1 P–Q4 | N–KB3 |

| 2 P–QB4 | P–K4 |

The Budapest Gambit, considered by experts to give Black an inferior position. This, of course, is only true if White knows how to proceed against it.

| 3 P×P | N–N5 |

4 P–K4   . . . .

A good alternative is 4 B–B4, N–QB3;
5 N–KB3, B–N5ch; 6 N–B3, Q–K2; 7
Q–Q5, B×Nch; 8 P×B, Q–R6; 9
R–B1.

4	N×KP
5 P–B4	B–N5ch!?

I had never seen this move before.
As it turned out in this game, the move
enabled White to gain precious time.
Usual here is 5 ... N–N3; 6 N–KB3,
B–N5ch; 7 N–B3, Q–K2; 8 B–Q3
with advantage.

6 B–Q2   **B×Bch**

6 ... KN–B3; 7 B×B, N×B; 8
Q–Q2, Q–K2; 9 N–QB3, O–O; 10
P–QR3, KN–B3; 11 B–Q3 followed by
N–Q5 is no improvement for Black.

7 Q×B	N–N3
8 N–QB3	P–Q3
9 N–B3	O–O
10 B–Q3	N–Q2
11 O–O	. . . .

Now that both sides have completed
their normal development, it becomes
clear that White's pieces enjoy much
greater mobility. For one thing, White
controls his very important Q5 square.
In addition, he has excellent attacking
possibilities with P–KB5–6. Black's
forces on the other hand, are inactive.
His position being sadly cramped, he
will be compelled to defend with the
utmost care.

11	N–B4
12 B–B2	P–QR4

To prevent White from driving the
Knight away with P–QN4. This turns
out to be only a temporary expedient.

13 N–Q4	P–KB3

Black's last move was necessary in
order to prevent P–B5–6 which, if
allowed, would have been disastrous
for Black. But the move created a
lasting, serious weakness at Black's K3
square. I soon started to concentrate on
this weakness.

14 QR–K1	B–Q2
15 K–R1	. . . .

Not having decided on any definite
action, I made a waiting move.

15	R–K1
16 R–K3	....

Making it possible to swing this Rook over to KN3 or KR3.

16	B–B3
17 P–QN3	....

The object of White's move was to remove pressure on his King-Pawn by driving the black Knight away later with P–QN4. To accomplish this it was first necessary to play P–QN3, then P–QR3. The immediate 17 P–QR3 would be answered by 17 ... P–R5.

17 N×B would be an inferior move because the recapture 17 ... P×N would deny White the use of his strategic Q5 square.

17	N–B1
18 P–QR3	K–R1
19 KR–K1	Q–K2
20 P–B5	....

White decides it is no longer necessary to drive away the Knight and begins to concentrate on his K6 and KN6 squares.

20	N(B4)–Q2

Black moves his Knight because his K4 square is now available to this piece. 20 ... N(B1)–Q2 would have been unwise for it would have taken away the seriously needed protection from his KRP.

21 N–Q5	....

White is making serious inroads into his adversary's territory.

21	Q–Q1

If 21 ... B×N; 22 KP×B, N–K4; 23 N–K6, N×N; 24 BP×N with the white Bishop becoming activated and the passed Pawn unbearable.

22 N–B4	N–K4
23 Q–K2	....

Aiming at KR5.

23	Q–K2

Preparing to meet 24 Q–R5 with 24 ... Q–B2.

24 R–R3	....

Lining the Rook up for possible future action.

24	Q–B2

A precautionary measure—to prevent Q–R5.

25 N(Q4)–K6	....

(See diagram on next page.)

I now felt that I was beginning to make substantial progress. Now being in a position to get rid of Black's Knight at his KB1, I had enhanced my attacking chances, for Black's Knight was a strong defensive weapon.

25	QR–B1
26 P–QN4	....

Now the purpose of this move was to get my Bishop to QN3 where it would be of great use in bolstering the attack.

26	B–Q2
27 N×N	R×N
28 P–B5	QP×P
29 P×BP	P–R5

Black's last move temporarily met the threat of 30 B–N3, Q–K1; 31 N–N6ch, N×N; 32 R×Pch, K×R; 33 Q–R5 mate.

30 B–N1   ....

Also good was 30 N–N6ch, N×N; 31 R×Pch!, K–N1 (31 ... K×R; 32 Q–R5ch, K–N1; 33 P×N and wins); 32 Q–R5 and Black is lost, for if 32 ... B–K1; 33 P×N, Q×P; 34 R–R8ch, K–B2; 35 Q×Qch, K×Q; 36 R×R. Or if 32 ... B×P; 33 P×B, KR–K1;

34 R–KN1 and Black must lose a piece.

30	Q–K1
31 N–N6ch	....

Now Black is at White's mercy. Everything is forced from now on.

31	N×N
32 R×Pch	K×R

If 32 ... K–N1; 33 B–R2ch, R–B2; 34 P×N.

33 Q–R5ch	K–N1
34 P×N	R–B2
35 P–K5	....

An important intermediate move. It threatens to open the King-file for the Rook. Insufficient was 35 B–R2, B–K3.

35 ....   B–K3

A very curious position. Black is lost in all variations. Instead of the text-move, the possibilities are:

(1) 35 ... P–B4; 36 P–K6, B×P; 37 B–R2, R–B3 (if 37 ... B×B; 38 Q–R7ch, K–B1; 39 Q–R8 mate, or if 37 ... R–Q2; 38 Q–R7ch, K–B1; 39 Q–R8ch, K–K2; 40 R×Bch, K–Q1; 41 Q×Q mate); 38 Q–R7ch, K–B1; 39 Q–R8ch, K–K2; 40 Q×Pch, K–Q1; 41 Q×Rch etc.

(2) 35 ... P×P; 36 Q–R7ch, K–B1; 37 Q–R8ch, K–K2; 38 R×Pch, K–B3; 39 R×Q, R×R; 40 Q–R4ch followed by P×R.

36 Q–R7ch   **K–B1**

37 Q–R8ch   **K–K2**
38 P×Pch   **K–Q2**

38 ... P×P is answered by 39 Q–R3 and if 39 ... P–B4; 40 P×R followed by B×P.

39 Q×Qch   **R×Q**
40 P×R   **B×P**
41 B–B5ch   **Resigns**

(See diagram at right.)

The final position. If 41 ... B–K3; 42 P×P etc. If 41 ... K–B3; 42 R×R B×R; 43 P×P, B–B2; 44 P–R4 etc.

And if 41 ... K–Q1; 42•R–Q1ch followed by mate.

Timidity Loses

While it is true that aggressiveness if often a fault, it is equally true that timidity loses many a chess game. If a player is apprehensive he plays too defensively. In the following game my opponent made two inferior opening moves, then insured his defeat by making a timidly defensive move on his 15th turn, apparently fearing the consequences of opening up the position. It is not customary for Larry Evans to play so faintheartedly in the opening, or at any other time, but in this game his weak opening moves gave him a lost position before the contest had barely started.

KING'S INDIAN DEFENSE

Wertheim Memorial Tournament
New York, 1951

S. RESHEVSKY   L. EVANS

1 P–Q4   **N–KB3**
2 P–QB4   **P–KN3**
3 P–KN3   **B–N2**
4 B–N2   **O–O**
5 P–K4   ....

More popular at present is to withhold the advance of this Pawn. Usual is 5 N–QB3, P–Q3; 6 N–B3 etc.

5 ....   **P–Q3**
6 N–K2   **P–K4**
7 P–Q5   **P–QR4**
8 O–O   **N–R3**
9 QN–B3   **N–B4**

10 P–KR3   **Q–K2?**

This is a waste of time. Correct was 10 ... N–K1 followed by ... P–B4.

11 B–K3   **B–Q2**
12 Q–Q2   **N–K1**
13 P–B4   **P×P**
14 P×P   ....

14 ....   R–Q1?

Imperative was 14 ... P–N3, and
if 15 P–K5, R–Q1. Black's objective
should have been to achieve ... P–KB4
in order to break up White's hold on
the center.

15 QR–K1   P–KB3??

This shuts in Black's King-Bishop.
Either 15 ... P–N3 or N–R3 followed
by ... P–KB4 was indicated.

16 P–B5   ....

Not only closing the door on Black's
King-Bishop but also making it possible
for White to get his Knight to his K6.

16 ....   R–N1

Black's position is hopeless and it is
just a matter of time.

17 N–B4	**P–KN4**
18 N–K6	**B × N**
19 QP × B	**P–B3**
20 R–Q1	**Q–QB2**
21 B–B3	**P–N3**
22 Q–N2	**B–R1**
23 P–K5	**....**

(See top of next column.)

The beginning of the end.

23 ....   P–R3

Position after 23 P–K5.

23 ... R–B1 would have offered
better resistance. If 23 ... BP × P; 24
Q × Pch, etc.

24 B × BP	**BP × P**
25 N–Q5	**Q–KR2**

Of course, if 25 ... Q × B; 26
N–K7ch.

26 P–KR4	**B–B3**
27 P × P	**P × P**
28 R–B3	**N–N2**
29 P–K7	**R–B2**

30 R–R3	**Q × P**
31 R–KB1	**Q–N3**
32 Q–R2	**N–K1**
33 R–R6	**Q–Q6**
34 B × N(K8)	**R × B**
35 R(R6) × B	**Resigns**

An Opening Variation Refuted

An unsound opening is inferior only if it is proven to be so. In other words, one must find the correct refutation to a bad variation. Quite often one can get away with a poor variation against a weaker opponent. Experts often take the risk of playing a defective opening, and get good results. Personally, I seldom take such chances.

In the following game my opponent employed an unusual form of the Nimzovich Defense. Mr. Kramer is quite original in the openings. I knew this, so I was not too surprised by the variation, but I took a long time to find the correct continuation and obtain a substantial advantage. I decided to play aggressively. My tenth and eleventh moves made it impossible for my opponent to castle. After the 14th turn, Mr. Kramer found himself completely tied up. In a desperate attempt to survive, he gave up his Queen for two Rooks. White's Queen proved much superior.

NIMZO-INDIAN DEFENSE

Wertheim Memorial Tournament
New York, 1951

S. RESHEVSKY	G. KRAMER
1 P-Q4	N-KB3
2 P-QB4	P-K3
3 N-QB3	B-N5
4 P-K3	P-QN3

Popular at the time. Recently, Keres has been experimenting with this variation.

5 N-K2 ....

To be able to recapture N×B after ... B×Nch. In my opinion, this move is the strongest.

5 .... **B-N2**

Better is 5 ... B-R3; 6 P-QR3, B-K2; 7 N-B4, O-O; 8 P-QN4, P-Q4; 9 P-N5, B-N2; 10 P×P, P×P; 11 B-N2, P-B4 with approximate equality.

6 P-QR3 ....

(See diagram.)

6 .... **B-K2**

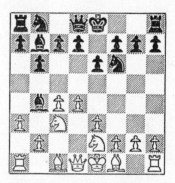

Position after 6 P-QR3

Black would have a better chance of getting a playable game with 6 ... B×Nch; 7 N×B, P-Q4; 8 B-K2, B-R3; 9 P-QN3, QN-Q2; 10 B-N2, P×P; 11 P×P, P-B4.

7 P-Q5 ....

This move gives Black difficulty because his Queen-Bishop is put out of play, at least temporarily.

7 ...	P-K4
8 N-N3	P-N3

Keeping White's Knight out of KB5 but at the same time considerably weakening his King-side.

9 B–Q3   **P–Q3**

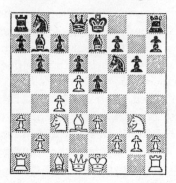

10 P–B4   ....

I decided on energetic action on the King-side. Quiet development would have enhanced Black's chances of equality. Thus, if 10 O–O, P–KR4!; 11 P–B4, P–R5; 12 KN–K4 (if 12 KN–K2, QN–Q2), N×N; 13 N×N, P–KB4 followed by ... P–K5 with a playable game. Neither was 10 P–K4 of any avail on account of 10 ... P–KR4; 11 B–N5 (11 P–KR4, N–N5!), P–R5; 12 KN–K2, N–R4; 13 B×B, Q×B with a good position.

10 ....   **QN–Q2**

Slightly better was 10 ... P×P; 11 P×P, O–O; and if White continues with 12 P–KB5, Black at least has a good square for his Queen-Knight at his K4.

11 P–KB5   **P–KN4?**

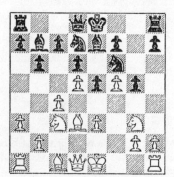

With the idea of continuing with ... P–KR4; but this threat can be met easily, as proven by White's next move. More prudent was 11 ... O–O; 12 P–K4, N–K1; 13 B–R6, N–N2; 14 Q–Q2, K–R1 with better chances than in the game.

12 B–K2   ....

Effectively preventing ... P–KR4. 12 N–R5 (to prevent ... P–KR4) would not be as good because of 12 ... N×N; 13 Q×N, N–B3; 14 Q×NP (14 Q–R6, N–N5; 15 Q–N7, B–B3 and the Queen is trapped), R–KN1 or ... N×P with excellent possibilities.

12 ....   **P–QR4**
13 R–QN1   **P–B3**

Being terribly cramped, Black must make an effort to free some of his pieces.

14 P–K4   **R–KN1**
15 P–R3   ....

Not permitting 15 ... P–N5 followed by ... P–KR4.

15 ....   **P×P**
16 KP×P   ....

An exception to the rule of capturing toward the center. The reason: to enable White to post a Knight at his K4.

16 ....   **B–R3**
17 B–K3   **P–R4**

This was the objective of Black's previous move.

18 N×P   ....

I accepted the offer of the exchange of Pawns.

18 ....   **N×N**
19 B×N   **B×P**
20 B–K2   **Q–B1**
21 R–QB1   ....

Black seems to have freed himself by the exchange of Pawns. However, the opening of the QB-file is to his detriment, as will soon become apparent.

| 21 .... | B × B |
| 22 Q × B | Q–N2 |

22 ... Q–R3 loses to 23 Q × Q, R × Q; 24 N–N5, K–Q1 (24 ... K–B1; 25 R–B7); 25 R–B6 and wins.

23 O–O ....

Getting my King in a safe position. White has plenty of time since Black is unable to undertake anything worth while.

23 .... **K–B1**

Black must attempt to get his King to safety.

24 Q–Q2 ....

Not allowing 24 ... K–N2, and forcing another weakness.

24 .... **P–B3**

Weakening his K3 square.

25 P–QN4 ....

Intending 26 N–N5.

25	P–N4
26 Q–K2	P × P
27 P × P	....

(See top of next column.)

27 .... **R–R1**

Inadequate was 27 ... R–N1 on

Position after 27 P × P

account of 28 R–R1 with the double threat of 29 R–R5 and 29 R–R7.

| 28 N × P | R–QN1 |
| 29 N–B7 | .... |

29 N–R7, Q × NP; 30 N–B6 does not win because of 30 ... Q–N4.

| 29 .... | Q × NP |
| 30 R–N1? | .... |

Missing the winning continuation in time trouble. Correct was 30 B–R7!, R–N2; 31 R–N1 and Black has nothing better than to take the two Rooks for the Queen.

30 .... **Q × R?**

Missing the only chance of survival. My opponent was also in time trouble. Correct was 30 ... Q–K5! and White would have had nothing better than 31

R×Rch, N×R; 32 R–B3, K–B2; 33
Q–N5, Q–B7 with an unclear position.

31 R×Q   R×Rch
32 K–R2   K–B2
33 Q–QB2   ....

Under ordinary conditions, two
Rooks are equal in value to a Queen.
In this position the Queen is much
superior, for three reasons: 1. The
Rooks are separated and cannot be
easily brought together. 2. Black's
King is in a dangerously exposed position. 3. Black's other pieces are
inactively posted.

33 ....   R–KB8

If 33 ... R(R1)–QN1; 34 B–R7,
R(N1)–N7 or N2: 35 Q–B6 and Black
is in trouble.

34 N–N5   N–N1

34 ... R–QN1 is met by 35 Q–B6!

35 B–N6   ....

Threatening 36 B–B7 winning the
Queen-Pawn.

35 ....   N–R3

Meeting the threat of B–B7, but
defending his QP is still a headache for
my opponent, as is indicated by White's
next move.

36 Q–B6   P–N5

Since the Pawn cannot be defended,
Black must take desperate measures.

37 Q–Q7   ....

Even stronger than 37 N×Pch.

37 ....   P–N6ch
38 K×P   R–N1ch
39 K–R2   R–N2
40 N×Pch   K–N1
41 Q–K6ch   K–R2
42 N–K8   ....

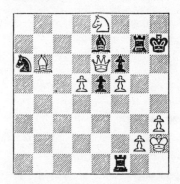

The final blow. Black now falls
apart rapidly.

42 ....   N–B4
43 B×N   B×B
44 N×Pch   K–R3
45 N–K8ch   K–N4
46 N×R   B–N8ch
47 K–N3   B–B7ch
48 K–B3   B–R5ch
49 K–K3   Resigns

Control of an Important Square

Kotov, one of the leading Russian veterans, is a tricky and dangerous adversary. His style being aggressive, he is always looking for an opportunity to bring about complications. He frequently tries to surprise his opponents in the opening, introducing a new move, good or bad. During a game he resorts to all kinds of psychological motions.

In this game, he set up the King's Indian Defense against my Queen-Pawn opening. He tried to confuse me by making a new move on his 9th turn. This soon turned out to be a costly waste of time. His 11th move gave me control of his Q4 square, which I never relinquished.

Kotov discovered he had the insurmountable problem of completing his development. His mishandling of the opening soon cost him a Pawn. He desperately attempted to create complications, hoping I would blunder in time trouble. Instead, I won two pieces by the 37th move. He finally resigned on his 42nd move. He could have done this comfortably on his 35th turn.

KING'S INDIAN DEFENSE

Candidates' Tournament
Switzerland, 1953

S. RESHEVSKY   A. KOTOV

1 P–Q4	N–KB3
2 P–QB4	P–Q3

More usual here is 2 ... P–KN3 if Black intends to play the King's Indian Defense. The text-move can innocuously lead into the same defense.

3 N–QB3	QN–Q2

Premature. Black should leave himself the option of developing this Knight at QB3, where it is better placed in case White decides to fianchetto his King-Bishop. Therefore 3 ... P–KN3 was correct.

4 N–B3	P–KN3
5 P–K4	....

Experience has shown that White's King-Bishop belongs at K2, rather than KN2, when Black's Queen-Knight is at Q2.

5	P–K4

6 B–K2	B–N2
7 O–O	O–O
8 R–K1	P–B3
9 B–B1	....

A well-known position has been reached. The usual continuation is 9 ... P×P, but Kotov had prepared a surprising new move!

9	N–K1!?

New, but is it good? The idea is to bring this Knight to K3 where it will exert pressure on White's important Q4 square.

10 R–N1	....

Preparing to start action on the Queen wing with P–QN4.

10 ....   **N–B2**
11 P–QN4   **P–QB4?**

Abandoning control of his Q4 square. This proved to be fatal. Kotov gave up his original idea of playing 11 ... N–K3 probably because of the reply 12 B–K3 followed by 13 P–Q5 driving the Knight back to QB2.

There is no promising continuation for Black. His Knights are awkwardly posted. White enjoys much greater scope for his pieces.

12 QP×BP   ....

Doubtful is 12 NP×P, QP×P (also playable is 12 ... KP×P; 13 N×P, P×P; 14 KN–N5, N×N; 15 N×N, N–K4); 13 P–Q5, N–K1 and Black will succeed in occupying his Q3 square with this Knight, thereby blocking the advance of the QP.

12 ....   **P×P**
13 B–R3   **N–K3**
14 P×P   **R–K1**

In order to play ... B–B1 and capture the Pawn with the Bishop. If Black had captured the Pawn with either of the Knights, 15 Q–Q5 would have subjected him to a dangerous pin.

15 N–QN5   ....

With the serious threat of N–Q6

followed by P–B6 and N×B, winning the exchange. Black is now compelled to regain his Pawn immediately.

15 ....   **N(Q2)×P**

15 ... N(K3)×P is not much better because of 16 Q–Q5, B–B1; 17 KR–Q1 Q–R4; 18 B–N4, Q–N3 (18 ... Q×P; 19 N–B7); 19 N–N5 and Black is in real trouble, for if 19 ... N–K3; 20 B×B, R×B; 21 N–Q6 and wins.

16 Q–Q5   **N–R5**

Exchanging Queens would of course cost Black a piece.

17 R–N3   ....

17 N–Q6 is met by 17 ... N–B6.

17 ....   **N–N3**
18 Q–Q1   ....

True, Black has succeeded in dislodging the Queen, but now the threat of P–B5 is most unpleasant for Black.

| 18 .... | B–Q2 |

To meet 19 N–Q6 with 19 ... B–R5,
but Black's 18th move allows White to
obtain a crushing pin on the Queen-file.
Relatively best was 18 ... B–B1; 19
N–Q6, B×N; 20 Q×B, B–Q2; 21
N×P, B–R5 with some counterplay.

| 19 P–B5 | .... |

| 19 .... | N–QB1 |

19 ... N–R5 fails on account of 20
N–Q6, N(R5)×P; 21 B×N, N×B;
22 N×R (also 22 R–B3, N–R5; 23
R–R3 suffices), N×R; 23 N×B,
N–B4; 24 N×P, K×N; 25 Q–Q4!

20 R–Q3	N–Q5
21 N(N5)×N	P×N
22 N×P	Q–R4

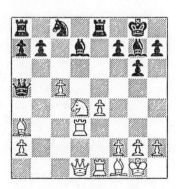

Black has no compensation for the
Pawn he was forced to give up.

| 23 N–N3 | Q×B |
| 24 R×B | .... |

Having a Rook on the seventh rank
is usually a sign of victory.

| 24 .... | N–K2 |

If 24 ... Q×RP; 25 B–B4, N–K2;
26 Q–B3 and the important KBP
cannot be defended.

25 R×P	Q×RP
26 B–N5	KR–Q1
27 Q–B3	B–B1
28 B–B4	....

The KBP cannot be defended any
more. My opponent could have resigned at this point, but Kotov is
always hoping for a blunder.

| 28 .... | Q–N7 |
| 29 Q×Pch | K–R1 |

| 30 P–K5 | .... |

Not 30 R×N, B×R; 31 Q×B on
account of 31 ... Q–B6; 32 R–QB1,
Q×B! After the text-move I was
threatening 31 R×N, B×R; 32 Q×B,
Q–B6; 33 Q–B6 mate.

30	Q–B6
31 K–B1	QR–N1
32 P–B6	QR–B1
33 B–K6	....

White threatens the Rook and also
intends 34 Q–B6ch, B–N2; 25 Q×N.

| 33 .... | Q–Q6ch |

34 K–N1   Q–K7

A superficial glance at the position

might lead one to believe that White is in trouble. If White plays 35 R–KB1, R–Q8 is very promising for Black. But I had a simple surprise for Kotov.

35 Q×Bch   ....

Making Kotov's face quite red.

35	R×Q
36 R×Q	R×QBP
37 R×N	P–QR4
38 P–KR4	P–R5
39 N–Q4	R–B8ch
40 K–R2	R–Q8
41 N–N5	R–QN8
42 N–Q6	**Resigns**

A Poor Opening

Years ago comparatively little importance was attached to the opening. The difference between the strength of masters was so great that the better player was able to extricate himself from an inferior position caused by a poor opening. The situation is quite different now. Very few players can afford to give a master an appreciable advantage in the opening and expect to survive.

In the seventh game of my match against Donald Byrne, he chose an inferior variation of the Hromadka System. The move 3 . . . P–K4, as played in this game, leads to a stagnant position if properly handled by White. Black's pieces were almost completely paralyzed after White's 14th move. At no point after that did Black have any opportunity for counteraction. White built up his advantage slowly, and after 29 Q–B4 Black was hopelessly lost.

HROMADKA SYSTEM

D. Byrne–S. Reshevsky Match
New York, 1957

S. RESHEVSKY   D. BYRNE

1 P–Q4   ....

The King's Pawn opening was not used in this match.

1	N–KB3
2 P–QB4	P–B4
3 P–Q5	....

Only with this move can White hope to obtain an opening advantage.

3 ....   P–K4

Black has better chances for equality with 3 . . . P–K3; 4 N–QB3, P×P; 5 P×P, P–Q3 followed by either . . . B–K2 or the fianchettoing of the KB. (See Bernstein–Reshevsky. Page 45.)

4 N–QB3   P–Q3

(See diagram on next page.)

5 P–K4   ....

Position after 4 ... P–Q3

Less effective is 5 P–KN3, P–KN3;
6 B–N2, B–N2; 7 P–K4, O–O; 8
KN–K2, N–K1; 9 O–O, P–B4 with
equal chances.

5 ....   B–K2

Fianchettoing this Bishop is even less
promising.

**6 B–Q3   O–O
7 KN–K2   N–K1**

Rearranging his pieces in case White
decides to attack with P–KR3 and
P–KN4.

8 B–K3   ....

White is leaving himself the option of
castling on either side.

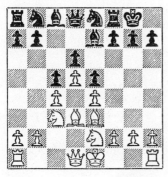

8 ....   N–Q2

Weak was 8 ... P–B4; 9 P×P, B×P
10 B×B, R×B; 11 N–N3, R–B2; 12

QN–K4 and Black's K3 square must
eventually come under the control of
White's forces.

**9 Q–Q2   P–QR3
10 N–N3   ....**

Seriously to be considered was 10
P–KN4 which would, of course, be a
declaration of war.

10 ....   N(Q2)–B3

11 P–KR3   ....

To prevent ... N–N5. A good alternative was 11 P–B3, P–KN3 (otherwise
12 N–B5); 12 B–R6, N–N2; 13 P–KR4
and P–KR5 with good attacking
possibilities.

**11 ....   P–KN3
12 B–R6   ....**

Among other things, this move
prevents ... P–KR4–5.

**12 ....   N–N2
13 O–O   ....**

13 ....   **B–Q2**

Overlooking the strength of White's next move. Correct was 13 ... K–R1 and then if 14 P–B4, Black can meet it successfully with 14 ... N–N1; 15 B×Nch, K×B; 16 P–B5 and Black's position, although cramped, is quite tenable. After 13 ... K–R1 White should abandon, at least temporarily, the advance of the KBP and begin action on the Queen-side with 14 P–R3 followed by P–QN4.

14 P–B4   **P×P**

Otherwise 15 P–B5 is most unpleasant

15 B×P   ....

Black must now reckon with the threat of P–K5. If 15 ... Q–B2; 16 QR–K1 and the threat remains.

15 ....   **N(B3)–R4**
16 N×N   **N×N**
17 B–R2   ....

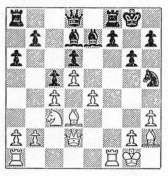

17 ....   **P–B3**

Best under the circumstances. If 17 ... Q–B2; 18 P–KN4, N–N2; 19 Q–R6 or QR–K1. The text-move not only weakened Black's King position and created a hole at his K3, but also completely shut in his KB. Black's only chance to free his pieces is to strive for an eventual ... P–KB4.

18 N–Q1   ....

White's obvious course is to bring all

his pieces to the King-side for a possible breakthrough. The Knight is heading for K3 and perhaps to KN4–R6.

18 ....   **P–QN4**

A desperate diversionary stroke which tends to weaken Black's Queen-side.

19 N–K3   **N–N2**

The beginning of the effort to effect ... P–B4.

20 R–B3   ....

In order to double Rooks on the KB-file.

20 ....   **P×P**

21 N×P   ....

Also good was capturing the Pawn with the Bishop, since Black would not have been able to improve his position by playing ... P–B4. After 21 B×BP, P–B4 there would have followed: 22 P–K5, P×P; 23 P–Q6ch, B–K3; 24 B×KP with the upper hand.

21 ....   **B–N4**

(*See diagram on next page.*)

22 P–QR4   ....

Best. 22 QR–KB1 is not as good on account of 22 ... P–B4; 23 P×P (if 23 P–K5, simply 23 ... P×P; 24 N or

Position after 21 ... B–N4

B×P, Q×P), B×N; 24 B×B, N×P
and Black's chances have improved
considerably.

22	B×N
23 B×B	....

23	K–R1

Preparing for ... P–B4. 23 ...
P–B4 is bad because of 24 P–K5, P×P
(otherwise P–K6); 25 P–Q6ch, K–R1;
26 P×B! (26 B×KP is, of course, sim-
pler) Q×Q; 27 P×R(Q)ch, R×Q;
28 B×KP, R–K1 (if 28 ... P–R3; 29
R–Q3 Q–QB7; 30 B–B3 followed by
R–Q7); 29 B–B3, Q–Q3 (29 ...
Q–QB7 is also ineffective because of 30
B–Q3, Q–N6; 31 B–N5 with the
double threat of B×R and B×Nch
winning the Queen); 30 R–Q3,
Q–B5 (30 ... Q–QB3; 31 QR–Q1
followed by R–Q7); 31 B–B7, R–KB1;
32 R–Q7 and wins.

24 P–KN4	....

So that if Black plays ... P–B4 his
King will be dangerously exposed to
attack.

24	P–B4

24 ... Q–Q2 was better but still
insufficient to hold on.

25 KP×P	P×P
26 QR–KB1	....

26	P×P

If 26 ... Q–Q2; 27 P–R5, P×P; 28
R×Rch, R×R (28 ... B×R; 29
Q–B4, as in the game); 29 R×Rch,
B×R; 30 Q–B4 followed by P×P with
an easily won end game, because the
QRP cannot be defended.

27 R×Rch	B×R
28 P×P	Q–Q2

Black is attacking two Pawns.

29 Q–B4	....

With the nasty threat of Q×Bch, R×Q; R×R mate.

29 ....   **B–K2**

29 ... K–N1 is no better because of the same reply as in the game.

30 B–Q3   ....

Threatening 31 Q–K4 followed by Q×P mate.

30 ....   **P–B5**

Giving up a Pawn for temporary relief.

31 B–B2   ....

31 Q×P is good enough but White wants more than a Pawn.

31 ....   **N–K1**

There is nothing better. If 31 ... Q–K1; 32 Q–K4, Q–N3; 33 Q×B, Q×B; 34 Q–B8ch.

32 K–R1   ....

In order that Black should not have a check. Inadequate is 32 Q–B7 on account of 32 ... Q×Pch; 33 K–R1, Q–N2 and White cannot make further progress. If 32 Q–K4, N–B3; 32 Q–Q4, K–N1; 33 B–B5 (threatening B–K6 ch), Q–R2 saves Black as White

is compelled to exchange Queens, thereby destroying his attack.

32 ....   **N–B3**

Q–R6 was White's immediate threat. 32 ... B–B3 fails on account of 33 P–N5, B–N2; 34 Q–K4, B×P; 35 R–B8ch, K–N2; 36 Q×Pch.

33 P–N5   ....

Now White must win a piece.

33 ....   **R–KB1**

If 33 ... N–N5; 34 Q–B7 wins. If 33 ... N–R4, the following neat finish could have come about: 34 Q–Q4ch, N–N2 (34 ... K–N1; 35 B–B5 etc.); 35 R–B7, R–KN1; 36 Q–R4, P–KR4; 37 Q×Pch, N×Q; 38 R–R7 mate.

34 P×N	B×P
35 Q×QP	Q–KN2
36 R–KN1	Q–R3
37 Q–B4	Q×Q
38 B×Q	B×P
39 B–KN3	R–K1
40 R–K1	R–KN1
41 K–R2	R–Q1
42 P–Q6	**Resigns**

Black must give up a piece for the passed Pawn.

Wasting Time in the Opening

My game with Mr. DiCamillo in the 1957–58 Rosenwald Tournament is a good example of winning against inferior opening moves. My opponent made a weak move on his 7th turn. The resulting loss of time gave me the chance to get slightly superior development. A gradual deterioration of my opponent's position induced him to sacrifice a Pawn, but this cost him the game.

The latter part of this contest illustrates the technique of winning when a Pawn ahead. Note that Black forces the exchange of the major pieces, the Rooks and then the Queens, and heads for the end game where his slight material superiority becomes proportionately greater. In the final stages Black gains another Pawn and then proceeds to cash in on his advantage. When White resigns Black has five connected Pawns against three. White cannot prevent the queening of a Pawn.

SICILIAN DEFENSE

Rosenwald Tournament
New York, 1957–58

A. DICAMILLO   S. RESHEVSKY

1 P–K4	P–QB4
2 N–KB3	P–Q3
3 P–Q4	P×P
4 N×P	N–KB3
5 N–QB3	P–KN3
6 B–K3	P–QR3

My latest attempt to defeat White's setup of P–KB3 followed by Q–Q2 and O–O–O (see Bisguier–Reshevsky, page 35). In my opinion, Black's plan of fianchettoing his QB, etc., is as effective as any known system.

3

7 P–KR3?   ....

Here the usual is 7 P–B3 In trying to avoid a well-known line White is wasting valuable time.

7	P–QN4
8 B–K2	B–QN2

8 ... P–N5; 9 N–Q5, N×P; 10 B–B3, P–B4; 11 B×N, P×B; 12 N×NP leads to an unclear position.

9 B–B3	QN–Q2

Also playable was 9 ... P–N5; 10 N–Q5, N×N; 11 P×N, B–N2.

10 O–O	B–N2

10 ... N–K4 was slightly better.

11 P–QR4

Attempting to weaken Black's Queen-side Pawns.

11	P–N5
12 N–Q5	....

(See diagram on next page.)

12	N–K4

Better than 12 ... N×N; 13 P×N, N–K4; 14 N–B6, N×Bch; 15 Q×N, Q–B2; 16 N×NP, B×NP; 17 QR–N1

Position after 12 N–Q5

B–N2; 18 N–B6 with a fine position. Black's two Bishops are not an asset.

13 N×NP   ....

13 ....   **N×P**

I was very much tempted to sacrifice a Pawn by playing 13 ... N×Bch; 14 P×N (14 Q×N, B×P would have given Black two Bishops without paying anything for them), Q–Q2; 15 K–N2, B–QB1; 16 R–R1—but it is unclear whether Black has sufficient compensation for the Pawn.

14 N(N4)–B6!?   ....

Also interesting was 14 N(Q4)–B6. There might have followed 14 ... N×Bch; 15 Q×N, Q–Q2; 16 Q×N, P–QR4 with complications—but 17 Q×Pch?, Q×Q; 18 N×Q, K×N; 19 B–N5ch, P–B3 loses a piece for White.

14 ....   **N×N**
15 B×N   **P–Q4**
16 B–B3   ....

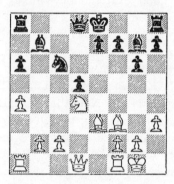

16 ....   **N–R4**

If 16 ... N×N; 17 B×N, P–K4; 18 B–B5 prevents Black from castling on the King-side. 16 ... N–K4 would have served approximately the same purpose as the text-move.

17 N–N3   ....

The purpose of this move was to meet the threat of ...N–B5. However, White is giving up a Pawn for which he mistakenly thought he would get adequate counterchances.

17 ....   **N×N**

Black could have won the Queen at the expense of three pieces as follows: 17 ... N–B5; 18 B–Q4, N×P; 19 B×B!, N×Q; 29 B×R, P–B3; 21 QR×N, K–B2; 22 N–B5, B–B3; 23

P–B4, Q×B (23 ... P–K3; 24 KR–K1
Q×B; 25 R×KP, R–QB1; 26 P×P,
B–R1; 27 N–K4); 24 P×P, B–K1; 25
P–Q6 with the better chances.

18 P×N   B×P
19 R–R2!   ....

If 19 R–N1, B–N2 and White has
nothing at all to show for the Pawn
sacrificed. With the text-move White
at least prevents his opponent from
castling.

19 ....   B–KB3

If 19 ... B–N2, White prevents
Black from castling by playing 20 R–Q2
(the purpose of White's 19th move now
becomes apparent), P–K3; 21 B–B5.

20 B–R6   P–K3

Now Black's problem is the effective
consolidation of his pieces. How to get
the KR into play is the most difficult
part of the problem.

21 R–K1   Q–Q3

21 ... B–N4; 22 B–N7, R–KN1; 23
Q–Q4 accomplishes nothing for Black.

22 R–B2   K–Q2

(See top of next column.)

Freeing the KR for action. Black's
King is quite safe here. Black's aim
will be to exchange Rooks as soon as
possible in order to reach the end game.

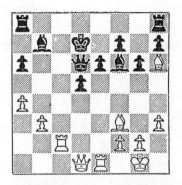

23 Q–Q2   QR–QB1
24 R(K1)–QB1   ....

White cannot avoid the exchange of
Rooks.

24 ....   R×R
25 R×R   R–QB1
26 R×R   B×R
27 P–QN4   Q–K4

Black is threatening to force the
exchange of Queens with ... Q–Q5.

28 B–K3   ....

If 28 P–N5, P×P; 29 P×P, Q–R8ch;
30 K–R2, Q–N7 and White is compelled
to exchange Queens because of the
threat of ... B–K4ch.

28 ....   Q–B6
29 Q×Q   B×Q
30 B–B5   ....

After 30 P–N5, P×P; 31 P×P,

K–Q3 followed by ... P–K4, White is
in bad shape.

30 ....   **K–B3**

Black is threatening to win a Pawn
with ... P–QR4.

31 B–K2   **B–K4**

Threatening ... B–Q3.

32 B–B8   **B–Q3**
33 P–N5ch   **P×P**
34 P×Pch   ....

34 B×Pch was slightly better.

34 ....   **K–B4**
35 B–R6   **B–Q2**
36 B–QB1   ....

White has no way of saving the
Pawn.

36 ....   **K–N3**

If 36 ... B×P; 37 B–R3ch, K–N3;
38 B×B(N5), B×B; 39 B–K8, P–B4;
40 B–B7 regaining the Pawn.

37 B–K3ch   **B–B4**
38 B–N5   **B×NP**
39 B–Q8ch   **K–B3**
40 B–Q1   **P–K4**
Resigns

Lack of Development

The principle of rapid and effective development of minor pieces in the
early stages of the game cannot be sufficiently stressed. Every good chess
player recognizes the importance of this principle. Occasionally, however,
every player becomes a victim of underdevelopment. The commonest
reason for this is the selection of an inferior opening line.

In the following game my opponent chose an unusual variation of the
Nimzo-Indian Defense. The choice of a rare or new line is obviously to
surprise one's opponent. This can often be extremely effective, especially
when the time element is such a significant factor in modern chess
competition. But extreme care is recommended in the selection of new or
rejected defenses.

After nine moves it was obvious that White's development was far
superior to Black's. By opening up the lines, the strength of White's two
Bishops became apparent. A gradual build-up against the black King

occupied my opponent's attention, preventing him from effectively developing his Queen-side pieces.

NIMZO–INDIAN DEFENSE

Rosenwald Tournament
New York, 1957–58

S. RESHEVSKY	G. KRAMER
1 P–Q4	N–KB3
2 P–QB4	P–K3
3 N–QB3	B–N5
4 P–K3	N–K5?

A move very rarely seen. I was surprised by it but not shocked. White proceeds to prove it to be a loss of time.

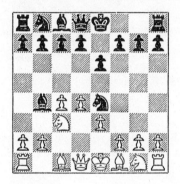

5 Q–B2 ....

Hasty action gets White nowhere. For instance: 5 Q–N4, N×N; 6 P–QR3, B–K2; 7 P×N (7 Q×NP?, B–B3), O–O; 8 P–K4, P–KB4 with an excellent game.

5	P–KB4
6 B–Q3	O–O!

(*See top of next column.*)

Is Black giving a Pawn for nothing? Not quite.

7 N–K2 ....

If 7 B×N, P×B; 8 Q×P, P–Q4!; 9 P×P (9 Q–Q3 is no better because of 9 ... Q–N4; 10 P–KN3, P–QN3; 11

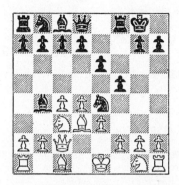

Position after 6 ... O–O

KN–K2, B–R3; 12 P–N3, P×P; 13 P×P, N–B3 with the serious threat of ... N–R4 winning the QBP), P×P; 10 Q–Q3, Q–N4; 11 P–KN3, B–KB4 with more than ample compensation for the Pawn.

7	P–Q4
8 P–QR3	B×Nch
9 P×B	P–QN3

A logical way of trying to develop the Bishop. As will be seen, however, this imperceptible error turns out to be the cause of Black's troubles. Better was the more solid 9 ... P–B3.

10 P×P	P×P
11 P–QB4	....

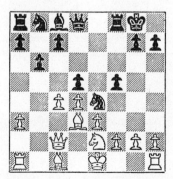

11	P×P

Black has difficulty in maintaining his Pawn at his Q4. For example, 11 ... P–B3; 12 P×P, P×P; 13 N–B4 (threatening 14 N×P, Q×N?; 15 B–B4), B–N2; 14 N–K6. Or if 13 ... K–R1; 14 P–KR4 (with the threat of P–B3) or 14 P–B3 immediately.

12 B×Pch	K–R1
13 N–B4	P–B3

To prevent B–Q5.

14 P–QR4   ....

Preventing ... P–QN4 and at the same time giving White the option of placing his Bishop at QR3.

14	N–Q3
15 B–N3	P–QR4

With the intention of anchoring his QN at his QN5.

16 P–R4   ....

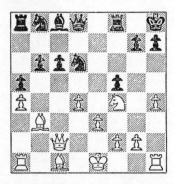

I would have had the better of it also after 16 O–O but the attacking possibilities offered by the text-move were too tempting. The immediate threat is 17 P–R5 followed by N–N6ch culminating in mate.

16 ....   **R–K1**

If White now plays 17 P–R5, the mate can be averted by 17 ... P–R3. The alternative 16 ... R–B3; 17 P–R5, R–R3 would also have parried the threat but the Rook would have been in an awkward position.

17 B–N2   **P–QN4**

Black must try to get rid of one of White's Bishops; otherwise he would succumb to an irresistible attack. In devoting his time to defensive measures Black is reluctantly unable to develop his pieces.

18 P–Q5	N–B5
19 B×N	P×B

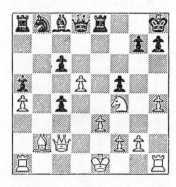

20 R–Q1   ....

Better than 20 Q×QBP, Q–N3; 21 Q–B3, Q–N5 resulting in an ending with some fighting chances for Black.

20 ....   **Q–Q3**

Best under the circumstances. If 20 ... P×P; 21 N×P with the nasty threat of N–B6.

21 Q×QBP   ....

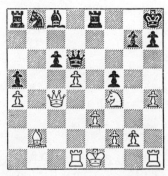

21 ....   **P×P**

Relatively best was 21 ... Q–N5ch but after 22 Q–B3 (22 Q×Q, P×Q would open up for Black's QR needlessly), Q×Q; 23 B×Q and Black's chances of survival would have been poor.

22 N×P   . . . .

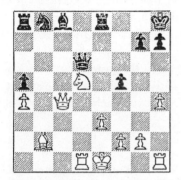

The threats of 23 N–B6 and 23 N–B7 are annoying.

22 . . . .   **B–R3**

There is nothing better. If 22 ... B–K3; 23 Q–B3, R–R2; 24 N–B6. If 22 ... R–Q1; 23 O–O, B–R3 (23 ... B–K3; 24 Q–B7 too); 24 Q–B7, Q×Q; 25 N×Q, R×R; 26 R×R and wins. If 22 ... Q–B1; 23 N–B7, R–K5; 24 Q–B5! winning a Rook, for if 24 ... Q×Q; 25 R–Q8ch leads to mate.

23 Q–B7   **Q–B1**
24 N–N6   . . . . .

Simple and sufficient.

24 . . . .   **P–B5**

There is no adequate defense. If 24 ... R–K2; 25 R–Q8 wins. Black is making a final desperate effort to save himself.

25 N×R   **P×P**
26 P–B4   **P–R3**
27 N–N6   **N–B3**

Pieces have no significance at this point.

28 Q×N   **Q×P**

Black threatens mate on the move.

29 B×Pch   . . . .

After 29 QxRch, K–R2 it looks offhand as if White had no defense against the threat of mate. But he had an adequate defense with 30 R–Q2, for after 30 ... P×Rch; 31 K–Q1, Q–N5ch; 32 K×P, Q×Pch; 33 K–B3 would avoid perpetual check. I chose the text-move, however, because it was a more pleasant way of finishing the game.

29 . . . .   **K–R2**

If 29 ... K×B; 30 R–Q7ch, K–R1 (30 ... K–B1; 31 Q–Q6ch); 31 Q–B3ch, R–K4; 32 R–Q8ch, K–N2; 33 Q–B7ch, K–N3; 34 P–R5ch, R×P; 35 R–N8ch, etc.

30 Q×Pch   **Resigns**

Faulty Development

Normal development of pieces is a basic requirement. Without it a player cannot hope to have equality. When selecting an opening variation one must be reasonably certain that the development of all the pieces will not be impeded or too long delayed.

In the following Nimzovich Defense, adopted by Pachman, my opponent played the opening somewhat mechanically. He soon discovered, to his surprise, that he was unable to complete development of his pieces satisfactorily. His main headache was his Queen-Rook. He was never able to make use of this piece.

After 16 moves Pachman's pieces were so badly posted that they got in each other's way. I continued to press my advantage and White's position improved with every move. After my 21st move Black had a completely lost game.

NIMZO–INDIAN DEFENSE

International Tournament
Buenos Aires, 1960

S. RESHEVSKY	L. PACHMAN
1 P–Q4	N–KB3
2 P–QB4	P–K3
3 N–QB3	B–N5
4 P–K3	O–O
5 N–K2	P–Q4
6 P–QR3	B–K2
7 P×P	N×P

While the text is not bad, Black has less difficulty with 7 ... P×P because Black's Queen-Bishop can be developed immediately.

8 Q–B2 ....

Making the freeing ... P–QB4 more difficult.

8 .... N×N

8 ... P–QB4 would be inadvisable on account of 9 P×P, B×P; 10 N×N, Q×N; 11 N–B4, Q–Q3; 12 B–Q3, P–KR3; 13 P–QN4, etc. and White has gained valuable time.

9 N×N P–QB4

A natural developing move but it gets Black into some trouble. Better was 9 ... N–Q2 followed by ... N–B3 and either ... B–Q2 or ... P–QB4.

10 P×P	B×P
11 B–K2	N–B3
12 O–O	Q–K2
13 P–QN4	....

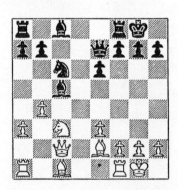

13 .... B–Q3

Black's position is already critical. After 13 ... B–N3; 14 B–N2, B–Q2; 15 N–R4, Black is also in trouble because he cannot save his KB by playing 15 ... B–B2 on account of 16 P–N5 winning a piece.

14 R–Q1   B–Q2

This Bishop must be developed some time.

15 B–N2   ....

White gains nothing with 15 Q–Q2. Black replies 15 ... B–K4.

15 ....   KR–Q1

15 ... QR–Q1 was better, but after 16 N–K4, B–N1; 17 P–N5, N–K4 (17 ... N–R4 loses to 18 Q–B3); 18 P–QR4 with a great plus.

16 N–K4   ....

Black is already lost. He must lose at least a Pawn.

16 ....   B–N1

16 ... B–B2; 17 P–N5 wins a piece. 16 ... B–K4; 17 B×B, N×B; 18 Q–B7 wins a Pawn. 16 ... B–K1; 17 P–N5, N–N1 (17 ... N–R4; 18 Q–B3) 18 N×B, R×N; 19 R×R, Q×R; 20 R–Q1, Q–K2; 21 Q–B8 and Black is strangled.

17 P–N5   N–K4
18 Q–B5   ....

(*See top of next column.*)

18 ....   K–B1

Position after 18 Q–B5

The only move. If 18 ... Q×Q; 19 N×Q wins at least a Pawn, for if 19 ... P–N3; 20 N×B, R×N; 21 R×R, N×R; 22 B–KB3.

19 QR–B1   P–B3
20 P–QR4   N–B2
21 B–R3   ....

Everything is forced from now on.

21 ....   Q×Q
22 N×Q   K–K1
23 N×NP   R–B1
24 R×Rch   B×R
25 B–B3   Resigns

The final position. If 25 ... N–N4; 26 R–Q8ch, K–B2; 27 R×B, N×Bch; 28 P×N, B×Pch; 29 K×B, R×R; 30 N–Q6ch.

2

OPENING INNOVATIONS

The importance of a knowledge of the openings was emphasized in the previous chapter. If you start out with a bad game it is difficult to recover later. And if you are unfamiliar with an opening, you waste valuable time. I can say this from personal experience because my knowledge of the openings was inadequate for many years and this handicap cost a great deal of time on the clock as I tried to find the best moves over the board.

Sometimes the study of openings reaps extra dividends. When going over the published variations of an opening, as played by masters and analyzed by experts, a new idea may occur to the student—a move or series of moves that has not been published. If analysis indicates that the new idea may be practical, it can then be tested in competition.

An opening innovation is something that every good chess player is constantly searching for. It not only satisfies one's ego, but also has an extremely useful purpose—surprising the opponent. If an opponent can be sufficiently disturbed by a new move, he might be compelled to consume a lot of time on his clock, which fact can often have an important bearing on the final outcome of the game. Dr. Alekhine was a genius at opening innovations. He was constantly looking for a new slant in known variations. I have seen him on many occasions take out his pocket set to try a new move.

In this section you will find some games in which opening innovations were successfully tested. Some of these new ideas were the result of pre-game analysis; others were found the hard way—over the board in actual competition.

A Crushing New Move

Stahlberg, the Swedish veteran, is an extremely tough opponent. His strength lies in his stubborn defense. He does not take any unnecessary chances. His objective is to draw. His style is similar to that of Eliskases. Both are difficult to defeat.

Playing the black pieces, Mr. Stahlberg adopted the Swedish variation of the Tarrasch Defense against my Queen-Pawn opening. I had suspected that he might use this favorite defense of his, and I was ready for it. My eleventh move, Q–B2, was brand new. My opponent was visibly perturbed and thought a long time before making his next move. He was unable to find a satisfactory reply. Most likely there is none. Within several moves my opponent's pieces were miserably tied up. My Queen-Pawn advanced to the seventh rank, adding greatly to Stahlberg's problems. Only his determined resistance enabled him to stay afloat as long as he did. In time trouble his defense crumbled, but his position was untenable in any case.

TARRASCH DEFENSE

Candidates' Tournament
Switzerland 1953

S. RESHEVSKY   G. STAHLBERG

1 P–Q4	P–Q4
2 P–QB4	P–K3
3 N–QB3	P–QB4
4 BP×P	KP×P
5 N–B3	N–QB3
6 P–KN3	....

Only by fianchettoing the Bishop can White hope to obtain an opening advantage.

6	P–B5

The Swedish Variation, a relatively recent contribution to the Tarrasch Defense. As can be judged from the results of this game, the Swedish Variation is no improvement over older lines. The most popular line is 6 ... N–B3; 7 B–N2, B–K2; 8 O–O, O–O; 9 P×P, P–Q5; 10 N–QR4, B–KB4; 11 B–B4 with the better prospects. Black has great difficulty in regaining the Pawn.

7 B–N2	B–QN5

Temporarily preventing P–K4.

8 O–O	....

8	KN–K2

8 ... N–B3 has the serious drawback of allowing 9 B–N5 with the threat of 10 B×N, Q×B (10 ... P×B weakens the King-side); 11 N×P. If, in this, 9 ... B–K3; 10 P–K4, B×N (10 ... P×P; 11 N×P, B–K2; 12 N×Nch, B×N; 13 P–Q5!); 11 P×B, P×P; 12 N–Q2 regaining the Pawn with much the superior position.

9 P–K4	....

White must strike at the center

if he wants to make any appreciable progress.

9 ....   P×P

Uninviting is 9 ... B×N; 10 P×B, P×P; 11 N–Q2, regaining the Pawn with excellent prospects because of the two Bishops and a powerful passed Pawn.

10 N×P   ....

Although White's Queen-Pawn is isolated, it is strong because it can be advanced with little difficulty.

10 ....   O–O
11 Q–B2   ....

An important innovation that probably ruins Black's defense in this variation. The point is that White allows the capture of the Queen-Pawn. If Black takes it, White regains the Pawn as follows: 11 ... N×P; 12 N×N, Q×N; 13 R–Q1, Q–N3; 14 B–K3, Q–R3 (if 14 ... Q–B2; 15 B–B4, Q–N3; 16 Q×P); 15 N–B5, Q–N4; 16 P–QR4 winning back the Pawn with the much better development.

The older continuation was 11 P–QR3, B–R4; 12 Q–R4, B–N5 with approximately equal chances.

11 ....   Q–Q4

Best. If 11 ... B–K3; 12 N(K4) –N5! 11 ... P–QN4 is effectively met by 12 P–QR4.

12 B–K3   ....

12 ....   N–N3

Better was 12 ... B–KB4 forcing the following simplification: 13 N–R4, N×P; 14 B×N, Q×B; 15 N×B, N×N; 16 KR–Q1, Q–N3; 17 Q×P, QR–B1; 18 Q–Q5 with good prospects for the end game because of the awkward position of Black's minor pieces.

13 N–R4   ....

Threatening to win the Queen with N–B6ch.

13 ....   Q–QN4

13 ... N×P would have cost a piece: 14 Q–Q1.!

14 N×N   RP×N
15 P–QR3   B–K2

14 ... B–R4 loses a Pawn after White plays 16 N–Q6.

16 P–Q5   ....

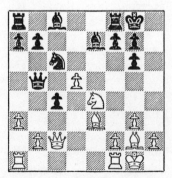

Obviously, the Pawn is immune to capture because of N–B6ch. The advance of this Pawn is going to be disconcerting to Black.

16 ....   N–R4

16 ... N–K4 was worse because of 17 B–Q4, N–Q6; 18 N–Q2 and the QBP is lost.

17 P–Q6   B–Q1
18 N–B3   Q–R3

The Queen seems to be well placed here. It protects the Bishop and Knight Pawns. In protecting the latter, the development of the Queen-Bishop is facilitated. Bad would have been 18 ... Q–N6 on account of 19 Q×Q, N×Q; 20 QR–Q1 threatening P–Q7. This would have yielded a Pawn at least.

19 QR–Q1   ....

At this point it is quite clear that White stands better; his pieces are well developed, especially his Bishops. Black, on the other hand, is obviously on the defensive. His pieces have poor mobility.

19 ....   B–N5
20 R–Q4   B–B4
21 Q–R4   R–N1

Intending ... P–QN4, thereby obtaining counterplay.

22 R–Q5   ....

Thwarting Black's plan.

22 ....   B–K3
23 R–K5   P–N3!

23 ... Q×P? loses to 24 R×N. The point of the text-move is to play 24 ... B–B3 to drive the Rook to an unfavorable square, K4.

24 P–Q7   ....

Preventing ... B–B3 in an interesting way: 24 ... B–B3; 25 R×B!, P×R; 26 N–N5 (threatening to win the Queen with N–B7), B–Q1. The Bishop is forced back to Q1 for if 26 ... QR–Q1; 27 N–B7, P–QN4; 28 Q–Q1 and wins.

24 ....   P–QN4

There is nothing better. If 24 ... B–B2; 25 R×B, P×R; 26 N–N5, B–K4; 27 P–B4, B×NP; 28 N–B7 etc.

25 R×P   R×R

25 ... B×P fails on account of 26 R×N, winning two pieces for the Rook.

26 Q×R   Q×Q
27 N×Q   P–R3

(See diagram on next page.)

28 N–B3   ....

Unclear was 28 N–Q6, B×P; 29 B–Q5, B–K3; 30 B×B, P×B; 31 R–B1, B–B3 and if 32 B–N6, B×P; 33 R–B2, B–K4!

Position after 27 ... P–R3

Forces the exchange of Bishops. This
enables White to post his Knight at
QB5 from where it can bear pressure on
the QRP.

| 31 .... | B×B |
| 32 N×B | .... |

| 32 .... | B–B4 |

In time trouble, Black selects the
worst move. 32 ... N–N6 was better,
but after 33 N×N, P×N; 34 B–Q5,
B–K3; 35 B×B, P×B; 36 R–Q6,
P–R4 (36 ... R–B1; 37 R–N6); 37
P–QR4! (threatening R–N6), R–N1;
38 R–R6 (if 38 R×P, R–N5 and Black
has fairly good chances of drawing),
R–QB1; 39 R–N6 and the ending is
won, but White has to play accurately
in this variation.

| 33 N×P | .... |

With a Pawn to the good, White has
no problems.

| 28 .... | B×P |
| 29 R–Q1 | .... |

Although Black seems to have come
out of the mess well, he has not solved
all of his problems by any means. For
one thing, his Rook is out of play. In
addition, his Pawn position on the
Queen-side is dangerously weak.

| 29 .... | B–B1 |

| 30 N–K4 | .... |

Tempting but leading to nothing was
30 R×B, R×R; 31 B–N6, N–B3!; 32
B×N, R–Q3; 33 N–Q5, B–K3; 34
N–K7ch, K–B1 and Black regains his
material. The text-move threatens 31
B–B5 followed by N–Q6.

| 30 .... | B–K2 |
| 31 B–B5 | .... |

33	R–K1
34 B–B3	N–N6
35 K–N2	B–B7
36 R–Q7	B–B4
37 R–Q1	B–B7
38 R–Q7	....

The repetition of moves was to gain
time.

38	B–B4
39 R–Q6	B–K3
40 N–B7	R–K2
41 N×B	Resigns

The final position. After 41 ...
P×N; 42 B–K2, N–R4; 43 R–R6
wins the QBP. If 41 ... R×N; 42
R×R, P×R; 43 B–K2, N–R4 (if 43
... N–Q7; 44 P–QR4 and the Black
King cannot stop the Pawn); 44
K–B3, K–B2; 45 K–K4, K–K2; 46
K–Q4 winning easily.

A New Idea Succeeds

In the second game of my match against Bisguier he used a setup
against the Dragon variation of the Sicilian Defense which has in the past
given Black a lot of trouble. White's plan is to castle on the Queen-side
and attack on the King-side. Some of the older lines for Black have not
proved completely satisfactory.

In this game I experimented with 7 ... P–QR3 and 8 ... P–QN4 to
prevent White from castling on the Queen-side, and with 10 ... P–KR4
to prevent White from playing P–KN4, which move is necessary for White
if he is to launch an assault against the black King. This new idea caused
White to castle on the King-side but he decided, nevertheless, to attack
with 18 P–KN4. This proved unsuccessful.

SICILIAN DEFENSE

Bisguier–Reshevsky Match
New York, 1957

A. BISGUIER   S. RESHEVSKY
1 P–K4   ....

Bisguier played P–K4 in every game
with White. I played P–Q4 with White
in four games and in one P–QB4 which
turned into the Queen's Gambit
Accepted.

1 ....   **P–QB4**

The Sicilian Defense tends to lead to
a real battle—much more so than the
Ruy Lopez.

2 N–KB3   **P–Q3**
3 P–Q4   **P×P**

4 N×P   **N–KB3**
5 N–QB3   **P–KN3**

The Dragon variation, which has
been a favorite of mine for a long time.
It has been my contention and still is,
that this is the best line for Black. Many
of the Russian experts, especially
Botvinnik, do not share this view; they
prefer 5 ... N–B3 and willingly submit
to the famous Richter Attack when
White plays 6 B–KN5.

6 B–K3   **B–N2**
7 P–B3   ....

To be followed by Q–Q2, O–O–O
and P–KN4, P–KR4–5. This setup is
troublesome for Black, because Black's
King safety is quickly threatened.

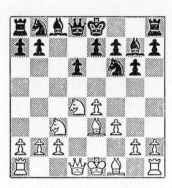

7 ....   **P–QR3**

7 ... N–B3; 8 B–QB4, B–Q2; 9 Q–Q2, Q–B1; 10 B–N3, N–K4; 11 P–N4, N–B5; 12 B×N, Q×B; 13 P–KR4 is one of the newer attempts for Black. An intense struggle would follow with White having the better chances.

8 B–QB4   ....

This Bishop will exert more influence at QN3 than at another square. It momentarily prevents Black from developing his Bishop at K3.

8 ....   **P–QN4**
9 B–N3   **B–N2**
10 Q–Q2   **P–KR4**

Preventing P–KN4, P–KR4–5, etc.

11 P–QR4   ....

In order to isolate Black's QRP.

11 ....   **P–N5**

12 N–R2   ....

On 12 N–Q5 Black can play simply ... P–QR4.

12 ....   **P–QR4**
13 P–B3   **P×P**
14 N×P   **N–R3**

From here this Knight has the option of going to Black's QB4 or QN5.

15 O–O   ....

Castling on the Queen-side is now out of the question since the White King could easily be subjected to a fierce attack.

15 ....   **O–O**

The opening phase is over and the mid-game battle is about to start. Neither side can boast of any advantage. Although Black's QRP is isolated, it cannot be easily attacked. On the other hand, the QN-file is accessible to Black.

16 KR–Q1   ....

If White intended to launch an attack, it would have been more logical to play 16 QR–Q1 and utilize the KR on the King-side. Apparently White desires to retain chances on the Queen-side by placing the QR on the QB-file.

16 ....   **K–R2**

Preventing B–KR6. Black's KB is an invaluable piece for defensive and attacking purposes.

17 Q–KB2 ....

18 .... **N(R3)–B4!**

Threatening 18 P–K5 with dire consequences for Black. For instance, 18 P–K5, N–K1 (18 ... P×P?; 19 N–K6 winning the exchange); 19 P×P N×P; 20 N(Q4)–N5 and Black may have to lose a Pawn.

17 .... **N–Q2**

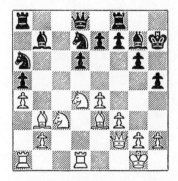

18 P–KN4!? ....

Too impetuous. 18 P–B4 is bad on account of 18 ... N–B3! threatening ... N×P and ... N–KN5. If 18 B–Q5, B×B; 19 N×B (19 P×B, N–K4 with a satisfactory position for Black), N–K4; 20 Q–R4, P–K3; 21 Q×Q (21 B–N5, P–B3!; 22 N×KP, P×B), KR×Q and White has made no progress.

Relatively best is 18 QR–B1, R–B1; 19 N(Q4)–N5 followed by N–Q5 with some pressure.

Black offers a Pawn which White unwisely accepts.

19 P×P? ....

Correct was 19 B–R2 and Black has to play very precisely to keep out of trouble. Black's only plausible reply would have been 19 ... P×P and there would have followed 20 Q–R4ch, K–N1; 21 Q×NP, N–K4; 22 Q–N3, Q–Q2 (in order to answer P–B4 with ... N–N5); 23 N–Q5, B×N (Black must get rid of this dangerous Knight); 24 B×B, QR–N1 with a complicated position.

19	N×B
20 P×Pch	**P×P**
21 N×N	**N–K4**

By giving up a Pawn, Black has the initiative. The two Bishops and the exposed position of the white King are

more than sufficient compensation for
the Pawn sacrificed.

22 N–Q4   ....

There is nothing better. 22 P–B4
would have weakened the KP and the
BP. There would have followed: 22
... N–B5; 23 Q–R4ch (23 B–Q4,
P–K4!), K–N1; 24 B–Q4, N×P; 25
R–Q2, N–B5 and if 26 R–KN2, P–K4
with the better chances.

22 ....   Q–Q2

Threatening ... Q–R6.

23 Q–R4ch   K–N1
24 Q–N3   R–B2

Simply intending to apply the maximum pressure on the KBP.

25 B–B1   ....

Attempting to meet 25 ... QR–KB1
with 26 P–B4 so that the Bishop cannot
be attacked by 26 ... N–B5, but Black
had a different idea.

25 P–N3, in order to answer 25 ...
QR–KB1 with 26 R–KB1, fails because
of 25 ... N×Pch; 26 N×N, B×N and
Black has regained his Pawn, and has
in addition a superior position. If in
this 27 QR–B1, B–N7; 28 R–B4 (28
R–B2, B×P), QR–KB1; 29 N–N5,
B–K4; 30 Q–R4 (30 Q×B?, R–B8ch),
B–B3.

25 ....   QR–KB1

26 P–B4   ....

On 26 R–B1, 26 ... P–Q4 is decisive.
For instance: 27 P×P (27 P–B4, P×P
and the KBP is pinned), B×P; 28
N×B (28 P–B4, B–B5; 29 R–Q1,
N–Q6), Q×N and if 29 B–K3, N–B5
is ruinous for White.

26 ....   N–N5

I had this move in mind for a long
time. From here the Knight is to go to
B3 where it will attack the KP, and from
B3 to R4 where it will simultaneously
attack the Queen and the KBP. White
is now playing with one Rook down,
for all practical purposes. His King is
perilously exposed. Add to this the fact
that all of Black's pieces are strategically
posted, and it becomes obvious that
White's extra Pawn means nothing.

27 P–R3   N–B3

28 Q×P . . . .

The only other possibility is 29 Q–N2 but after 29 ... Q×Qch; 30 K×Q, N×P Black should have no difficulty in winning the end game.

29 . . . .   **N–N5**
Resigns

A better try, but still inadequate, was 28 P–B5, N×P; 29 Q×NP (29 N×N, B×N; 30 P×P, B×Nch; 31 R×B, R–B8ch; 32 K–R2, R–R8 mate), N×N; 30 P×N, B–K5; 31 B–R6, P–K4; 32 P×P e.p., B×Q; 33 P×Q, B×B; 34 N–K6, R×P and wins.

28 . . . .   **Q×KRP**
29 R–R3   . . . .

The final position. The dual threats of ... Q–R7ch followed by ... Q–B7 mate, and .... Q–N6ch followed by a Knight check winning the Queen, cannot be met.

Bishop for Knight

Many players do not like to give up a Bishop for a Knight, especially if there is some expectation of reaching an ending in which two Bishops may be invaluable. This feeling may explain the opening innovation made in the following game. On his 8th turn White introduces a new move which secures an opening advantage for him. The move exchanges a Bishop for a Knight, but the gain in development is more than sufficient compensation. Later, with 17 N–Q6, White limits the coordinated development of Black's Rooks. On his 27th turn White wins the Queen for a Rook and Knight.

NIMZO-INDIAN DEFENSE

International Tournament
Dallas, 1957

S. RESHEVSKY   M. NAJDORF

1 P–Q4	N–KB3
2 P–QB4	P–K3
3 N–QB3	B–N5
4 P–K3	P–B4

5 N–K2   **P×P**

Best. 5 ... P–Q4; 6 P–QR3, BP×P; 7 P×B, P×N; 8 N×P, P×P; 9 Q×Qch, K×Q; 10 B×P, N–B3; 11 P–N5, N–K4; 12 B–K2 gives White too much of an opening advantage.

6 P×P	P–Q4
7 P–B5	N–K5
8 B–Q2	. . . .

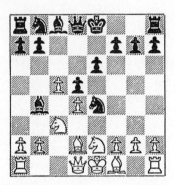

Giving up a Bishop for a Knight but gaining in development. This is a new wrinkle in an old line which had been considered as completely equalizing for Black.

8	N×B
9 Q×N	P–QN3
10 P–QR3	B×N
11 N×B	P×P
12 P×P	P–QR4

Temporarily preventing P–QN4.

13 B–N5ch	B–Q2
14 O–O	....

14 ....   **O–O**

14 ... P–R5, intending to prevent P–QN4, is interesting, but after 15 Q–Q4, Q–B3; 16 Q–QN4, N–B3; 17 B×N, B×B; 18 Q–N6, P–K4; 19 N–N5, O–O; 20 N–Q6, White has the upper hand.

15 P–QN4   ....

White's passed Pawns, being further advanced than Black's, and having greater support, give White the much better prospects.

15	B×B
16 N×B	N–R3

16 ... N–B3 is no better.

17 N–Q6   ....

Dislodging this Knight from its favorable post is almost an impossibility.

17	Q–Q2
18 P–B4	....

Threatening to demolish Black's King-position with P–B5–6.

18	QR–N1
19 P–B5	KP×P

20 QR–N1   ....

Interesting, but perhaps insufficient, is 20 N×P(B5), P×P; 21 N×P, P–B4 (not 21 ... K×N; 22 Q–N5ch, K–R1;

23 Q–B6ch, K–N1; 24 R–B3 etc.); 22 N–R5, N×P and if 23 R–B3, N–K5.

and the advance of the two passed Pawns cannot be halted.

| 20 .... | P×P |
| 21 P×P | .... |

| 21 .... | K–R1 |

27 R–K8ch	Q×R
28 N×Q	R×N
29 P–N5	....

Black cannot protect the threatened Pawn with 21 ... P–N3. There follows 22 N×P(B5), P×N; 23 Q–N5ch, K–R1; 24 Q–B6ch, K–N1; 25 R×P and wins.

22 Q–B3	N–B2
23 N×P(B5)	N–K3
24 N–Q6	P–B3
25 Q–KR3	....

Threatening to win a piece with KR–K1.

| 25 .... | KR–Q1 |
| 26 KR–K1 | N–Q5 |

This loses the Queen but there is hardly anything better. The only square available for the Knight where the loss of the Queen would be avoided was B1, but after 26 ... N–B1; 27 Q×Q, R×Q (27 ... N×Q; 28 N–B7ch); 28 P–N5 followed by P–N6

| 29 .... | N×P |

29 ... R×P is no better; there follows 30 R×R, N×R; 31 Q–Q7, R–QN1; 32 P–B6.

30 Q–Q7	N–B6
31 R×R	R×R
32 P–B6	N–K5

The last hope

| 33 P–R4 | Resigns |

Determined to Win

When I sat down to play William Lombardy in the 1958–59 Rosenwald Tournament, I could not help but remember that he had beaten me the previous year in the same tournament. I was determined to get my revenge.

Lombardy played the King's Indian Defense. On the ninth move he chose a line that was played by Geller against Smyslov in the 1953 Candidates Tournament in Switzerland. The former lost because he misplayed it in the middle game, and not because of a bad opening. As a matter of fact, Geller had at least an even position in the opening stage. I was, therefore, confronted with the difficult task of finding an improvement for White over the board. I spent approximately half an hour for my tenth move. The move I chose seems to be much superior to the one Smyslov used. Lombardy soon found himself in insurmountable difficulties.

KING'S INDIAN DEFENSE

Rosenwald Tournament
New York, 1958–59

S. RESHEVSKY   W. LOMBARDY

1 P–QB4   **P–KN3**

Years ago players would have looked at this move with amazement, but recently it has been accepted as playable by experts.

2 P–Q4	**B–N2**
3 N–KB3	**P–Q3**
4 N–B3	**N–KB3**
5 P–KN3	**O–O**
6 B–N2	**QN–Q2**

Other moves which lead into playable lines are 6 ... P–B4 and 6 ... N–B3.

7 O–O	**P–K4**
8 P–K4	**P–B3**
9 P–KR3	**....**

This position has been seen many times in the past. The usual continuation has been 9 ... P×P; 10 N×P, R–K1; 11 R–K1, P–QR4; 12 B–K3, N–B4; 13 Q–B2, P–R5 with an inter-

esting struggle in which White has slightly the better prospects.

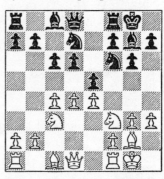

9 ....   **Q–N3**

An interesting move which requires attention.

10 R–N1 ....

In the game mentioned in the introduction above, Smyslov played 10 R–K1 and the continuation was 10 ... P×P; 11 N×P, N–N5; 12 P×N, B×N with complete equality. The purpose of the move I selected was to protect the QNP in order to be able to continue with B–K3.

10 .... **P×P**
11 N×P **N×P**

This was the move I had to consider seriously before I made my tenth move.

12 N×N ....

12 .... **B×N**

If 12 ... Q×N; 13 N×P, Q×Q; 14 R×Q, N–B4; 15 P–N3 with advantage.

13 P–QN4 ....

This move gives White excellent prospects. The natural 13 N×P, P–QB4; 14 N×B, QR×N leads to nothing. White's advantage of the two Bishops would be sufficiently offset by Black's well-posted Bishop.

13 .... **N–K4**

There is nothing better. For example 13 ... P–Q4; 14 P–B5, Q–Q1 (14 ... B×QBP; 15 N×B, N×N; 16 B–K3 winning a piece); 15 Q×B, P×N; 16 B–N2, P–B3; 17 B×P with a big plus. If 13 ... P–QB4 (trying to keep the Pawn); 14 B–R6 followed by P×P.

14 P–B5 ....

The key move to White's strategy. The alternative is 14 N×P but this is satisfactorily met by 14 ... R–Q1 when 15 P–B5 fails on account of 15 ... B×QBP. The text-move wins the exchange by force.

14 .... **P×P**
15 P×P ....

(See diagram on next page.)

15 .... **Q–Q1**

Why not 15 ... Q×R? The answer is not 16 Q×B because Black would have an adequate defense in 16 ... P–B3; 17 N×Pch, R×N; 18 Q×N, Q–B4 with the better of it; and if 17 B–R6, Q–Q6 with equality. The

Position after 15 P×P

winning line after 15 ... Q×R is 16
N–B6ch, K–R1 (16 ... K–N2; 17
B–R6ch wins the Queen); 17 Q×B,
Q–B4; 18 B–B4!

16 B–R6   ....

And not 16 B–N5 on account of 16
... P–B3; 17 N×Pch?, R×N; 18
B×R, Q×B; 19 Q×B, N–B6ch
winning the Queen.

16 ....   **P–QN4**

There is no way of saving the exchange; for if 16 ... R–K1; 17 B–N5
wins outright.

17 B×R   **K×B**

Although White is the exchange
ahead, it is by no means an easy win.
Black's two Bishops can become dangerous if White should relax.

18 Q–K2   ....

Threatening KR–Q1 with a nasty
pin.

18 ....   **Q–K2**

There is no adequate defense against
White's serious threat. If 18 ... B–K3;
19 KR–Q1, B–B5; 20 Q–Q2, N–Q6
(20 ... B–Q6; 21 R–N3) 21 B–B1 and
wins.

19 KR–Q1   **B×QBP**
20 N×B   **Q×N**
21 QR–B1   ....

21 ....   **N–B5**

Neither is 21 ... Q–K2 of any avail,
for after 22 R–K1, P–B3; 23 P–B4, the
Knight is lost.

22 R–Q8ch   **K–N2**
23 Q–K8   **Q–R6**
24 R–K1   **N–N3**
25 Q–R8ch   **K–R3**
26 R–N8   **Resigns**

Mate cannot be stopped.

The Hromadka System

The Hromadka System, like many other variations, has gone through various stages of popularity. It has been experimented with considerably in the last few years. Its major exponents have been Keres and Tal. I have also used it on occasions. To gain an opening advantage, White has to play exceedingly well against the variation.

In the following game against Sidney Bernstein I decided to use this variation. My opponent proceeded cautiously against the controversial Hromadka System. Everything seemed to be under control for both sides until my 18th turn. At this point I found an unusual maneuver for my Queen-Knight, bringing it from an unfavorable location to a very active square. My opponent was visibly baffled by this sudden strategy.

Black's position gradually improved. Mr. Bernstein became impatient. On his 26th turn he began to counterattack, bringing one of his Rooks into my territory. He thought he could force simplification and thus draw the game. Obviously overlooking the stunning reply 33 ... N–Q2, he resigned.

HROMADKA SYSTEM

Rosenwald Tournament
New York, 1959–1960

S. BERNSTEIN   S. RESHEVSKY

1	P–Q4	N–KB3
2	P–QB4	P–K3
3	N–KB3	P–B4
4	P–Q5	....

The only move with which White can hope to obtain an opening advantage. 4 N–B3, P×P; 5 N×P, N–B3; 6 P–KN3, B–B4 or B–N5 leads to complete equality.

4	....	P×P
5	P×P	P–Q3
6	N–B3	P–KN3

6 ... B–K2 is also a plausible continuation which has been tried. Fianchettoing the Bishop, however, is more logical since it gives the piece more scope and mobility. The objection to the fianchetto is that the Bishop does not protect Black's Queen-Pawn.

7 P–KN3	....

The quiet and conservative continuation. More energetic is 7 P–K4, leading to complicated problems for both sides. Botvinnik, in his first match against Tal, experimented with 7 B–N5 with unsatisfactory results.

7	....	B–N2
8	B–N2	O–O
9	O–O	P–QR3

This is necessary, sooner or later, to prevent N–QN5, attacking the QP.

10 P–QR4	....

White must not allow the freeing ... P–QN4–5.

10	....	QN–Q2
11	B–B4	Q–K2

(*See diagram on next page.*)

12 Q–B1	....

In order to play B–KR6. It is questionable, however, whether Black's King-Bishop is more valuable than White's Queen-Bishop. To be considered was 12 N–Q2, N–K4; 13 P–R3

Position after 11 ... Q–K2

(to prevent ... N–N5 after 13 ...
N–R4; 14 B–K3), R–N1; 14 P–R5,
P–QN4; 15 P×P e.p., R×P; 16
R–R2.

| 12 .... | R–K1 |
| 13 B–R6 | R–N1 |

I could have safely avoided the exchange of Bishops by playing 13 ...
B–R1 but I felt that gaining a tempo
was more essential.

| 14 B×B | K×B |
| 15 P–R5 | .... |

Otherwise 15 ... P–QN4–5 would
be too strong.

| 15 .... | P–QN4 |

It is imperative that Black try to
obtain control of the Knight-file.

| 16 P×P e.p. | .... |

Forced. Otherwise Black plays 16
... P–N5, causing unpleasantness for
the Knight.

| 16 .... | N×NP |

I considered 16 ... R×P but discarded it because of 17 N–Q2 (threatening the annoying N–B4–R5–B6), N–K4,
18 P–R3 followed by P–B4 and N–B4.

| 17 N–Q2 | P–KR4 |

Threatening ... P–R5.

| 18 P–R3 | .... |

| 18 .... | N–R1 |

I spent a long time trying to find a
plausible continuation. My Knight at
QN3 prevents White from playing
N–QB4. Other than that, this Knight
is not favorably utilized here. I
decided, therefore, to bring it to a
better square, QN4, but I had to make
certain that my opponent would be
unable to cause me any discomfort
during the next three moves.

19 N–B4	N–B2
20 Q–B4	R–Q1
21 R–R3	....

Intending 22 P–QN3, to free the
Queen-Knight for action. 21 R–R2
would have been a little better, and if
21 ... R–N5; 22 Q–K3.

| 21 .... | R–N5 |
| 22 P–N3 | N–N4 |

23 N×N	P×N
24 Q–K3	Q×Q
25 N×Q	R–Q5

Black's chances in the end game are better because White has a weak Pawn structure. His Queen-Pawn is under fire and his QNP is isolated. His only compensation is control of the QR-file.

26 R–R8 ....

Better was 26 R–Q1, R×Rch (if 26 ... R–QN5; 27 N–B2 and the Rook is trapped); 27 N×R, B–N2; 28 N–K3 and White might be able to hold his own. In this line, 28 P–K4 is not playable because of 28 ... R–K1; 29 P–B3 (or R–R7), B×P followed by ... R–K8ch.

26	R–K1
27 R–N8	R–QN5

28 R–N1 ....

On 28 R–N6 I had the choice of two promising continuations:
(1) 28 ... R×P; 29 R×QP, P–B5 with two powerful passed Pawns.
(2) 28 ... R–Q1; 29 R–N1, B–B4!; 30 N×Bch, P×N and the threat of ... P–QB5 cannot be met satisfactorily.

28 .... **B–B4**

28 ... N–Q2; 29 R–R8, P–B5 was also good.

29 N×Bch ....

If 29 R×R, B×R; 30 R–Q8, R×P; 31 R×P, P–B5; 32 R–Q8, R–N7; 33 P–Q6, R–Q7 wins.

29 .... **P×N**

30 R–N6 ....

Better was 30 R×R, N×R; 31 K–B1, N–B3; 32 K–K1, N–K5; 33 B×N, R×B and although Black should win the ending it is by no means simple.

30	P–QB5
31 R×QP	R×NP
32 R×R	P×R
33 R–N6	N–Q2

The move undoubtedly overlooked by Mr. Bernstein. White resigns because after 34 R×P, R–QN1 the Pawn must queen, or White must lose his Rook.

Shift of Plan

When I played Hector Rossetto in the 1960 Buenos Aires Tournament I had to win in order to keep up with Korchnoi, the Russian champion. However, Rossetto had been doing extremely well. He had not been beaten for eight rounds, although he had some very strong opponents. I knew my task was a difficult one.

My opponent played the perplexing Hromadka System against my Queen-Pawn opening. Rossetto's 7th move, B–N5, was a radical deviation from the usual continuation. I countered with a move which virtually forced him to give up castling. In compelling his King to move I lost two tempi. At the time I was not quite sure whether I benefited by this exchange, but it proved to be decisive. Black did not get his King-Rook into play until late in the game—too late. Rossetto's opening innovation backfired.

After castling on the King-side, I began building up all my forces in the center with the obvious intention of effecting a breakthrough there. My opponent brought all his pieces to the King-side, anticipating an attack there or in the center. On my 27th turn I suddenly shifted the attack to the Queen-side. Rossetto was unable to regroup his pieces in time to meet all threats on that wing successfully. I won a Pawn by force on the 33rd move, then a piece on the 35th.

HROMADKA SYSTEM

International Tournament
Buenos Aires, 1960

S. RESHEVSKY	H. ROSSETTO
1 P–Q4	N–KB3
2 P–QB4	P–K3
3 N–QB3	P–B4
4 P–Q5	....

On 4 P–K3 Black can easily equalize with 4 ... P–Q4 or 4 ... P×P; 5 P×P, P–Q4. After 4 N–B3, P×P; 5 N×P, N–B3; 6 P–KN3, Q–N3 or ... B–B4, Black has no particular opening difficulty.

4	P×P
5 P×P	P–Q3
6 P–K4	....

Whether this is better than the fianchettoing of the KB is debatable. My preference is for the text-move because it is more aggressive and poses more problems for Black in completing his development.

6	P–KN3
7 N–B3	B–N5!?
8 Q–N3	....

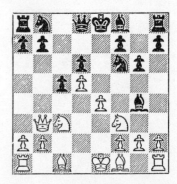

Obviously, the purpose of Black's last move was to get rid of White's Knight.

Since Black's Queen-Bishop has limited mobility in this variation, the idea of the contemplated exchange seems justified. However, Black's QN-Pawn becomes an immediate target for White's Queen.

8 ....   Q–K2

Relatively best. 8 ... Q–Q2 is out of the question because of 9 B–QN5. 8 ... Q–B2 is inadvisable because of the possible N–QN5 attacking the Queen and the Queen-Pawn. 8 .... Q–B1 is unattractive on account of 9 P–K5, B×N (if 9 ... P×P; 10 N×P gaining valuable time for an attack with B–N5ch); 10 P×N, B–N5; 11 B–N5ch followed by O–O with a terrific position. Finally, 8 ... P–N3 is quite unappetizing after 9 B–N5ch, QN–Q2; 10 N–Q2 with the unpleasant threat of P–B3 followed by P–KN4 winning the Bishop.

9 N–Q2   B–N2
10 Q–N5ch   ....

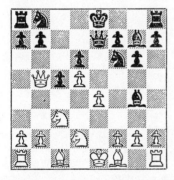

Compelling Black to move his King. In doing so White must lose some time because the white Queen can easily be driven away from this square. I felt that the prevention of Black's castling was sufficient compensation for the loss of time.

10 ....   K–B1

10 ... Q–Q2 loses to 11 P–B3, Q×Q, 12 N×Q followed by N–B7ch. Of course if 10 ... B–Q2; 11 Q×NP wins material.

11 P–B3   ....

Not best, since the Bishop has to retreat to QB1 anyway; otherwise Black would not be able to develop his Queen-Knight. Wiser was 11 Q–N3, P–QR3; 12 P–QR4 (preventing the freeing ... P–QN4), B–B1; 13 B–K2, QN–Q2; 14 O–O.

11 ....   B–B1
12 N–B4   QN–Q2
13 B–B4   N–K1

13 ... N–K4 loses a Pawn after 14 B×N, P×B; 15 P–Q6.

14 Q–N3   ....

Black was threatening to grab the initiative with 14 ... P–QR3 followed by ... P–QN4.

14 ....   N–K4
15 B–K2   P–KR4

Trying to discourage White from castling on the King-side by the indication of a contemplated attack.

16 O–O   ....

Not heeding the warning.

16 ....   P–R5
17 B–K3   ....

17 ....   N×N

17 ... P–KN4 is satisfactorily met by

18 P–B4, P×P; 19 B×KBP, N–N3;
20 B–K3. Opening of the KB–file
would have been to Black's detriment.

18 Q×N	B–Q2
19 P–QR4	P–R3
20 Q–Q3	R–B1
21 Q–Q2	....

The Queen is now better posted. If
a King-side attack is undertaken it can
be used advantageously from this
square. At QN3 the Queen was out of
play.

| 21 .... | N–B3 |
| 22 QR–K1 | .... |

All of White's pieces are ostensibly
ready for an onslaught in the center.

| 22 .... | N–R4 |

| 23 B–QB4 | .... |

Black's last move was a good one,
with a very serious threat!

If 23 B–KN5, B–Q5ch; 24 K–R1 (24
Q×B, P×Q; 25 B×Qch, K×B with
a fine game), N–N6ch; 25 P×N,
P×Pch with mate to follow. If 23
P–R5, N–N6!; 24 P×N, P×P; 25
B–KN5 (otherwise ... Q–R5 with mate
to follow), Q×B!; 26 Q×Q, B–Q5ch
with mate to follow.

But after the text-move, if Black
plays 23 ... N–N6, White simply
replies 24 R–B2 and the Knight stays
there inactivated.

| 23 .... | R–K1 |

Black now has all his forces ready for
any action in the center.

| 24 P–R5 | .... |

I decided to turn my attention to the
Queen-side with the specific intention
of effecting P–QN4.

| 24 .... | Q–Q1 |
| 25 N–K2 | .... |

26 P–QN4 is an immediate threat.
If allowed, it would endanger Black's
Queen-side Pawn solidarity.

| 25 .... | P–QN4 |

Black is vainly attempting to get the
punch in first.

| 26 P×P e.p. | Q×P |
| 27 R–R1 | .... |

| 27 .... | B–N4 |

If 27 ... R–R1, White would proceed
quietly with 28 R–R2 followed by
KR–R1 and Black's QRP would be
under dangerous fire. 27 ... Q×P
was bad on account of 28 Q–R5
(threatening Q–B7), Q–N5; 29 Q×Q,
P×Q; 30 R×P, K–K2; 31 R–N1,
R–QN1; 31 N–Q4 with the upper
hand.

| 28 B×B | P×B |

28 ... Q×B was no better. After 29
N–B3, Q–N2; 30 P–B4 with the threat
of either 30 P–K5 or 30 P–B5 was not
too attractive for my opponent.

29 R–R2   . . . .

The double threat of 30 P–QN4 and doubling the Rooks on the QR-file was too much for Black. His position suddenly begins to crumble.

29 . . . .   **B–B3**

Trying to get his King–Rook into play by getting the King to KN2.

20 P–QN4	Q–B2
31 P×P	P×P
32 Q–R5	. . . .

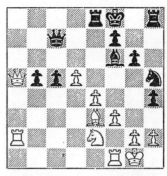

(See diagram at right.)

Both Pawns are now under fiery attack. He can save only one of them.

| 32 . . . . | R–B1 |
| 33 Q×P | K–N2 |

Black's King-Rook is finally freed, but too late to be of any help.

| 34 P–B4 | KR–K1 |
| 35 P–K5 | B×P |

Forced, for if 35 . . . B–Q1; 36 P–Q6 followed by P–Q7 winning a Rook.

36 P×B	R×P
37 Q–Q3	R(B1)–K1
38 B–B1	K–N1
39 P–Q6	Q–Q2
40 N–B4	Resigns

Attack and Defense

It does not happen too often that one side attacks and defends simultaneously. Usually, one side attacks and the other defends.

Against Mr. Wade in the 1960 Argentine Tournament, I made a new move in the opening. The purpose of 12 . . . P–R5 was to keep the King-side open for action. This necessitated having my King near the center of the board, enabling my opponent to sacrifice a Pawn and obtain attacking possibilities. I was faced with the difficult task of putting up an adequate defense on the Queen-side and at the same time nursing my attack on the opposite wing. This required an exact distribution of forces.

After the 23rd move, White appeared to have excellent attacking chances. He had most of his forces mobilized in the center, where my King was considerably exposed. It took accurate and calm defensive tactics to neutralize the situation. On my 27th turn I won another Pawn. My 28th move brought the King to a safe square and White's chances disappeared.

KING'S INDIAN DEFENSE

International Tournament
Buenos Aires, 1960

R. WADE   S. RESHEVSKY

1	P–Q4	N–KB3
2	P–QB4	P–KN3
3	N–QB3	B–N2
4	P–K4	P–Q3
5	B–K2	O–O
6	N–B3	P–K4
7	O–O	N–B3
8	P–Q5	N–K2
9	N–K1	N–Q2
10	P–B3	P–KB4
11	P–KN4	....

Usual here is 11 N–Q3, P–B5 etc. Or 11 B–K3, P–B5; 12 B–B2, P–KN4. In either case, Black will attack on the King-side and White on the opposite wing. Experience has shown that Black has the better chances. The text-move is designed to block the King-side as follows: 11 ... P–B5; 12 P–KR4, and if 12 ... P–KR4; 13 P–N5, and Black has no counterplay on the King-wing.

11	....	P–KR4
12	P–N5	P–R5

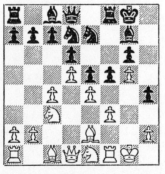

The purpose of this new move is to keep things alive on the King-side by preventing 13 P–KR4. I had to consider the consequences if my opponent chose to go after this isolated Pawn.

13 N–Q3   ....

Preparing for an eventual P–QB5.

13 ....   **P–B5**

Preventing B–K3 and at the same time isolating White's KNP.

14 Q–K1   **K–B2**

Also playable was 14 ... P–R6, for if 15 Q–R4, K–B2; 16 Q×RP, R–R1; 17 Q–N2, R–R4; 18 K–R1, N–B1, followed by 19 ... N–R2 regaining the Pawn.

15 K–R1   ....

Inadvisable was 15 Q×P, R–R1; 16 Q–B2, R–R4; 17 P–KR4, Q–R1, winning the KRP with great positional advantage.

15	....	R–R1
16	R–KN1	N–B1

With the intention of continuing 17 ... R–R4, followed by ... N–R2 and ... N×NP.

17 P–B5   ....

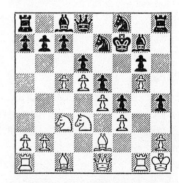

White has achieved his main objective. Without counterplay on the Queen-side he would be theoretically lost because his KNP must eventually fall.

17 ....   **B–Q2**

Preventing an eventual N–QN5 which, if allowed, could be cumbersome for Black. The drawback of driving away the Knight at QN5 by

... P–QR3 would have been the weakening of Black's QN3 square. White could take advantage of this weakness by playing N–QR3–QB4. I did not like 17 ... R–R4 (with the intention of continuing with 18 ... N–R2) because of 18 P×P, P×P; 19 B×P!, P×B; 20 N×P, R–R1; 21 N–Q3 followed by P–B4 and P–K5 with a promising attack.

18 P–N3   ....

Making it possible for his Queen-Bishop to get to QR3—a strategic square.

18 ....   **R–R4**

Black cannot afford to stall any longer. Forceful action has become necessary. Winning White's KNP is Black's objective.

19 B–R3   ....

If 19 P×P, P×P; 20 B×P, P×B; 21 N×P, R–B1; 22 R–QB1, Q–R4 and White is kept busy protecting his pieces.

19 ....   **N–B1**

Protecting the QP and attacking the KNP at the same time.

20 P–B5   ....

Although this move was forced (otherwise Black simply wins the KNP) it was nevertheless an interesting idea. Black must proceed cautiously.

20 ....   **P×P**
21 P×P   **B×P**

21 ... B–K3 looks safer but after 22 N–N4, R×P; 23 R×R, Q×R; 24 N–R6, Q–K2; 25 N–N5 and Black's QBP cannot be defended.

22 N–N4   **B–Q2**
23 B–B4ch   ....

By giving up a Pawn, this Bishop was able to get into action.

23 ....   **N–K3**

Not as good was 23 ... B–K3 on account of 24 B–Q5, B×B (if 24 ... R–N1; 25 N–B6); 25 P×B, R×P; 26 N–K4, R×R; 27 Q×R with better chances than with the text-move.

24 B–Q5   **R–N1**
25 R–QB1   **P–B4**

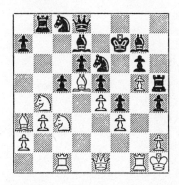

A strong defensive move. It serves the important function of restricting the influence of White's Queen-Rook. Without the cooperation of this piece, White's hopes begin to wane.

26 B×Nch   ....

26 N–R6, R–N3; 27 B–B4, N–K2 followed by ... K–B1 or ... Q–B1 gives White little hope.

26 ....   **K×B**

Not 26 ... B×B?; 27 N–B6.

27 N(N4)–Q5 ....

White now has complete control of his Q5 square, but at the expense of two Pawns.

| 27 .... | **R×KNP** |
| **28 Q–K2** | .... |

With the devastating threat of 29 Q–B4 followed by a discovered check.

| 28 .... | **K–B2** |
| **29 Q–R6** | .... |

29 Q–B4 can be effectively met by either 29 ... B–K3 or 29 ... K–B1.

| 29 .... | **P–R6** |
| **30 Q–Q3** | .... |

An admission that White has run out of ideas. Being two Pawns down with no visible compensation for them, the game is theoretically over—but to score the point still requires some effort.

30	**R×R**
31 R×R	**Q–R5**
32 Q–K2	....

Preventing ... Q–B7.

32	**R–N2**
33 B–B1	**P–R4**
34 B–Q2	**N–R2**
35 B–K1	**Q–R4**
36 B–B2	**P–N4**
37 Q–Q1	**N–B3**
38 Q–K2	....

White is just waiting for the end. That is all he can do.

38	**N–Q5**
39 B×N	**KP×B**
40 N–Q1	**B–N4**
41 Q–KB2	**P–B5**
42 P×P	**B×P**
43 R–N4	**B–Q6**
44 Q–K1	**K–N1**

44 ... R–N8; 45 Q–Q2, B–B8; 46 Q–QB2 would have given White some drawing chances, unnecessarily.

| **45 K–N1** | **R–N8** |

| **46 K–B2** | .... |

If 46 Q–Q2, Black continues with 46 ... Q–K1; 47 Q×B, Q–R5 and wins.

| 46 .... | **K–R2** |

Getting the monarch to a safe spot.

47 N–K7	**Q–K1**
48 Q–Q2	**B–QR3**
49 R×NP	**Q×N**
50 Q×BP	**R×N**
51 Q–B5ch	**K–N1**
52 Q–Q5ch	**Q–B2**
53 Q–R8ch	**K–R2**
54 Q×B	**Q–KB5**
55 R–R5ch	**K–N3**
56 R×P	**Q–K6ch**
Resigns	

Mr. Wade put up a good fight.

3

TAKING ADVANTAGE OF MISTAKES

If all chess games were played perfectly by both sides, every game would end in a draw. The fact that White makes the first move gives him a slight edge, but this initiative is not sufficient to win against perfect defense. For a chess game to end in a win, a mistake must be made by one of the players, or the loser must make more or worse mistakes than the winner.

All chess players, good and bad, know the meaning of a blunder. It is most common among average players, but even grandmasters make an occasional blunder. It occurs when one least expects it. The odd thing about it is that one usually sees the blunder right after making it. In the Candidates Tournament of 1953 I allowed Szabo the opportunity to mate me in two moves, but he overlooked it in time trouble and the game ended in a draw. Usually, however, one is a dead duck after pulling a boner like that.

Almost any good player can win a game in which his opponent makes an outright blunder. In most games, however, the mistakes are almost imperceptible. It may require several inferior moves to cause a player's position to crumble. Sometimes, on the other hand, one seemingly slight error may allow the opponent to break through with a winning attack.

The games in this chapter illustrate the technique of capitalizing on tactical and positional mistakes. These examples underline the importance of looking for weaknesses created by the opponent's moves, and then taking advantage of these weaknesses.

Falling for a trap

Sometimes it is a mistake to win material! If your opponent offers you the chance to win something for nothing, take a good look at the consequences before accepting the gift. It may be a trap. If so, swallowing the bait would be a mistake and might cost the game.

In the following contest my opponent played the opening much too cautiously and got into a bad position. On my 27th move I set a trap, giving Black the opportunity to play a Pawn fork, attacking Queen and Rook simultaneously. My opponent fell for the trap, "won" my Queen, and resigned five moves later.

SEMI-SLAV DEFENSE

Wertheim Memorial Tournament
New York, 1951

S. RESHEVSKY   G. SHAINSWIT

1 P–Q4	P–Q4
2 P–QB4	P–QB3
3 N–KB3	N–B3
4 N–B3	P–K3
5 P–K3	QN–Q2
6 Q–B2	....

An effort to avoid the complications arising out of the Meran Variation: 6 B–Q3, P×P; 7 B×BP, P–QN4; 8 B–Q3, P–QR3; 9 P–K4, P–B4, etc.

6	P–QR3

6 ... P×P; 7 B×P, P–QN4; 8 B–Q3, P–QR3; 9 P–K4, P–B4 leads to lively play for both sides.

7 P–QN3	P–QN3

Black is obviously reduced to passivity. To be considered was 7 ... P–QN4, and if 8 P–B5, Q–B2 in order to effectuate ... P–K4.

8 B–K2	B–N2
9 O–O	B–K2
10 B–N2	O–O
11 QR–Q1	....

To obtain play on the King-side, I left the King-Rook where it could be used for aggressive purposes. Otherwise I would have played 11 KR–Q1.

11	Q–B2
12 P–KR3	QR–B1

13 B–R1	....

I discarded 13 P–K4, P×KP; 14 N×P, P–B4; 15 P–Q5, P×P; 16 P×P, N×P, for White then has insufficient compensation for the Pawn.

13	B–N5

14 N–K5   **P–B4**

14 ... N×N; 15 P×N, N–Q2 (15
... Q×P?; 16 N×P); 16 P–B4
would have promoted White's aggressive intentions.

15 N×N   **N×N**

15 ... Q×N; 16 QP×P, B×P; 17
N–R4 with a big plus. White is
threatening B×N and N×B.

16 QP×P   ....

16 ....   **QP×P**

If 16 ... Q×P; 17 P–K4, N–B3 (17
... P–Q5?; 18 N–R4 winning a Pawn);
18 KP×P, P×P; 19 B–B3, KR–Q1;
20 Q–B5!

17 NP×P   ....

17 P×NP is adequately met by 17
... N×P; 18 P×P, N×P; 19 Q–N3,
P–QR4.

17 ....   **B×BP**

17 ... P×P; 18 N–K4 (threatening
N–Q6) is in White's favor. 17 ...
N×P; 18 Q–N2 (threatening N–Q5
and mate) compels Black to give up his
King-Bishop.

18 Q–N2   **N–B3**

(See top of next column.)

19 Q–N3   .....

If 19 N–R4, Q–B3; 20 B–B3, Q×N;

Position after 18 ... N–B3

21 B×B, QR–Q1 and although White
has the two Bishops, Black has sufficient
compensation in White's isolated Pawns.

19 ....   **Q–B3**

19 ... B–B3 was better.

20 B–B3   **Q–B2**
21 B×B   **Q×B**
22 N–R4   **Q–B3**
23 N×B   **Q×N**

23 P×N; 24 R–Q3 followed by
KR–Q1 is not better for Black.

24 R–B1   **P–K4**
25 P–B4   ....

25 ....   **N–K5**

If 25 ... P×P; 26 B–Q4 followed by
R×P.

26 Q–Q3   **N–N6**

Threatening ... P–K5. Black seems

to be recovering, but I had something up my sleeve.

27 R–B3!   **P–K5?**

Black fell for the trap, forking the Queen and Rook with his Pawn. Relatively best was 27 ... P×P; 28 B–Q4, Q–B3; 29 R×P, but White would then have the initiative.

28 R×N!   ....

28 Q–B3 is met by 28 ... N–B4; 29 P–N4 (29 R–N3, P–B3), P×R; 30 P×N, P–B3.

28	P×Q
29 R×Pch	K–R1
30 R×BPch	K–N1
31 R–N7ch	K–R1
32 R–N3ch	Resigns

Loss of Time

According to Tarrasch, a tempo is "the time value of a move." A player loses a tempo when he makes two moves to accomplish something that could have been done in one move, or when he moves a piece twice in the opening and thereby falls behind in development, or when he makes a meaningless or irrelevant move. In general, a move loses a tempo if it threatens nothing, gains no positional advantage, or does not meet the defensive requirements of the position on the board.

There are occasions when a player can afford to lose time, being in a much stronger position than his opponent, or when it is to his advantage to lose a tempo, but in most situations a serious loss of time may be disastrous. A tempo-losing move may be just as grave a mistake as a more obvious blunder which loses material immediately.

In this game Mr. Bisguier attempted to create a weakness on my King-side, in preparation for an attack. In forcing this weakness, however, he had to lose two very important tempi. As a result of this loss of time I was able to get my opponent into an annoying pin. After an exchange of the remaining minor pieces, White was compelled to give up a Pawn. He tried hard to get some counterplay on the Queen-side, but to no avail. I finally won another Pawn. Being confronted by a mating threat, White resigned.

SEMI-TARRASCH DEFENSE

Wertheim Memorial Tournament
New York, 1951

A. BISGUIER	S. RESHEVSKY
1 P–Q4	N–KB3
2 P–QB4	P–K3
3 N–KB3	P–Q4
4 N–B3	P–B4

Other usual moves are 4 ... B–N5,
4 ... P–B3 and 4 ... B–K2. The text-
move leads to more lively play.

5 BP×P   N×P

Best. 5 ... KP×P; 6 P–KN3 gives
White a considerable opening advantage.

6 P–K4   ....

Only with 6 P–K3, N–QB3; 7 B–Q3
or 7 B–B4 can White hope to get the
better of it. This line gives attacking
chances, so I was surprised that Mr.
Bisguier did not chose the variation.

6	N×N
7 P×N	P×P
8 P×P	B–N5ch

Quite necessary. White's Queen-
Bishop is stronger than Black's King-
Bishop. White's Bishop at QN2 would
have been strongly posted. Therefore
it was wise for Black to force the
exchange of Bishops.

9 B–Q2   B×Bch

9 ... Q–R4 would not be as good on
account of 10 R–QN1, B×Bch; 11
Q×B, Q×Qch; 12 K×Q with the
better end game, White's King position
being very favorable.

10 Q×B   O–O

(See top of next column.)

11 R–B1   ....

11 B–N5 is slightly better, for this

Position after 10 ... O–O

makes it more difficult for Black to play
... N–B3, but Black could reach
equality with 11 ... P–QN3; 12 O–O,
B–N2; 13 KR–K1, N–B3; 14 QR–B1,
R–B1, or with 11 ... N–Q2; 12 O–O,
N–B3; 13 Q–B4 (or 13 KR–K1),
P–QN3 etc.

11	N–B3
12 B–K2	....

I prefer 12 B–N5. There might have
followed 12 ... B–Q2; 13 O–O, R–B1
(13 ... N×P?; 14 B×B); 14 KR–Q1.

12 ....   Q–B3

With the purpose of provoking P–K5.

13 P–K5   ....

Forced, either now or on the next
move, for if 13 O–O, R–Q1; 14 P–K5
(not 14 KR–Q1, N×P!; 15 N×N,
P–K4).

13 ....   **Q–K2**

Black's plan of slightly weakening White's QP has been successfully carried out.

14 O–O   **R–Q1**
15 KR–Q1   **B–Q2**

16 N–N5   ....

Provoking ... P–KR3, but in doing so White loses too much time. Wiser was 16 B–Q3, N–N5; 17 B–N1, B–R5; 18 R–K1, QR–B1; 19 P–QR3, N–Q4; 20 Q–Q3, P–KN3; 21 P–N3.

Bad was 16 P–Q5, P×P; 17 Q×P, B–K3; 18 Q–K4, B×P; 19 B–Q3, P–KN3 and White has insufficient compensation for the Pawn.

16 ....   **B–K1**

It looks as though Black could win a Pawn with 16 ... N×QP but this loses as follows: 17 Q×N, Q×N; 18 P–B4!, Q–R5; 19 P–N3, Q–R6 (if 19 ... Q–K2; 20 R–B7); 20 R–B7, B–K1; 21 Q×R, R×Q; 22 R×R and wins.

17 B–Q3   **P–KR3**

Dangerous was 17 ... R×P; 18 B×Pch, K–R1; 19 Q–K3 with the eventual threat of Q–KR3. Thus, if 19 ... R×Rch; 20 R×R, P–B3; 21 Q–KR3, P×N; 22 B–N6ch, K–N1; 23 Q–R7ch, K–B1; 24 Q–R8 mate; and if, in this, 20 ... P–KN3; 21 P–B4 with the annoying threat of Q–KR3.

18 N–B3   **N–N5**

18 ... N×QP?; 19 N×N, R×N; 20 B–R7ch winning the exchange. There was no point to keeping up pressure on White's Queen-Pawn for it was amply protected. Therefore I changed my strategy. The main purpose of the text-move was to get my Bishop activated.

19 B–N1   ....

White cannot afford to give up his Bishop. Without it he has absolutely no aggressive prospects.

19 ....   **B–B3**

Threatening to cripple White's Pawn structure with ... B×N.

20 N–K1?   ....

20 Q–K3 was better, but after 20 ... N–Q4; 21 Q–Q3, P–KN3, I prefer Black's chances.

20 ....   **B–R5**

Causing White to get into an unpleasant pin, leading to the loss of a Pawn.

21 B–B2 ....

If 21 N–B2, B×N; 22 B×B, N×P; 23 R–N1, QR–B1 and if 24 B–K4?, N–B6; 25 R×P, N×B and wins.

21 .... **N×B**

White had to give up his Bishop after all.

22 N×N **QR–B1**
23 R–K1 **R–B5**

I decided to win the Pawn my way. Taking it immediately might have given White some drawing chances: 23 ... B×N; 24 R×B, R×R; 25 Q×R, R×P; 26 R–Q1 and the ending is not clearly won.

24 N–K3 ....

My opponent was compelled to give up the Pawn this way. Otherwise he would have been slowly strangled.

24 .... **R(B5)×P**
25 Q–R5 ....

25 .... **B–B3**

25 ... P–QN3 would not be as good because after 26 Q–R6 or 26 Q–B3, my Bishop could not have been posted at QB3.

26 Q×P **R–QR5**

27 Q–N6 **R×P**

Black is a Pawn ahead. In addition, he has a passed Pawn and a powerfully posted Bishop. White has no compensation for all this.

28 KR–Q1 ....

If 28 N–B4, Q–N4; 29 P–N3, R(Q1)–R1; 30 N–Q6, Q–N5, making inroads at KR6 or KB6.

28 .... **R(Q1)–Q7**
29 R×R **R×R**
30 P–R3 **Q–N4**

Black begins vigorous action aimed at the opposing King.

31 N–N4 **R–Q4**

31 ... P–R4 is met by 32 Q–K3 avoiding the loss of another Pawn. The text-move wins a Pawn by force.

32 R–B4 ....

Intending to meet 32 ... P–R4 with 33 P–B4, Q–R5; 34 N–B2 or 34 Q–B2.

Rook—but White is in for a real surprise!

32 ....   R×P

Surprise! Mr. Bisguier apparently overlooked the following continuation. However, the position was untenable.

33 P–B4   R–K8ch
34 K–B2   Q–Q4

If 34 ... Q–R5ch; 35 P–N3, Q×RP 36 K×R, Q×N; 37 Q–Q8ch, K–R2; 38 Q–Q3ch and Black is not well off.

35 R–Q4   ....

It looks as though Black had blundered and White was going to win a

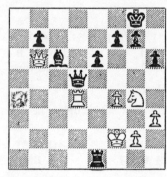

35 ....   R–QN8!
36 Q×R   ....

There is nothing better.

36 ....   Q×Rch
37 K–N3   P–R4
38 N–K5   P–R5ch
39 K×P   Q×Pch
40 N–N4   P–B4
41 P–N3   Q–Q5
42 Q–R2   Q–Q1ch
Resigns

After 43 K–R5, B–K1 is mate.

Stepping into a Pin

In this second game of my first match with Najdorf, Black chose a slightly inferior move on his 13th turn. This led to a position in which White had threats that were hard to meet. Then Najdorf, on his 21st move, made an outright blunder. He moved his Knight to a square on which it could be pinned against his Queen. It was relatively easy to take advantage of this mistake. Pinning the Knight soon won material and the game.

QUEEN'S GAMBIT ACCEPTED

Najdorf–Reshevsky Match
New York, 1952

. S. RESHEVSKY   M. NAJDORF
1 P–Q4   P–Q4

2 P–QB4	**P–QB3**
3 N–KB3	**N–B3**
4 N–B3	**P–K3**
5 P–K3	**P–QR3**
6 B–Q3	**P×P**
7 B×BP	**P–QN4**
8 B–N3	**.....**

8 B–Q3 is equally as good.

8	P–B4
9 O–O	B–N2
10 Q–K2	QN–Q2
11 R–Q1	Q–B2
12 P–K4	P×P
13 N×QP	....

13	B–Q3

If 13 ... P–N5; 14 N–Q5!, P×N; 15 P×Pch with sufficient compensation for the piece. 13 ... B–B4 is best.

14 P–N3	B–K4
15 P–B3	O–O
16 B–K3	N–B4
17 B–QB2	QR–B1
18 R–Q2	P–N5
19 N–R4	KN–Q2
20 QR–Q1	....

Black's position is suddenly becoming precarious. If Black continues with the normal 20 ... KR–Q1, there follows: 21 N×N, N×N (21 ... Q×N, 22 N×P); 22 Q–B4 and Black is faced with the problem of defending his QNP. 22 ... P–QR4 fails on account of 23 N–N5, winning a piece. 22 ... Q–N3 is bad because of 23 N–N3, R×R; 24 R×R, N×N; 25 B×Q, R×Q; 26 R–Q8 mate. The only try would have been 22 ... Q–R4. There would have followed: 23 N–K2, N–Q2; 24 Q–N3, B–QB3; 25 N–Q4 with the upper hand.

20	N×N
21 B×N	N–B4?

This gets Black into a nasty pin. The only playable move was 21 ... N–B3. If 21 ... N–N3; 22 R–B2, Q–N1; 23 N–B6, B×N; 24 B×B, B×QNP; 25 Q×P with the upper hand.

22 R–B2	B–Q3

22 ... Q–R4 fails as a defense on account of 23 R×N!, R×R; 24 N–N3, Q×B (24 ... R–B7; 25 N×Q, R×Q; 26 N×B, R×B; 27 K–B2!); 25 N×R, Q–B3; 26 N–Q7 and wins.

23 N–N3 ....

(*See diagram on next page.*)

Threatening 24 R×B. If 23 ... Q–K2; 24 N×N, B×N; 25 R–Q7 winning a piece.

23	N × B

There is no adequate defense.

24 R × Q	B × R
25 N–B5	N × N
26 B × N	KR–Q1
27 R × Rch	B × R
28 Q–Q3	P–R3
29 B–K3	B–R4
30 Q–Q7	R–B2
31 Q–R4	**Resigns**

Time Pressure

Time pressure is something that every chess expert has had the displeasure of getting into at one time or another. Even grandmasters like Alekhine, Botvinnik, Fine and others are no exceptions. The two principal reasons for time trouble are complicated positions and the desire to find the perfect move in every position.

Years ago I used to get into terrific time pressure quite often. Some chess critics claimed that I deliberately got myself short of time to induce my opponents to move rapidly. The real explanation, however, was the fact that I had acquired that bad habit during the period when my knowledge of the openings was limited. This had necessitated my spending excessive time in search of the correct moves in the openings.

To get short of time occasionally is unavoidable and even necessary, but to get into it often is inexcusable and fatal. It is one of the commonest causes of blunders.

In the fifth game of my match against Arthur Bisguier time pressure was the deciding factor. I had worked up such an excellent position that it took two blunders (my 28th and 35th moves) to throw away the win, then one deafening blunder (my 37th move) to lose the game.

NIMZO–INDIAN DEFENSE

Bisguier–Reshevsky Match
New York, 1957

S. RESHEVSKY   A. BISGUIER

1 P–Q4	N–KB3
2 P–QB4	P–K3
3 N–QB3	B–N5
4 P–K3	P–QN3

This defense has recently been adopted by Smyslov and Keres. It is easier for Black to achieve equality with the normal continuation than with this setup.

5 N–K2   ....

If 5 B–Q3, B–N2; 6 N–B3, O–O; 7 O–O, P–B4 with no advantage for either side.

5 ....   **B–R3**

The main idea being to exert pressure on the QBP and to trade this Bishop for White's KB if possible.

6 P–QR3   **B–K2**

Better than 6 ... B×Nch; 7 N×B, P–Q4; 8 P–QN3 in which Black has no compensation for White's two Bishops.

7 N–B4   ....

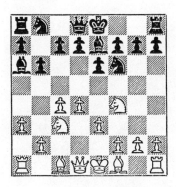

7 ....   **O–O**

7 ... P–Q4 is better. It has been proven that sacrificing a piece is unsound for White: 8 P×P, B×B; 9 P×P, B–R3; 10 P×Pch, K×P. If necessary, Black can give back a piece for two Pawns and emerge with the superior position. Consequently, White's best reply against 7 ... P–Q4 is 8 P–QN3.

8 P–K4   ....

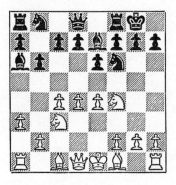

White now has established a strong center threatening to stifle the mobility of Black's pieces.

8 ....   **P–Q3**

Comparatively best. If 8 ... P–B4; 9 P–Q5, P×P (9 ... P–K4; 10 N–R3); 10 BP×P, B×B; 11 K×B with the better prospects. Or if 8 ... P–Q4; 9 BP×P, B×B; 10 K×B, P×P; 11 P–K5 wins Black's Queen-Pawn.

9 B–K2   **QN–Q2**
10 O–O   **P–B3**

10 ... P–K4; 11 P×P, N×P; 12 P–QN3 does not give Black's pieces more freedom.

11 P–Q5   **BP×P**
12 BP×P   **B×B**
13 Q×B   **P–K4**
14 N–Q3   ....

White is now threatening to get his Knight to QB6 via QN4. The only way to prevent this is to play 14 ... P–QR4, but after 15 P–QN4 Black is practically forced to play P×P (otherwise his pieces become completely immobilized because QB4 cannot be occupied) and after 16 N×NP White again achieves his objective of getting his Knight to QB6.

14 ....   **N–B4**
15 N–N4   **N–N6**
16 N–B6   **Q–Q2**

17 R–N1	N–QR4

To dislodge White's Knight is necessary at all cost.

18 N×Bch   ....

By playing N×N White could give Black a doubled Pawn but in itself this is not too significant. The text-move is better because it gives Black some concern about his misplaced Knight at his R4.

18	Q×N
19 P–QN3	KR–B1
20 B–Q2	P–QR3

Intending ... P–QN4.

21 N–R4	Q–Q1

Better than 21 ... Q–N2; 22 B–N4, N–K1; 23 Q–K3, QR–N1; 24 N×P etc. winning a Pawn.

22 B×N	....

There is nothing better. 22 Q–K3, P–QN4; 23 N–N6, N–N5; 24 Q–N3, Q×N; 25 Q×N, N–N2; 26 B–R6, P–N3 leads to nothing tangible for White. If 22 B–K3, N–Q2 followed by ... P–QN4 with a good position.

22	P×B
23 KR–B1	QR–N1
24 R–B6	....

24 Q×P, N×KP improves Black's position.

24	R×R

Forced. Otherwise comes 25 R×RP.

25 P×R	Q–B2
26 Q–B4	R–QB1
27 R–QB1	Q–R2

28 P–R3?	....

The first blunder. 28 N–B3! with the intention of playing N–Q5 would have made Black's task of holding on almost impossible. I was under the wrong impression that I would be able to get my Knight to Q5 any time I desired to do so.

28	K–B1

Now 29 N–B3 is bad because of 29 ... Q–B4; 30 N–Q5, simply R×P. With the King at N1, 30 ... R×P could not have been played on account of 31 N–K7ch.

29 P–N3	R–B2
30 R–Q1	....

To prevent 30 ... Q–Q5.

30	N–K1
31 K–B1	Q–N1
32 R–B1	N–B3

32 ... Q–N4; 33 Q×Q, P×Q; 34 N–N6, followed by N–Q5 is bad for Black.

33 K–N2 ....

On 33 N–B3, intending N–Q5, Black plays 33 ... Q–B1 attacking two Pawns.

| 33 .... | Q–N4 |
| 34 K–B3 | P–Q4 |

The only way to freedom.

35 P×P? ....

White misses his last chance to play for a win. Correct was 35 Q–B5ch, Q×Q; 36 N×Q with much the better ending, for Black cannot capture the QBP because of N–Q7ch winning the exchange.

If, after 35 Q–B5ch, Black plays 35 ... K–K1, then 36 Q–Q6 and Black is in trouble. For if 36 ... Q×Pch; 37 K–N2, R–B1; 38 Q×Pch, K–B1; 39 N–B5 with the unpleasant threat of N–Q7ch. And if 36 ... P×Pch; 37 K–N2, R–B1; 38 R–B5 followed by R×Pch.

| 35 .... | N×P |
| 36 Q–B5ch | .... |

36 Q×Q, P×Q; 37 N–B5, K–K2; 38 K–K4 gives White better chances.

| 36 .... | K–K1 |
| 37 Q–Q6?? | .... |

A real time-pressure blunder. With 37 Q×Q, P×Q; 38 N–N2 White could still have held his own.

| 37 .... | Q–Q6ch |
| **Resigns** | |

After the King moves, a Knight check wins White's Queen.

A Rook on the Seventh

William Lombardy is one of the most promising young American masters. In his match against me he proved he possesses qualities that may carry him far in the chess world. He is calm, confident, has a sufficiently good theoretical background, and, perhaps most important of all, he does not get discouraged easily.

In our match, the first five games, although ending in draws, were well fought and interesting throughout. In the sixth and last game I was finally able to score a point. The opening proceeded normally up to White's 11th move. Instead of castling, I played 11 P–N5, immediately presenting Black with the problem of how to avoid a deterioration of his Queen-side Pawn position. Black decided to remain with a QP weakness. On his 16th, Lombardy made an inferior move and I was able to build up a strong position, eventually placing a Rook on the 7th rank. His pieces badly bottled up, my opponent went into a faulty combination.

NIMZO-INDIAN DEFENSE

Lombardy–Reshevsky Match
New York, 1957

S. RESHEVSKY	W. LOMBARDY
1 P–QB4	N–KB3
2 P–Q4	P–K3
3 N–QB3	B–N5
4 P–K3	O–O
5 N–K2	P–Q4
6 P–QR3	B–K2
7 P×P	....

The only move that promises White an opening initiative. If 7 N–B4, P–B3; 8 P×P, BP×P; 9 B–K2, N–B3; 10 O–O, P–QN3 with complete equality.

| 7 .... | P×P |

7 ... N×P is also playable.

| 8 P–QN4 | .... |

To prevent ... P–QB4.

| 8 .... | R–K1 |
| 9 N–N3 | .... |

9 N–B4 is a good alternative.

9	QN–Q2
10 B–Q3	P–B3
11 P–N5	....

Otherwise Black would obtain active play on the Queen-side with 11 ... P–QN4 followed by N–N3–B5.

| 11 .... | P–B4 |
| 12 O–O | P–QN3 |

| 13 B–Q2 | B–B1 |
| 14 P–QR4 | P–QR4 |

Wisely preventing P–R5.

| 15 P×P e.p. | B×P |

| 16 N–N5 | .... |

Since White's KB is more active than Black's QB, it would have been disadvantageous for White to have exchanged Bishops.

| 16 .... | N–K5 |

A natural looking move which turns out badly. 16 ... P–N3 followed by B–KN2 was more promising.

17 N×N	P×N
18 B–B4	Q–R5
19 Q–N3	....

19 N–B7 fails because of 19 ... B–Q3 threatening mate and the capture of the Knight.

| 19 .... | Q–R4 |

20 P–R3 . . . .

Threatening N–B7.

20 . . . . **QR–B1**
21 KR–B1 . . . .

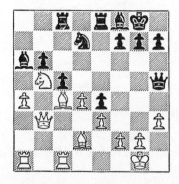

It is becoming increasingly clear that Black's pieces are not working harmoniously. Black's Queen is out of place; his Bishops are practically inactivated and his Knight is awkwardly placed. White's pieces, on the other hand, enjoy freedom and scope. White's control of the QR file cannot be denied.

21 . . . . **R–B3**
22 B–K1 . . . .

Serving a double purpose—protecting the KBP and freeing the Q-file for the Rook.

22 . . . . **R–Q1**

23 R–Q1 . . . .
6

23 B–Q5 does not win a Pawn because of 23 ... B×N; 24 P×B, R–Q3; 25 B×KP, P×P; 26 B–N4, N–B4 and Black's game has improved considerably. The text-move is a bid for the control of the vital Q-file.

23 . . . . **B×N**

Handing over control of the Rook-file but removal of the Knight was eventually unavoidable.

24 P×B **R–Q3**
25 R–R7 . . . .

25 . . . . **N–K4**

This turns out disastrously but Black is badly tied up anyway.

26 P×N **Q×R**

26 ... R×R is out of the question because of 27 B×Pch.

27 P×R **Q×Bch**
28 B–B1 . . . .

My opponent must have overlooked
the seriousness of his position after this
move.

28	K–R1
29 Q×P	Q–Q8
30 P–Q7	Q–Q3

31 P–N3   ....

If 31 Q–K8 (a plausible-looking
move), Q–N1! and wins. For if 32
Q×P, Q×R; 33 B–Q3, Q–R8ch;
followed by ... P–N3 and wins.

31	P–R3
32 B–B4	K–R2
33 Q–K8	....

33 ....   **B–K2**

There is nothing better. For if 33
... Q–K2; 34 R–R8, R×P; 35 Q×B.
If 33 ... Q–KB3; 34 R–R8, B–K2; 35
R×R, B×R; 36 B–N8ch, K–R1; 37
B–B7ch, K–R2; 38 Q–N8 mate. And
finally, if 33 ... Q–N1; 34 Q×Pch,
K–R1; 35 R–N7, Q–Q3; 36 Q–K8
and Black is defenseless.

34 B–N8ch	K–R1
35 B–Q5ch	Resigns

For if 35 ... K–R2; 36 B×Pch,
P–N3; 37 Q–B7ch, K–R1; 38 B×P.

An Unpleasant Position

Occasionally even the best players emerge from the opening with an
inferior game. It is too much to expect from anyone always to obtain
satisfactory results from experimental variations. Even the Russian
experts, who devote great attention and time to the analysis of the openings,
sometimes get themselves into awkward positions.

Do not give up when you get into a bad position. Keep calm and play
with confidence. Your opponent may make the common mistake of
relaxing when he has the upper hand. He may blunder and give you the
opportunity to win. This is what happened to me in the following game
against Arthur Bisguier. I played a variation of the Sicilian Defense with
which the Russians have experimented recently. My opponent, playing
with precision, had a distinct advantage after 12 moves. My position
being unpleasantly cramped, I decided to sit and wait for developments.

My patience was rewarded when on move 18 Bisguier plunged into a risky continuation. Then on move 22, in his anxiety to win a Pawn, White overlooked a winning reply.

SICILIAN DEFENSE

Rosenwald Tournament
New York, 1957–58

A. BISGUIER   S. RESHEVSKY

| 1 P–K4 | P–QB4 |
| 2 N–KB3 | P–K3 |

I decided to experiment with this revived variation. The Russian masters have obtained satisfactory results with it in the last year or so. My favorite in the past has been the Dragon Variation starting with 2 ... P–Q3.

| 3 P–Q4 | P×P |
| 4 N×P | P–QR3 |

Allowing White to get a bind on the center by playing 5 P–QB4 if he wishes.

| 5 N–QB3 | Q–B2 |

With the possibility of ... B–N5 and at the same time preventing White from playing P–K5.

6 B–Q3	N–QB3
7 N×N	NP×N
8 O–O	....

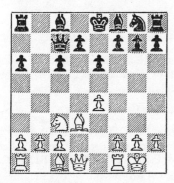

White handled the opening with logical simplicity. His pieces are better developed. He undoubtedly has the better prospects.

| 8 .... | N–B3 |
| 9 Q–K2 | P–Q3 |

I decided on passive strategy. However, 9 ... P–Q4 was better, for if 10 P–K5, N–Q2; 11 P–B4, P–QB4 with good counterplay. What I did not like too much was 10 B–N5 threatening to win a Pawn with 11 B×N followed by P×P, etc. But after 10 ... B–K2; 11 B×N, P×B, Black has a promising position despite the fact that he has the problem of castling satisfactorily.

| 10 P–B4 | .... |

| 10 .... | N–Q2 |

Preventing P–K5, On 10 ... B–K2 White proceeds with 11 P–K5 and Black has three possible replies. If 11 ... P×P; 12 P×P, N–Q2; 13 B–KB4, N–B4; 14 Q–N4 with good attacking chances. Neither is 11 ... N–Q2 very promising on account of 12 P×P, B×P; 13 N–K4, B–K2; 14 P–B5! and Black is in trouble. Finally, if 11 ... N–Q4; 12 N–K4, P×P; 13 P×P, Q×P; 14 P–B4, N–N5; 15 B–N1 (threatening to win a piece with P–QR3), P–QR4; 16 B–B4 with excellent attacking possibilities.

| 11 B–K3 | B–K2 |
| 12 R–B3 | .... |

Preparing an onslaught against the King if Black should dare to castle on the King-side.

12 ....   **R–QN1**
13 N–R4   ....

13 P–QN3 is answered by 13 ... B–B3.

13 ....   **B–B3**
14 R–N1   **P–QR4**

14 ... Q–R4 is met by 15 P–QN3.

15 P–B4   ....

Preventing an eventual ... P–Q4 which would free Black's position considerably.

15 ....   **B–R3**

The logical place for this Bishop. The only other useful square would be QN2, but to get any use out of the Bishop there, ... P–QB4 would be necessary. In that event White would have an excellent square for his Knight at his QN5.

16 R–QB1   **P–R4**

An admission that Black has given up hope of castling.

17 R(B3)–B1   **B–K2**

(See top of next column.)

18 B–Q4?   ....

Position after 17 ... B–K2

Ignoring Black's plan. Correct was 18 K–R1 followed by B–Q2–B3.

18 ....   **P–K4**
19 B–B3   ....

19 P×P, N×P would have given Black a strong bind in the center.

19 ....   **P×P**

Unquestionably risky but I decided that the complications involved offered some chances of success for me.

20 B×P   ....

Better than 20 R–N1 (20 R×P?, B–N4 winning the exchange), N–K4; 21 R×P, B–N4; 22 R(B4)–B1, R–R3 with good prospects.

20 ....   **R–R2**

Also playable was 20 .... R–N1; 21 B–R6, N–K4; 22 B×P, B–N4.

21 B–B3	N–K4

22 B–Q2?   . . . .

Too anxious to win a Pawn. White apparently overlooked Black's rejoinder. Relatively best was 22 P–QN3, B–QB1; 23 B–N1, B–N5; 24 Q–Q2, P–B6 with interesting complications.

22	Q–R2ch
23 K–R1	Q–Q5

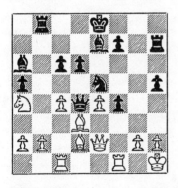

24 R–KB3   . . . .

White must lose the exchange. If 24 R–QB3, N×B; 25 R×N, Q×BP. Equally bad is 24 B–N1, B×P; 25 Q–B2, Q×Q; 26 R×Q, B–QN4; 27 N–B3, B–KR5; 28 R×P, B–N4; 29 R–B2, N–N5 and wins.

24	N×R
25 Q×N	R–R3

White was seriously threatening to open lines with 26 P–K5.

26 B×BP	R–B3

With the exchange to the good, Black should encounter no serious difficulties from here on.

27 P–KN3   . . . .

Parrying the threat of 27 . . . R×B followed by Q×B.

27 . . . .   B–QB1

Placing the Bishop on a useful diagonal.

28 K–N2	B–N5
29 Q–B1	P–R5
30 P–N3	P×P
31 P×P	K–Q2

To get the QR into active play.

32 B–K2	B×B
33 Q×B	R×B!

Forceful and irrefutable.

34 P×R	R–N1ch
35 K–B3	....

If 35 K–R1, R–R1ch; 36 K–N2, Q–N2ch; 37 K–B3, R–R6ch; 38 K–B2, Q–N6ch; 39 K–B1, R–R8 mate.

35	B–R5
Resigns	

See final position at right.

Mate cannot be avoided. If 36 Q–R2, Q–Q6 mate. If 36 Q–Q1, R–N6ch; 37 K–K2, Q–K6ch; 38

K–B1, R–N8 mate. If 36 Q–B1, R–N6 ch; 37 K–K2, R–K6 mate.

What does he Threaten?

Putting or leaving a piece *en prise* is the kind of blunder that is made often by beginners, and occasionally by masters, but there are other kinds of blunders. For instance, when your opponent makes a move you should always examine the move carefully and ask yourself, "What does he threaten?" Failure to do so may result in making a reply which can be classed as a blunder because it does not meet your opponent's threats.

In the following game, my opponent seemed to be holding his own up to the 25th move, but on the 26th it suddenly became apparent that his position was hopelessly lost. Where did he go wrong? Did he blunder? Of course, he did not put a piece *en prise* but he made the fatal mistake of not examining my threats thoroughly. When he made his 22nd move he apparently did not see that White was threatening to win at least a Pawn. Three moves later Black could not avoid the loss of a Pawn, but again he did not visualize White's more serious threats. His 25th move was a real blunder, allowing mate or win of the Queen.

RETI OPENING

Rosenwald Tournament
New York, 1957–58

S. RESHEVSKY   A. FEUERSTEIN

1 N–KB3	N–KB3
2 P–KN3	P–KN3
3 P–QN3	....

The double fianchetto is not too popular.

3	B–N2
4 B–QN2	O–O
5 B–N2	P–Q3
6 P–Q4	P–QR4

6 ... QN–Q2 is more usual. But the text-move has a point: to provoke P–QR4, enabling Black's Knight to occupy more easily his QN5 square.

| 7 P–QR4 | .... |

Otherwise 7 ... P–QR5.

7	N–B3
8 O–O	P–K4
9 P×P	N–KN5
10 N–R3	N(5)×KP
11 N×N	N×N
12 K–R1	R–K1

The position is approximately even. White has slightly better development.

13 N–N5	Q–K2
14 P–KB4	....

This Knight must be dislodged if White is to hope for any progress.

| 14 .... | N–B3 |

If 14 ... N–N5; 15 B×B, K×B; 16 P–K4 and 16 ... N–K6 is impossible because of 17 Q–Q4ch.

15 B×B	K×B
16 P–K4	P–B4
17 R–K1	Q–B2
18 Q–Q2	P×P
19 B×P	B–K3

To have been considered was 19 ... B–B4; 20 B–Q5, Q–Q2; 21 Q–B3ch, K–R3, and although Black's King seems to be in a dangerous position, there is no immediate threat.

| 20 P–B4 | .... |

Preventing ... P–Q4.

20	QR–N1
21 R–K3	N–N5

Threatening ... P–Q4 again.

| 22 N–B3 | B–B4? |

Black was apparently oblivious to White's threats. 22 ... P–QN3; 23 QR–K1, B–Q2 was better.

23 QR–K1	B–Q2
24 N–Q5	N×N
25 B×N	B–B3??

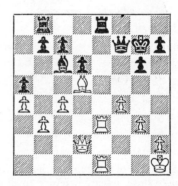

If 25 ... Q–B3 White wins a Pawn with 26 Q×P. After the text-move Black was expecting 26 B×B, P×B; 27 Q×P, R×R; 28 R×R, R–K1; 29 R×R, Q×R; 30 Q×Pch, K–R3 with a chance for perpetual check—but ...

| 26 Q–Q4ch | Resigns |

An unexpected finish. If 26 ... K–B1; 27 Q–R8ch followed by mate. If 26 ... Q–B3; 27 R–K7ch winning the Queen. If 26 ... K–R3; 27 P–KN4 threatening R–R3 mate.

No Luck in Chess?

Unlike most other games, chess is not supposed to be affected by luck. The two contestants are dealt the same number and kind of pieces and Pawns, and there is no partner to blame for bad moves. But a player may win a game he deserved to lose or draw if his opponent blunders in a winning or drawing position. Is this luck? Perhaps not, but the kibitzers will not fail to tell the winner that he was lucky.

The following game is not presented as an example of perfect play on the winner's part. On more than one occasion I failed to make the best move. My 25th was certainly questionable because it gave White the opportunity to equalize. It was "lucky" for my opponent that I did not make the right move, but he immediately returned the compliment and presented me with the game by failing to make the simple, drawing move. Again, on his 29th move, White made it easy for me. In time trouble he allowed a quick win instead of the long drawn-out winning battle that might have ensued.

SICILIAN DEFENSE

Israeli International Tournament
Tel Aviv, 1958

S. BURSTEIN   S. RESHEVSKY

1 P–K4	P–QB4
2 N–KB3	P–Q3
3 P–Q4	P×P
4 N×P	N–KB3
5 N–QB3	P–QR3
6 B–K2	P–K4
7 N–B3	....

Some are of the opinion that 7 N–N3 gives White a better chance to obtain an opening advantage.

7	B–K2
8 O–O	O–O
9 B–KN5	....

9 B–K3 is more usual.

9	QN–Q2
10 Q–Q2	P–R3
11 B–K3	....

11 B–R4 would be more consistent with White's 9th move.

11	P–QN4

12 QR–Q1	P–N5
13 N–Q5	....

If 13 N–QR4, P–QR4; 14 B–Q3, B–N2 wins a Pawn.

13	N×N

14 Q×N	....

If 14 P×N, P–QR4 followed by ... P–KB4 with the nasty threat of ... P–B5.

14	R–N1
15 N–Q2	B–N2
16 Q–N3	N–B3
17 P–KB4	....

Possible was 17 Q×NP, B×P; 18
Q–R4, B–N2 with equal chances.

17 ....   **Q–B2**

17 ... P×P; 18 B×BP, N×P; 19
N×N, B×N; 10 Q–N3 leads to very
little for Black. I chose to keep the
position fluid.

18 P×P   **P×P**
19 B–QB4   **N–N5**

My opponent admitted that this
move never occurred to him.

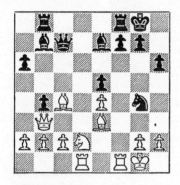

20 R×P   ....

Best. After 20 B×Pch, K–R1; 21
K–R1 (what else?), N×B; 22 Q×N,
B–N4; 23 Q–QN3, QR–Q1 Black wins
a piece, for if 24 B–Q5, B×N; 25
R×B?, R×R mate.

20 ....   **R×R**
21 B×Rch   **K–R1**
22 N–B1   ....

The only possibility.

22 ....   **B–B4**
23 B–Q5   **Q–N3**
24 R–K1   **B×B(Q4)**
25 P×B   **P–K5?**

Allowing White to equalize. 25 ...
N×B; 26 N×N, P–K5 was much
better.

26 P–KR3?   ....

Up to now, White put up stiff resistance in a precarious position, but now
he slips. Indicated was 26 B×B,
Q×Bch; 27 N–K3 with an even game.

26 ....   **N×B**
27 N×N   **Q–N3**

27 ... R–KB1 was even stronger.

28 Q–B4   ....

White's position is critical. If 28
K–R2, B–Q3ch; 29 K–N1, Q–N6; 30
R–K2 (30 R–KB1, B–B4), Q–R7ch; 31
K–B1 (31 K–B2, B–N6ch), Q–R8ch;
32 K–B2, R–B1ch.

If 28 K–R1, Q–N6; 29 R–K2,
R–KB1 threatening ... B×N followed
by ... R–B8ch.

If 28 P–N4, R–KB1; 29 K–N2,
R–B6 with a fatal pin.

28	Q–N6
29 Q–K2	....

29 Q×B, Q×Rch; 30 K–R2 was, of course, much better, but Black would have won after a long struggle. The text-move loses immediately. My opponent was in terrific time trouble at this point.

29	R–KB1
30 K–R1	B×N
Resigns	

After 31 Q×B, R–B8ch wins.

The Danger of Complacency

R. Blumenfeld, one of the young Israeli prospects, is ambitious, enterprising, and fearless. He likes a fighting type of game, avoiding drawing positions. His aggressive style is dangerous for any opponent.

In this game I turned Mr. Blumenfeld's English Opening into the King's Indian Defense. He chose a line which requires exact and fine play by Black to acquire equality. On his eighth turn White made a dubious move, P–K4, relinquishing control of his Q4 square. This gave me a distinct positional advantage but I became too complacent. Instead of following up vigorously I made one or two slightly inaccurate moves. After 21 moves the position was even and the game should have ended in a draw. But on his 24th turn White made the mistake of trying to complicate the position instead of continuing conservatively. Then White's inferior 25th move gave me the opportunity to attack. Getting into a nasty pin, White's position became precarious. Being faced with the loss of a Pawn and the exchange, my opponent tried to get a perpetual check. This attempt was easily thwarted.

KING'S INDIAN DEFENSE

Israeli International Tournament
Tel Aviv, 1958

R. BLUMENFELD	S. RESHEVSKY
1 P–QB4	P–KN3

There is no disadvantage to this move. The only drawback, if any, is Black's early declaration of intending to play the King's Indian Defense.

2 P–KN3	B–N2
3 B–N2	P–QB4
4 N–KB3	N–QB3
5 N–B3	P–QR3
6 P–QR3	R–N1

Intending 7 ... P–QN4.

7 R–QN1	P–Q3

I rejected 7 ... P–QN4; 8 P×P, P×P; 9 P–QN4, P×P (9 ... P–B5; 10 P–QR4! with the better prospects because Black's QRP would become undefended); 10 P×P, because I wanted to discontinue the symmetry.

8 P–K4?	....

Unnecessarily creating a weakness at his Q4 square. Wiser was 8 P–Q3, N–B3; 9 O–O, O–O; 10 P–QN4.

8	N–B3
9 O–O	O–O
10 P–QN4	B–N5

With the obvious intention of occupying Q5 with the Knight.

11 P–KR3   **B×N**

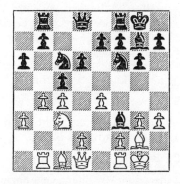

12 B×B   ....

12 Q×B gets White into difficulties as follows: 12 ... P×P; 13 P×P, R–B1 (threatening to win a Pawn with ... N–K4); 14 P–Q3, P–QN4, again threatening ... N–K4, and if 15 P×P?, N–K4 wins a piece.

12 ....   **N–Q2**

White has to proceed cautiously. 13 P–N5, for instance, loses a Pawn after 13 ... N–R4; 14 B–K2, N–N3.

13 B–K2   ....

This saves the Pawn but takes the Bishop away from its normal location at KN2.

13 ....   **N–Q5**

The well-posted Knight is more than sufficient compensation for the two Bishops.

14 B–N2   **P–K3**

Preventing N–Q5. Also giving more space for the black Queen. Black definitely stands better.

15 R–K1   ....

Apparently wanting to play B–KB1–KN2.

15 ....   **P–B4**

With the serious threat of ... P–B5 with rapid exposure of White's King.

16 KP×P   ....

16 P–B4 is ineffective because of 16 ... P–K4; 17 BP×P, B×P.

16 ....   **NP×P**
17 P×P   **P–B5**
18 N–K4   ....

18 BP×P?, P×P; 19 P×P, Q–N3!; 20 K–N2, Q–B3ch; 21 K–N1, N–K4 with the fatal threat of ... N–B6ch. 18 P–N4 loses to 18 ... Q–R5.

18 ....   **N×P**

18 ... P–B6; 19 B–KB1 leads to very little for Black. However, 18 ... QP×P was very promising, giving White the problem of finding an adequate defense against ... N–K4–B6ch, etc.

19 N×N   **P×P**

Hoping White would try to retain the piece. I would have had sufficient compensation for the piece after 20 N–K4, P×Pch; 31 N×P, Q–R5 (also 21 ... Q–N4ch; 22 B–N4, P–KR4 was a promising possibility); 22 N–R1!, Q×RP; 23 B–KB1, Q–R5 with fine attacking chances.

20 P×P   ....

Wisely refusing the gift.

20 ....   **P×N**
21 K–N2   ....

My opponent so far has defended staunchly. Due to my slight inaccuracies, he has emerged with an approximately even position. Had my opponent proceeded cautiously and conservatively from here on, the just result would have been a draw.

21 ....   **Q–N4**
22 B–N4   **QR–Q1**

23 P–Q3   ....

Naturally, 23 B×Pch, N×B; 24 R×N, R×Pch loses for White. 23 B–QB3 is also bad on account of 23 ... N–B4! (threatening ... B×B); 24 B–QR5 (the only plausible defense), R–Q6 and White is in real trouble.

23 ....   **K–R1**

Getting out of the check after White captures the KP with his Bishop.

24 B–B1   ....

At this point Mr. Blumenfeld apparently overestimated his position. He must have overrated the strength of his two Bishops. Consequently, he abandons the idea of giving up his QB for the Knight and the resulting drawish position of Bishops of opposite colors.

The sound and correct continuation was 24 B–QB3 followed by Q–Q2 and then R–KB1.

24 ....   **Q–K2**
25 Q–Q2?   ....

25 B–K3 was necessary.

25 ....   **P–N4**

White is beginning to have problems because of his 25th indifferent move. For instance: 26 P×P, P×P; 27 B–N2 (relatively best), Q–N2ch; 28 K–R2 (28 R–K4, P–B5; 29 B×N, R×B), P–B5 with the threat of N–B6ch or N–N6 which is difficult to meet.

26 Q–N5	Q–N2ch
27 R–K4	....

The only move. 27 K–N1 loses after 27 ... N–B7; 28 R–K4 (... B–Q5ch was the threat, with mate to follow), R × P and White is hopelessly lost. 27 K–R2 leads to mate: 27 ... R–B7ch; 28 K–N1, Q–N7 mate.

27	N–B4

The dual threat of ... R × P and ... N–Q3 winning the exchange is impossible to meet.

28 B–N2	....

If 28 B–B3, R × P; 29 R–B4, R × B; 30 R × R, N–Q5 or N–R5ch wins. If 28 Q–Q2, N–Q3; 29 B–B3, R × B; 30 K × R, N × R.

28	B × B
29 R × B	R × P
30 R–K2	....

30	N × P

30 ... R × Pch is tempting but treacherous, e.g., 31 K–R2, Q–QB2; 32 Q–B4!, Q × Q; 33 R × Q and Black is in difficulties; and if 31 ... R × QRP; 32 B × N, R × B (32 ... P × B; 33 R–K7 and Black is forced to take the perpetual check: 33 ... Q–N1ch; 34 R(K2)–K5, R–R7ch; 35 K–R1, R–R8ch; 36 K–R2, R–R7ch, etc.); 33 Q–Q8ch, K–N2; 34 R–N2ch, K–B2; 35 Q–N8ch and wins.

31 Q × P	....

The only move that offered any hope was 31 Q–K5ch. There would have followed: 31 ... Q–N2; 32 Q × Qch, K × Q; 33 R(K2)–K3 (33 R(K4)–K3 loses because of 33 ... N × R; 34 R × R, N–B5ch), N × R; 34 R × R, P × P; 35 R–K3, R–B5; 36 B × P, and although Black should win he must continue cautiously.

31	R–B2

31 ... Q–N2 would also have been adequate. White had to lose the exchange.

32 Q–K5ch	R–N2
33 Q × KP	....

This loses immediately but there was no promising continuation. White had to get out of the pin with 33 K–R2, N × R(K7); 34 R × N (34 B × N, R–K6!; 35 R × R, Q–N7 mate), Q–QB2; 35 Q × Q, R × Q; 36 P × P, P × P; 37 B × P, R × QRP and wins.

33	N×R(K7)
34 Q–K8ch	R–N1
35 Q–K5ch	Q–N2
36 Q×Qch	....

This loses a piece, but after 36 R × N, Q×Q; 37 R×Q, P×P there is no hope either.

36	R×Q
37 R×N	P–KR4
Resigns	

The Temptation of a Pawn

Winning a Pawn is usually enough to win a game between two good players. It is understandable, therefore, that a player is often tempted to grab a Pawn when the opportunity arises. But this can be a serious mistake if the gain in material is more than offset by positional disadvantages. In the opening, Pawn-grabbing at the expense of development is a violation of principles. In the later stages, the win of a Pawn in some positions can result in the loss of a won game. Great self-restraint and self-control are necessary in such tempting situations.

In the following game, my opponent chose the King's Indian Defense and gained approximate equality. Then Black played a weak 15th move which gave White a distinct advantage. On the 21st move I could have chosen a normal continuation which would have retained my superior position. Instead, I made the mistake of playing to win a Pawn. As a result, my King's position became unsafe and my opponent's pieces were given greater mobility. Positionally, I lost more than I gained in material.

Fortunately, Black was not able to take full advantage of my mistake. After a long struggle I again built up a strong position against my opponent's attempts to force a draw. On his 42nd turn, in order to avoid the exchange of Queens, Black sacrificed the exchange. The resulting ending was theoretically won for me, but my opponent held out tenaciously until the 60th move.

KING'S INDIAN DEFENSE

Israeli International Tournament
Tel Aviv, 1958

S. RESHEVSKY   A. ROSENBERG

1 P–Q4	N–KB3
2 P–QB4	P–KN3
3 P–KN3	B–N2
4 B–N2	P–Q3
5 N–KB3	QN–Q2

More precise is 5 ... O–O retaining the option of playing other lines, such as 6 ... P–B4 or 6 ... N–B3.

6 O–O	O–O
7 Q–B2	....

In order to answer 7 ... P–K4 with 8 R–Q1.

7	P–B3
8 P–K4	P–K4
9 N–B3	R–K1
10 P–KR3	....

This is the normal line of this variation. It is usually continued: 10 ... P×P; 11 N×P, P–QR4; 12 B–K3, N–B4, etc. White has the better chances.

10	Q–B2

This is a less committing move than 10 ... P×P. Another move that has been experimented with is 10 ... Q–K2, but with little success.

11 B–K3	N–B1
12 KR–Q1	....

It is difficult to say at this point whether 12 QR–Q1 is preferable. I thought that the action would be mainly concentrated on the Queen-side. Therefore I kept the QR on that side.

12	N–R4

Intending an eventual ... P–KB4.

13 P–B5	....

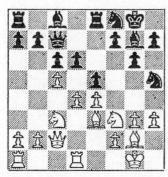

13	KP×P

If 13 ... QP×P; 14 P×KP! (threatening the win of a piece with 14 P–KN4); B×KP; 15 N×B, Q×N;

16 P–B4, Q–B2; 17 Q–B2, P–N3; 18 P–K5 with an excellent position.

14 P×P	Q×P
15 B×P	Q–K2?

Better was 15 ... B×B; 16 R×B, Q–K2. The gaining of the tempo with the Rook would have been insignificant. The move played allowed White to cut off Black's KB from active play.

16 P–K5	B–K3
17 N–K2	....

Threatening 18 P–KN4.

17	B–R3
18 B–B5	Q–B2
19 B–Q6	....

The Bishop is now excellently posted, hindering the mobility of Black's Rooks.

19	Q–B1
20 K–R2	N–Q2

White's position is much superior. His pieces are, by far, better posted.

21 P–KN4?   ....

I decided to win a Pawn. In doing so, I allowed my opponent's pieces too much freedom, and also exposed my King-position. The logical, positional continuation was 21 N(B3) followed by N–Q4.

21	N–B5

The only move. 21 ... N–N2 loses a piece after 22 P–N5.

22 Q–Q2   P–KN4

Forced, for if 22 ... N×N; 23 Q×B followed by N–N5, winning.

23 N×N   P×N
24 P–N5   B–N2
25 Q×P   N–N3
26 B–B1   N–Q4

The Knight is well posted here.

27 Q–KR4   B–B4
28 R–K1   N–K2

29 B–B4   ....

Tempting but ineffective is 29 B×N, R×B; 30 P–N6, Q–K3; 31 Q×Pch, K–B1 and Black regains his Pawn with an improved position.

29 ....   N–N3
30 Q–N3   ....

White is a Pawn ahead but it is still very difficult to make progress. The main reason is the fact that White's King position is unsafe.

30 ....   B–K3
31 B–Q3   ....

To exchange Bishops would free Black's Queen from its inactivity.

31 ....   B–B4

Black is, of course, content to repeat moves.

32 B–B1   N–K2
33 P–KR4   B–K3

34 Q–B4   ....

If 34 P–R5, N–B4; 35 Q–B4, N×B; 36 P×N, B×NP; 37 QR–N1, B–R1 and Black would have improved his chances considerably.

34 ....   N–Q4
35 Q–Q4   B–N5

Black's tactics are to keep White busy defending his pieces.

36 Q–K4   B–B4
37 Q–Q4   B–N5
38 K–N3   ....

The King is also a piece!

38 ....   B×N
39 K×B   Q–B4ch
40 K–N3   QR–Q1
41 B–Q3   Q–K3
42 Q–KN4   ....

The adjourned position. After the exchange of Queens Black's chances in the end game would be very poor. The other alternative, which my opponent chose, was the sacrifice of the exchange.

42	R×B
43 P×R	Q×Pch
44 K–B3	R–Q1
45 QR–Q1	....

If 45 Q–B5, B×P; 46 Q×RPch (46 QR–N1, Q–R6 and the pin is uncomfortable for White), K–B1; 47 QR–Q1, Q–B5ch; 48 K–N2, Q–N5ch with a perpetual check.

| 45 .... | B×P |
| 46 P–R5 | .... |

If Black now plays 46 ... Q–R6, White wins with 47 Q–B5, N–N5; 48 R–K7!, R×Bch (if 48 ... Q×P; 49 B–B4, Q–R6ch; 50 K–N2 or R–K3); 49 K–N2, Q×P; 50 R–K8ch, K–N2; 51 P–R6 mate.

| 46 .... | B–N2 |
| 47 P–R6 | .... |

47 Q–B5 yields nothing because of 47 ... K–B1.

| 47 .... | B–B6 |

(See top of next column.)

| 48 R–K2 | .... |

48 Q–B5 is met by 48 ... Q–N3 (not

7

Position after 47 ... B–B6

---

48 ... B×R on account of 49 Q×RPch, K–B1; 50 Q–N7ch, K–K2; 51 R×Bch, K–Q2; 52 Q×Pch, K–B1; 53 P–R7, etc.); and after 49 Q×Q, RP×Q the ending is still difficult.

| 48 .... | Q–R7 |
| 49 Q–N3 | Q×Qch |

Forced, for if Black attempts to avoid the exchange of Queens with 49 ... Q–R4ch, White replies 50 K–N2 and the threat of 51 R–KR1 is decisive.

| 50 K×Q | B–N5 |
| 51 B–B4 | .... |

This pin eventually leads to Black's downfall.

51	P–N4
52 B–N3	K–B1
53 K–N4	B–B6
54 K–B3	P–R4

Black must lose a Pawn. On 54 ...
B–R4 (to release the Knight) comes 55
B×N, P×B; 56 R–K5.

55 R–K3	P–N5
56 R(K3)–Q3	K–K2
57 B×N	P×B
58 R×P	....

(See diagram at right.)

| 58 .... | R×R |

After 58 ... R–QR1; 59 R–Q7ch,
K–K1; 60 R–N7, P–R5; 61 R(Q1)–
Q7, P–N6; 62 P×P, P–R6; 63 R–R7,
R–N1; 64 R(Q7)–QB7, Black is hope-
lessly lost.

| 59 R×R | P–R5 |
| 60 R–R5 | Resigns |

Position after 58 R×P

The ending is easily won. One
method would be (after Black plays 60
... P–R6) to play 61 R–R6 and bring
the King to QB4. This would be
followed by giving up the Rook for the
Bishop and Black's QNP.

Determined Resistance

In the fourth round of the 1958 Rosenwald Tournament I was pitted
against Mr. Kalme. He is one of our most promising young players who
may go very far. He is fearless, confident, and his style is aggressive. He
is not prone to blunders. However, he lacks experience.

The opening was a King's Indian. Up to the ninth move the position
was symmetrical. Mr. Kalme was visibly disturbed by my tenth move,
N–Q5, which took us out of the symmetry. Black's problem was how to
keep his Queen out of trouble. My opponent found the correct continuation. But Black had one difficulty—how to develop his Queen-Bishop.

On my 19th turn I forced the exchange of Queens. This made it
possible for my Rooks to gain control of the Queen-file. Although the
position was exceedingly difficult for Mr. Kalme, he fought on with great
determination. He met every tactical threat perfectly. In doing so,
however, he consumed too much time. On his 32nd turn my opponent
made an error, due to time pressure.

KING'S INDIAN DEFENSE

Rosenwald Tournament
New York, 1958–59

S. RESHEVSKY   C. KALME

| 1 P–QB4 | N–KB3 |

2 P–Q4	P–KN3
3 P–KN3	B–N2
4 B–N2	O–O
5 N–KB3	P–B4
6 O–O	....

6 P×P, Q–R4ch is unpleasant for

White. 6 P–Q5, P–Q3; 7 O–O, N–R3; 8 N–B3, N–B2, etc., leads to a well-known variation, difficult for both sides.

6	P–Q3
7 N–B3	N–B3
8 P×P	P×P
9 B–K3	....

White must find some way to get out of the symmetry. Another possibility is 9 B–B4.

| 9 .... | Q–R4 |

9 ... B–K3, continuing the symmetry, has been tried with little success.

10 N–Q5 ....

A good alternative is 10 Q–B1 with the intention of B–KR6 at some point.

| 10 .... | B–B4 |

10 ... R–Q1 loses on account of 11 B–Q2, Q–R3; 12 N–B7.

11 B–Q2 **Q–Q1**

12 N–R4 ....

12 B–B3 looks like the correct and natural continuation, but after 12 ... B–K5; 13 N×Nch, P×N; 14 N–R4, B×B; 15 N×B, P–B4 with approximate equality. The text-move tends to keep the position alive.

| 12 .... | B–Q2 |

12 ... B–K3 is an alternative, but

Black intends to drive White's Knight with ... P–K3.

13 B–QB3 ....

Arriving at the position contemplated when playing 10 N–Q5. White's position is slightly better. Black's problem is to drive White's Knight from Q5 and at the same time avoid shutting in his Queen-Bishop.

| 13 .... | N–KN5 |

If 13 ... N×N; 14 B×B, K×B; 15 Q×N, P–N3 (15 ... N–Q5; 16 P–K3); 16 KR–Q1 and Black is in serious trouble.

| 14 B×B | K×B |
| 15 P–KR3 | .... |

15 .... **N–R3**

Perhaps safest. 15 ... N–B3; 16 N×N, P×N; 17 Q–Q6 was difficult for Black. Neither was 15 ... KN–K4 to be recommended, on account of 16

P–B4, N×P; 18 Q–B1, or 16 Q–B1 immediately threatening to win a piece with 17 P–B4.

16 Q–Q3   P–K3

Driving away this Knight was imperative; otherwise, Black's development would have remained incompleted.

17 N–QB3   Q–K2
18 KR–Q1   KR–Q1

Black seems to be holding his own despite his undeveloped Bishop.

19 Q–Q6   ....

Realizing that, after the exchange of Queens, I would be in a position to control the Queen-file advantageously.

19 ....   Q×Q
20 R×Q   B–K1
21 N–K4   ....

The only move that gives Black any

problem at all. 21 QR–Q1 is met by 21 ... R×R; 22 R×R, K–B1; 23 N–K4, K–K2 and Black has nothing to worry about.

21 ....   P–N3

Forced. For if 21 ... R×R; 22 N×R, R–N1; 23 R–Q1, K–B1; 24 N–K4, P–N3; 25 N–B6!

22 QR–Q1   KR–B1

22 ... K–B1 loses because of 23 N–B6. Equally bad is 22 ... P–B4 on account of 23 N–N5.

23 R(Q6)–Q2   R–B2
24 N–Q6   K–B1
25 N–B3   P–B3

Necessary, in order to prevent N–KN5.

26 P–KN4   ....

Threatening 27 P–N5, P×P; 28 N×P and the defense of Black's KP would have been difficult.

26 ....   N–B2

Or 26 ... P–KN4; 27 P–KR4, P×P; 28 P–N5, P×P; 29 N×P, K–K2; 30 N×KP, K×N: 31 N×B, R×N; 32 R–Q6ch, etc.

27 P–N5   ....

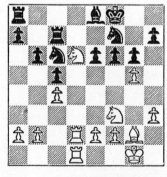

27 ....   P×P

27 ... P–B4 was insufficient. There would have followed: 28 N×N, K×N

(28 ... R×N or B×N; 29 N–K5
leads to the same thing); 29 N–K5ch,
K–B1 (29 ... N×N; 30 B×R); 30
N×N, B×N; 31 B×B, R×B; 32
R–Q7 and wins.

28 N×N	K×N
29 N×Pch	K–B3
30 P–B4	....

Seriously threatening 31 R–Q6.

30	P–KR3
31 N–K4ch	K–K2
32 N–Q6	R–Q1?

A blunder made during severe time
pressure. Correct was 33 ... B–Q2.
White's position was clearly better but
not clearly won.

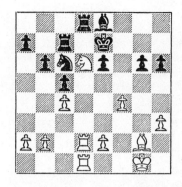

33 B×N	B×B
34 N–B5ch	KP×N

Black loses on time—but after 35
R×R White has an easy win.

Positional Judgment

It is not easy to define positional judgment. Not many have it; very
few acquire it. That feeling or intuition one has for a position is something
one is usually born with. The ability to be able to appraise positions
without having to resort to lengthy analysis is an attribute distinguishing
great players.

In the following game my opponent, Larry Evans, played the opening
correctly, obtaining complete equality. On my 13th turn I decided to
pursue an aggressive course. On my 16th I made a slightly inferior move
which gave Evans the better chances. On his 23rd move he committed a
tactical error which could only be attributed to a lack of positional judgment. This is not to imply that Evans usually lacks good positional
judgment.

It soon became evident that Evans's troubles resulted from his 23rd
move. By sacrificing a Pawn with 27 P–B5 my opponent's position
deteriorated rapidly. Black's staunch resistance soon collapsed.

NIMZO-INDIAN DEFENSE

Rosenwald Tournament
New York, 1958–59

S. RESHEVSKY   L. EVANS

1 P–Q4	N–KB3	
2 P–QB4	P–K3	
3 N–QB3	B–N5	
4 P–K3	O–O	
5 N–K2	P–Q4	
6 P–QR3	B–K2	
7 P×P	P×P	
8 N–B4	....	

To prevent Black from playing the freeing ... P–QB4. The same purpose would be accomplished by 8 P–QN4 but this has the drawback of weakening White's QB4 square. 8 N–N3 enables Black to equalize immediately with 8 ... P–B4.

| 8 .... | P–QR4! |

Preventing P–QN4.

9 B–Q3	R–K1
10 O–O	P–B3
11 P–B3	....

Preparing for either P–K4 or P–KN4. With passive play White cannot hope to get anywhere.

| 11 .... | N–R3 |
| 12 Q–B2 | P–KN3 |

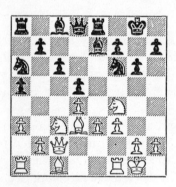

| 13 P–KN4 | .... |

I decided against 13 QN–K2 (in order to play 14 P–K4) because of 13 ... P–B4; 14 B×N, R×B; 15 P×P, Q–B2 regaining the Pawn with a good position. 16 N–Q3 is met by 16 ... B–KB4.

| 13 .... | N–B2 |
| 14 Q–N2 | P–QN4 |

Black simply ignores White's preparations on the King-side and proceeds to create activity on the other wing.

| 15 B–Q2 | N–K3 |

| 16 N(B4)–K2? | .... |

Taking away an important square from the QN. Logical was 16 N×N, B×N; 17 N–K2 and then to B4 with chances for both sides.

| 16 .... | B–R3! |

Threatening to win material with 17 ... P–N5; 18 B×B, P×N.

| 17 N–Q1 | .... |

This forced retreat proves that White's 16th move was weak.

| 17 .... | P–B4 |

Threatening to strengthen his position considerably with 18 ... P–B5 followed by ... P–N5.

| 18 P×P | .... |

Forced.

18	B×P
19 P–N4	B–N3
20 K–R1	P×P
21 P×P	....

(*See diagram on next page.*)

This might be called the critical position of the game. White's threat was to win a Pawn with 22 R×B, R×R; 23 B×QNP.

21 ....   N–B2

Black had two other continuations that were preferable:

(1) 21 ... Q–Q2; 22 B–B3, P–Q5; 23 B–N2, N–Q4!

(2) 21 ... Q–Q3; 22 N(Q1)–B3 (if 22 B–B3, P–Q5; or if 22 R×B, R×R; 23 B×QNP, R–R7; 24 B×R, R×B followed by Q×NP), P–Q5! 23 P×P (23 N×NP?, Q–Q2), N×P; 24 N×N, Q×N; 25 B×QNP, B×B; 26 R×R (26 N×B, Q×R!), B×R; 27 R×Rch, N×R; 28 Q×B, Q×B with a piece ahead.

22 N–Q4   ....

Shielding the KP and at the same time giving protection to the weak BP.

22 ....   N–Q2

Intending ... N–K4–B5.

23 P–B4   .....

Preventing ... N–K4 but at the expense of weakening my K4 square. There was the promising alternative of 23 N–B6, Q–B3; 24 R–B1, N–K4 (24 ... R–K3; 25 P–N5, Q–N2; 26 B–B3, Q–B1; 27 N–Q4, R(3)–K1; 28 P–B4 with an overwhelming position); 25 P–N5, Q–K3; 26 N×N, Q×N; 27 P–B4, Q–Q3; 28 P–B5 with the better prospects.

23 ....   B×N?

Giving up one of his best pieces. Correct was 23 ... N–B3; 24 N–QB3, Q–K2 with the intention of playing ... N–K5. If in this, 25 N(Q4)×P, N×N; 26 B×N, B×B; 27 N×B, R×R; 28 R×R, B×P with a fine game.

The text-move allows White's pieces too much mobility. As a result, I was able to launch a severe attack against Black's weakened King-position.

24 P×B   ....

White's QB is now ready for action.

24 ....   Q–B3

24 ... N–B3; 25 P–B5, N–K5; 26 B–KB4 is no more promising for Black.

25 Q–B2   P–R3

Hoping to prevent 26 P–N5 followed by P–B5, but Black is in for a surprise.

26 P–N5   P×P

27 P–B5   ....

This must have come as a complete
surprise to my opponent. He must have
expected 27 P×P, Q×Q; 28 R×Q,
N–K3; 29 B–K3, N–N3 with an even
position. If White tries to win a Pawn
with 30 R×B he would get into trouble
as follows: 30 ... R×R; 31 B×NP,
R(K1)–R1; 32 B×R, R×B and Black
has more than ample compensation for
the Pawn, mainly because the white
Bishop is immobilized, being compelled to protect the KN and Q Pawns.
In addition, Black's immediate threats
of ... R–R8 and ... N–QB5 are
difficult to parry. The move I chose
demolishes Black's King-position. The
immediate threats are 28 P×P and 28
Q–N3.

27 ....   **N–B1**

Both threats could not be met. Black
did the next best thing—answer the
first threat mentioned above. 27 ...
P×P was out of the question because of
the ruinous 28 B×KNP, Q×B?; 29
R–KN1.

28 Q–N3   ....

With three significant threats.

28 ....   **Q×QP**

My opponent decides on do-or-die
tactics. 28 ... Q–N3 would have
parried temporarily the most serious
threats, but after 29 B×KNP followed

by either B–KB4 or B–R6, White would
have had a crushing attack.

29 P×P   ....

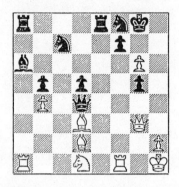

29 ....   **P×P**

Black would have been no better off
with 29 ... N×P. There would have
followed: 30 Q×N, Q×B; 31 Q×Pch,
K–R1; 32 R–B3 and if 32 ... R–KB1,
then 33 Q×Rch followed by R×Q.

30 Q×N   ....

I discarded 30 B–B3, Q–N3; 31
R–B6 R–K3 with some chances of
survival. The move selected is crushing.

30 ....   **Q×B**
31 Q–B7ch   **K–R1**
32 R–B3   ....

The whole point. Black's Queen is
lost. 32 ... Q–K5 fails on account of
33 N–B2 followed by R–R3ch.

32	Q×R
33 Q×Q	P–Q5

Losing another piece but not affecting the outcome of the game.

34 Q–B6ch	K–R2
35 R×B	R×R

36 Q×R	R–K7
37 Q–R7ch	K–R3
38 Q×P	N–K3
39 Q–R8 mate	

A game ending in mate is an unusual occurrence among grandmasters.

One Bad Move

It is unusual for a player to build up a good position and then throw away the game by making one bad move, but that is what happened in this contest. My young opponent played well and made it necessary for me to weaken my King position so that my pieces could obtain more mobility. Then, on his 21st move Weinstein blew the game by making a tactical error which created serious weaknesses in his position. I was able to take immediate advantage of these weaknesses. By giving up a Pawn I conducted a violent attack and White resigned a few moves later.

KING'S INDIAN DEFENSE

Rosenwald Tournament
New York, 1959–60

R. WEINSTEIN   S. RESHEVSKY

1 P–Q4	N–KB3
2 P–QB4	P–KN3
3 P–KN3	B–N2
4 B–N2	O–O
5 N–KB3	P–B4
6 P–Q5	P–Q3
7 N–B3	N–R3
8 O–O	N–B2
9 B–B4	P–QR3

The opening play on both sides is quite well known. Black's aim is to open the QN-file for future operations.

10 P–QR4	R–N1
11 P–R5	P–QN4
12 P×P e.p.	R×P

The net result of this variation is that both sides have weak Pawns.

13 P–N3	N–R4

13 ... P–R3 was safer in order to prevent N–KN5.

14 B–Q2	....

Threatening 15 N–QR4 followed by B–R5 and Black would be in an uncomfortable pin.

14	P–K3
15 P×P	B×P
16 N–KN5	B–Q2
17 N–R4!	....

Well played! For if 17 ... B×R; 18 N×R, B–N2; 19 N×B, Q×N; 20 B–K3 with the better of it; and if 17 ... B×N; 18 R×B, Q–N1; 19 B–R5 winning material.

17	R–N1
18 R–R3	P–R3
19 N–K4	P–B4

Driving this Knight out of play but at the expense of slightly weakening my King-position. I felt that this weakness had to be made so that my pieces would have more mobility.

20 N(K4)–B3   ....

Obviously, 20 N×QP loses material after 20 ... B×N.

| 20 .... | B–K3 |
| 21 P–K4? | .... |

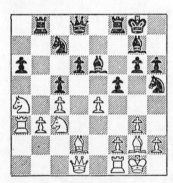

Relinquishing control of his vital squares KB4, Q4, and K5. The significance of this tactical error soon becomes apparent. Correct was first 21 P–B4 (preventing Black's next move) then followed by P–K4.

21 ....   **P–B5**

This involves giving up a Pawn. For the Pawn offered Black obtains a deadly attack.

22 P–KN4   ....

Closing his eyes to the lurking danger.

22 ....   **P–B6**

White suddenly finds himself in a hopeless situation.

| 23 B×BP | Q–R5 |
| 24 K–N2 | .... |

The only try to stay alive, for if 24 P×N, B–K4; 25 R–K1, B×Pch; 26 K–B1 (26 K–N2, Q–R6ch; 27 K–R1, B–N6ch; 28 K–N1, Q–R7ch followed by Q×P mate), R×B; 27 Q×R, B–R6ch; 28 K–K2, B–N5.

| 24 .... | N–B5ch |
| 25 B×N | R×B |

(See diagram on next page.)

26 B–K2   ....

Black was threatening 26 ... QR–KB1. If 26 N–K2, R×B; 27 K×R, Q–R6ch; 28 N–N3 (28 K–B4, P–N4 mate), B×Pch winning the Queen.

Position after 25 ... R×B

The final position. If 28 Q–K1, B×NP; 29 B×B, R×Bch; 30 P×R, Q–R7 mate. If 28 P–B3, R×Pch; 29 BP×R, Q–N6ch; 30 K–R1, Q–R7 mate.

26	B–K4
27 P–R3	QR–KB1
Resigns	

Discounting the Threat

Failure to see a threat is a chronic fault with the average player. Masters also become victims of oversights. Among experts, however, a threat is usually seen, but its importance may be discounted. To minimize an opponent's idea without thorough analysis is folly and costly. One reason for this mode of thinking is overoptimism; another is disrespect for the opponent's strength.

In the following game, Mr. Mednis played a well-known variation of the King's Indian Defense. On my tenth turn I played a new move which seemed to upset my opponent. This came as no surprise. Whenever a new move is introduced in the opening, the opponent will invariably be affected by it.

Later, Black completely disregarded my threat of 19 P–KN4 which tied up his men so badly that he was compelled to give up a piece. The move was a bold one, since it exposed the King somewhat. Mr. Mednis probably thought that this would deter me from making the move. As a result, he discounted the effectiveness of the threat.

KING'S INDIAN DEFENSE

Rosenwald Tournament
New York, 1959–60

S. RESHEVSKY   E. MEDNIS

1 P–Q4	N–KB3
2 P–QB4	P–KN3
3 N–QB3	B–N2
4 P–K4	....

(See diagram on next page.)

| 4 .... | P–Q3 |

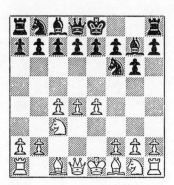

Position after 4 P–K4

4 ... O–O might be dangerous for Black. Donovan against Evans played 5 P–K5, N–K1; 6 B–B4, P–Q3; 7 P×P, N×P; 8 Q–Q2, N–B3; 9 N–B3, N×QP; 10 N×N, P–K4; 11 B–N5, P–KB3; 12 N–B3, P×B; 13 P–B5, N–B2; 14 Q×Q, R×Q; 15 B–B4 with advantage.

5 B–K2 ....

This setup by White against the King's Indian is at the present time preferred to the fianchetto of the King-Bishop. It is held that the Bishop at K2 serves better than at KN2 because it protects White's Queen-Bishop Pawn.

5 ....   **O–O**
6 N–B3   **P–B3**

6 ... P–K4 is more usual here.

7 O–O   **P–K4**
8 R–K1   ....

8 P×P, P×P; 9 Q×Q, R×Q; 10 N×P, N×P leads to equality.

8 ....   **Q–N3**

This move is more effective and logical when White fianchettoes his King-Bishop.

9 P–Q5   ....

Best. White threatens to gain a tempo after making provision for the protection of his QNP.

9 ....   **P–B4**
10 N–KR4   ....

A new idea, making immediate provision against Black's anticipated ... P–KB4. 10 P–QR3 and 10 P–QR4 have been tried here.

10 ....   **Q–Q1**

An admission that Black's 8th move, Q–N3, was a loss of time.

11 P–KN3   ....

The protection of the King-Knight was necessary.

11 ....   **N–K1**
12 B–B1   ....

Preventing ... B–KR6.

12 ....   **N–R3**
13 P–QR3   ....

Preventing ... N–QN5 and also preparing for action on the Queen-wing with P–QN4, if necessary.

13 ....   **P–B4**

Without this advance, Black would have no counterchances against White's inevitable thrust on the Queen-side.

14 P×P   ....

Forced. Otherwise 14 ... P–B5 with a devastating attack.

14 ....   **P×P**
15 P–B4   ....

Again to prevent 15 ... P–B5.

15 ....   **P–K5**

Black seems to be well off. He has a passed Pawn, and his King-Bishop is potent, controlling his Q5 square. However, the picture is deceptive. Black's passed Pawn cannot be advanced. It might become weak if the KBP can be attacked. White is in a position to undertake action on either wing.

16 B–K3   **B–B3**
17 N–N2   **N–N2**
18 P–R3   **....**

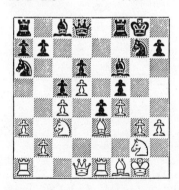

With the serious threat of 19 P–KN4 which cannot be ignored!

18 ....   **N–B2?**

But Black pays no attention to the threat. Correct was 18 ... P–R4 and if 19 B–K2, Q–K1; 20 N–N5, B–K2 (20 ... B×P; 21 R–N1 followed by N×QP with a winning position) and

although White stands better, Black can hold on.

19 P–KN4   **N(B2)–K1**
20 P–N5   **....**

This virtually immobilizes Black's forces. White's plan becomes obvious. He is going to advance his KN and KR Pawns until it hurts.

20 ....   **B×N**

Better than 20 ... B–K2 where the Bishop would be completely inactive. In addition, the text-move relieves pressure on Black's KP.

21 P×B   **Q–R4**
22 B–Q2   **K–B2**

My opponent obviously anticipated the advance of the KRP. The King must attempt to escape.

23 P–KR4   **....**

23 ....   **R–KN1?**

Black misses his only chance of survival. 21 ... R–R1 was forced, and if White continued with 22 P–R5 (threatening P–R6), P–R3!. If 22 B–K2 (threatening B–R5ch), P–R4. This defense would have made it difficult for White to progress with the attack.

24 P–R5   **....**

The threat is P–R6 winning the Knight.

24	N–B3

Desperation. However, if 24 ... N–B2; 25 P–R6, N(N2)–K1; 26 Q–R5ch, K–K2; 27 N–R4 followed by K–R2 and P–N6!

25 P×N	N–K1

Although White is a piece ahead, he must proceed carefully because his King is exposed.

26 R–K3	N×P
27 B–K1	B–Q2
28 B–R4	....

I wanted to get rid of Black's active Knight.

28	Q–R5

By offering the exchange of Queens Black is virtually tendering his resignation. More logical was 28 ... N–N5; 29 R–N3, R–N2 followed by doubling the Rooks.

29 Q×Q	B×Q
30 B×N	K×B
31 K–B2	B–Q2

Apparently my opponent's hope was that I would be unable to break through the seemingly closed position. It turned out to be a false hope.

32 R–N3	R×R
33 K×R	R–N1ch
34 K–B2	B–K1
35 B–K2	B–Q2

36 N–K3	B–R5
37 B–Q1	B–Q2

Now White is ready to penetrate the Black position.

38 P–R4	B–B1
39 P–R5	R–N2
40 R–N1	R–N1
41 B–K2	R–N2
42 N–B2	Resigns

The final position. If 42 ... R–KB2, the simple method to win would be as follows: 43 N–R3, P–QR3 (if anything else, White plays 44 N–N5 followed by N–R7 and wins); 44 R–N6, and if 44 ... R–Q2 White brings his Bishop to KR3 and his Knight to K3, when Black must lose a Pawn because he is in "zugzwang." Against 44 ... K–K2, White also brings his Bishop to KR3 and his Knight to K3, attacking the KBP. When Black defends the Pawn with his Rook at KB2, White plays B×P, B×B; R×Pch, etc.

4

SACRIFICES, GOOD AND BAD

Frequently, the way to win a chess game is to sacrifice material in order to gain a positional advantage or an immediate attack on the King. A great many of these sacrifices are of a temporary nature. They have been called pseudo sacrifices. The material given up is promptly regained by force, and with a profit. On the other hand, there are many "real" sacrifices which do not regain material but pave the way to a winning attack.

When a sacrifice is sound, and particularly when it involves giving up a major piece, the artistry of the combination arouses admiration. But there are many sacrificial combinations which prove to be unsound. The cause may be the player's inability to analyze correctly the resulting combinations, or the sacrifice may have been made in desperation in an attempt to win a drawn game or to save a lost game.

In this chapter there are several examples of games in which the key play involved a sacrifice of material. Some of these sacrificial combinations were sound; others were not.

A Knight for Three Pawns

In this fourth game of the Najdorf–Reshevsky match the first eight moves followed a well-known line of the King's Indian Defense. My opponent's ninth move was somewhat irregular. His tenth, which had an aggressive idea behind it, proved to be a serious loss of time.

On my 15th turn I sacrificed a Knight but then captured three Pawns by force in the succeeding moves. A Knight for three Pawns is an approximately even swap, but in addition I gained excellent attacking possibilities. In fact, within a few moves Black's position became untenable.

KING'S INDIAN DEFENSE

Najdorf–Reshevsky Match
New York, 1952

S. RESHEVSKY   M. NAJDORF

1 P–Q4	N–KB3
2 P–QB4	P–KN3

My opponent's favorite defense against the Queen's Pawn opening. Most of the Russian grandmasters also show a preference for this defense.

3 N–QB3	B–N2
4 P–K4	O–O

4 ... P–Q3 is more usual but the text-move is equally as good.

5 N–B3	....

5 P–K5 is unwise because Black is able to break up White's control of the center with 5 ... N–K1; 6 P–B4, P–Q3; 7 N–B3, P×P; 8 BP×P, B–N5; 9 B–K2, P–QB4.

5	P–Q3
6 P–KN3	....

Another major line is 6 B–K2, P–K4; 7 O–O, N–B3 or QN–Q2.

6	P–K4
7 B–N2	QN–Q2
8 O–O	P–B3
9 P–KR3	N–R4!?

More usual and better is 9 ... P×P; 10 N×P, R–K1; 11 R–K1, P–QR4;

12 B–K3, N–B4, etc. This line is a solid continuation requiring utmost patience by both players. But my opponent has aggressive intentions in mind.

10 B–K3	Q–K2

The immediate 10 ... P–KB4 may have been playable. After 11 KP×P, NP×P; 12 P×P, P×P; 13 N×P, N×N; 14 Q×N, N×P, the position is full of possibilities for both sides. Najdorf was obviously preparing for this push. The loss of one tempo gets him into serious trouble.

11 R–K1	....

Making 11 ... P–KB4 impossible because of 12 KP×P, NP×P; 13 N×P, P×N; 14 Q×N and if 14 ... P×P; 15 B×QP and the Queen is under attack.

11	K–R1

A waiting move of little significance.

12 Q–K2	Q–K1

Protecting his Knight at KR4 in order to play ... P–KB4.

13 QR–Q1	....

White, having fully developed his pieces, is ready and waiting for Black to break.

13	P–KB4

Finally the planned advance.

14 KP×P	P–K5

After 14 ... NP×P; 15 P×P, P×P; 16 N×P!, N or B×N; 17 B–Q4 regaining the piece with a clearly won position.

15 N×P!	....

This sacrifice must have been overlooked by Najdorf. That is to say, he did not overlook its existence but must have misjudged its effectiveness.

15	Q×N
16 N–R4	Q–K1
17 P×P	....

The important point being that Black cannot regain a Pawn by playing 17 ... P×P. There would follow: 18 Q–B2, R–B3 (18 ... K–R2; 19 N×P, Q×N; 20 B–K4 winning the Queen); 19 B–N5, R–K3; 20 R×R, Q×R; 21 N×Pch, K–N1; 22 P–Q5!, Q–B2; 23 P×P and Black is in a hopeless state.

The result of White's sacrifice is that he winds up with three Pawns for the piece. In addition, Black's King is in a dangerous situation, being subjected to immediate attack.

17	N(R4)–B3
18 Q–B2	....

Threatening, among other things, B–B4.

18	Q–Q1
19 B–B4	N–N3
20 P×P	R–K1

20 ... R–B2 loses the exchange: 21 N–N6ch, K×P; 22 N–K5ch.

(*See diagram on next page.*)

21 B–N5	B–Q2
22 P–N3	....

White is in no particular hurry to

Position after 20 ... R–K1

With the threat of R–R4ch. If 28 ... N×R; 29 N–N6ch wins the Queen

rush into anything. Black's pieces are almost completely immobilized.

22	R×Rch
23 R×R	B–K1
24 B–K4	N(N3)–Q2
25 B–N6	B×B
26 N×Bch	K×P
27 N–K7ch	K–R1
28 R–K4	....

28	B–R3
29 R–R4	....

29 B×B, N×R; 30 Q×N, N–B3 would have kept Black alive a little longer.

29	Q×N
30 R×Bch	K–N1
31 Q–N6ch	Q–N2
32 B×N	Resigns

Sacrifice by Analysis

It is not often that one can execute a sacrifice analyzed as sound before the game begins. This is what happened in the 16th game of the Najdorf–Reshevsky match. Before the game was played I went over different variations of the Slav Defense. In one of these lines I found that White could sacrifice a Knight if Black made a certain move in the opening. Sure enough, Najdorf made this move and I was able to sacrifice a Knight for two Pawns and a winning position.

SEMI-SLAV DEFENSE

Najdorf–Reshevsky Match
Buenos Aires, 1952

S. RESHEVSKY   M. NAJDORF

1 P–Q4	P–Q4
2 P–QB4	P–QB3
3 N–KB3	N–B3
4 N–B3	P–K3

5 P–K3	P–QR3
6 B–Q3	P×P
7 B×BP	P–QN4
8 B–N3	P–B4
9 O–O	B–N2
10 Q–K2	QN–Q2
11 R–Q1	Q–N3

Varying from Game No. 2 of the match in which Najdorf played 11 ... Q–B2. (See Page 56.)

12 P–Q5	P–K4

12 ... P×P; 13 P–K4! leads to many complications which favor White.

13 P–QR4	P–B5
14 B–B2	R–B1?

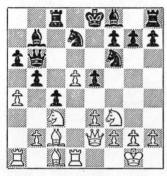

Allowing White to sacrifice a piece successfully. Correct was 14 ... B–N5 and the position becomes difficult to assess.

15 P×P	P×P
16 N×NP	....

I would venture a guess that Najdorf completely overlooked this possibility.

16	Q×N
17 B–R4	Q–B4
18 N×P	....

The net result of the sacrifice: White has two Pawns for the piece and will be able to prevent Black from castling.

18	Q–B2

19 N×N	N×N
20 Q–N4	P–R4
21 Q–R3	....

Better than the tempting 21 Q–K4ch, B–K2; 22 B–Q2, Q–Q3 followed by castling.

21	B–Q3
22 B–Q2	....

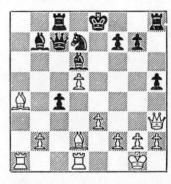

The only plausible way Black can attempt to castle is to protect his Knight with ... R–Q1. That is now impossible because of 23 B–R5!, Q×B?; 24 B×Nch, etc. As a matter of fact, White is threatening to play this move now.

22	R–R1
23 B–B3	P–B3

Reluctantly weakening his K3 square. In view of what follows, 23 ... R×B; 24 R×R, O–O was better.

24 B–B6	....

After this, Black's collapse is imminent.

24 ....   R×R

There is nothing better. If 24 ...
R–QN1; 25 B–R5, Q–B1; 26 Q–K6ch,
B–K2; 27 P–Q6. If 24 ... B×B; 25
P×B, N–N3 (25 ... R×R; 26
P×Nch, etc.); 26 R×Rch, N×R; 27
Q–K6ch, B–K2; 28 R–Q7 and wins.

25 R×R   B×B
26 Q–K6ch   ....

The right *zwischenzug*. For if 26
P×B, N–N1 and Black might defend
successfully.

26 ....   K–B1

If 26 ... B–K2; 27 P×B, N–N3 (27

... N–N1; 28 R–R8 followed by
B–R5); 28 B–R5, K–B1; 29 B×N,
Q×B; 30 R–R8ch, B–Q1; 31 Q–Q7
and wins.

27 P×B   N–N1

27 ... N–N3 is met by 28 B–R5. If
27 ... Q×P; 28 B–N4!

28 R–R8   Q–K2

28 ... Q×P; 29 R×Nch.

29 Q–Q5   P–N3
30 B–N4   Resigns

The final position. If 30 ... B×B;
31 R×Nch, K–N2; 32 R–N7. If 30
... K–N2; 31 Q×B, Q×Q; 32 B×Q,
R–Q1; 33 P–B7!, R×B; 34 P–R3 and
wins.

A Tempting Sacrifice

The first game of a match is of great importance. The psychological
effect of a win or loss can very well decide the final outcome. Therefore, I
proceed cautiously in my first encounter in order to feel out my opponent
as to his choice of opening, his extent of aggressiveness and his general
ability.

Arthur Bisguier is well known for his combinative ability and aggressive
style. That he would grab the first opportunity to sacrifice a piece was,
however, a surprise to me, but I can see that the temptation was great
since Black was getting two Pawns and what looked like a promising
attack against the unprotected King by giving up a Knight.

In the opening a well-known line was followed up to the seventh move. Instead of the usual 7 ... P×P, Black played ... N×P and continued on his eighth and ninth moves in the same way as I did against Larry Evans several years before. Here I experimented with 9 B–Q2 which tested Bisguier's ability to meet a new move. He found the right continuation. On his 21st move Bisguier, instead of simplifying with ... R–B1, threw all caution to the wind.

NIMZO-INDIAN DEFENSE

Bisguier–Reshevsky Match
New York, 1957

S. RESHEVSKY   A. BISGUIER

| 1 P–Q4 | N–KB3 |
| 2 P–QB4 | P–K3 |

I was always of the opinion that the Nimzo-Indian is the best defense against the QP opening. Most of the leading American players are slowly adopting that view.

| 3 N–QB3 | B–N5 |
| 4 P–K3 | O–O |

There are three other playable moves: ... P–Q4, ... P–B4 and ... P–QN3. Each leads to a different type of position. Which is best, each player must decide for himself according to his own taste.

5 N–K2	P–Q4
6 P–QR3	B–K2
7 P×P	N×P

More usual is 7 ... P×P; 8 P–QN4 (8 N–N3, P–QB4 equalizes), P–B3; 9 N–N3, P–QN4; 10 B–Q2, P–QR4 with chances for both sides.

| 8 Q–B2 | .... |

(See top of next column.)

Preventing ... P–QB4. For instance, 8 ... P–QB4; 9 P×P, B×P; 10 N×N, Q×N; 11 N–B4, Q–B3; 12 B–Q3, P–KR3; 13 B–K4 followed by castling on the K-side with the superior development.

| 8 .... | N–Q2 |
| 9 B–Q2 | .... |

In order to answer ... N×N with B×N, placing the Bishop on a favorable square. 9 P–KN3 is also to be considered.

| 9 .... | N(Q4)–B3 |

Black took a long time for this move and rightly so. Black must strive for ... P–QB4 in order to release the tension in the center. 9 ... P–QB4 is inadvisable because of 10 N×N, P×N; 11 B–B3 leaving Black with a weak QP. 9 ... P–QN3 fails on account of 10

N×N, P×N; 11 Q–B6 winning a Pawn. If 9 ... N(Q2)–B3; 10 N–R4, P–QN3; 11 P–K4. And 9 ... N(Q4)–N3 stops Black from developing his QB via QN2. The text-move (not obvious) is the correct one.

10 N–N3   ....

If 10 P–KN3, P–K4; 11 B–N2, P×P; 12 N×P, N–K4; 13 O–O, P–B4; 14 N–B3 with chances even.

10 ....   **P–B4**
11 P×P   ....

Forced. Otherwise Black plays ... P×P and White remains with an isolated Pawn.

11 ....   **N×P**

11 ... B×P is inferior because it enables White to gain a tempo with either Knight to K4, forcing the Bishop to retreat.

12 B–K2   **P–QN3**
13 O–O   **B–N2**

Black has played the opening well and has achieved equality. All his minor pieces are well posted and there are no weaknesses in his position.

14 KR–Q1   **R–B1**
15 QR–B1   **Q–B2**

15 ... N(B4)–K5; 16 B–K1, Q–B2; 17 Q–N1 improves White's position slightly.

16 Q–N1   ....

If 16 P–N4, N(B4)–K5; 17 B–K1, N×QN; 18 Q×N, Q×Q; 19 R×Q, R×R; 20 B×R, R–Q1 with little left for either side to play for. The text-move prepares for P–QN4 and invites Black to play 16 ... N–N6.

16 ....   **Q–N1**

16 ... N–N6 is tempting but White gains the upper hand as follows: 17 N–Q5, Q–Q2 (17 ... N×B?; 18 R×Q, N×Q; 19 N×Bch, etc.); 18 N×Bch, Q×N; 19 B–N4, N–B4; 20 R–Q4 followed by R–KR4 with excellent prospects for an attack.

17 P–N4   ....

A committing move since it weakens somewhat White's Q-side, especially his QB4 square. If Black is able to post one of his Knights on this square it would make White extremely uncomfortable. Much as I disliked making the move, I had practically no choice because the unpleasant ... N–N6 was the immediate threat. 17 Q–R2 (preventing ... N–N6) is unsatisfactory because of 17 ... N(B3)–K5; 18 B–K1 (18 N(N3) × N, N × N; 19 N × N, B × N and there is no life left in the position), N × N(B6); 19 B × N, B–Q4; 20 Q–N1 (not 20 B–B4?, N–Q6 winning the exchange), N–N6 and Black has the initiative.

| 17 .... | N(B4)–Q2 |
| 18 N–N5 | .... |

It is very difficult to find a promising continuation in this even position. The text-move has a double purpose, to find a better post for this Knight and to provoke ... P–QR3 and ... P–QN4 giving my Knight the square QR5.

18	P–QR3
19 N–Q4	P–QN4
20 N–N3	....

While it is true that I have attained my objective of having QR5 accessible for my Knight, it is equally true that Black can utilize his QR5 for his Knight. White is one tempo ahead but it is doubtful if this is important.

| 20 .... | R × R |
| 21 R × R | .... |

(See top of next column.)

| 21 .... | Q–R1 |

Position after 21 R × R

Black decided to go into complications involving the sacrifice of a piece. With 21 ... R–B1 he had nothing to fear. For example, 22 N–R5, B–R1 (Black must avoid giving up one of his Bishops); 23 P–QR4?, P × P; 24 B × P, R × R; 25 Q × R, B × QNP; 26 B × B, Q × B; 27 Q–B8ch, Q–B1 and White has nothing for the Pawn given up.

| 22 P–B3 | P–KR4 |

Threatening to demolish White's King-side with ... P–R5–R6.

| 23 N–B1 | .... |

Now ... P–R5 is met by P–R3.

| 23 .... | N–K4 |

Threatening 24 ... B × BP, 25 P × B, N × Pch; 26 B × N, Q × B; 27 N–Q4, Q–N5ch; 28 K–R1 (28 N–N3, P–R5),

N–K5; 29 B–K1, P–K4 with sufficient compensation.

24 P–K4   ....

Threatening to consolidate my position with N–B5. If 24 ... R–Q1; 25 B–N5 followed by N–B5 or R5.

24 ....   **N×KP?**

This is what Black was playing for when he made his 21st move, and this is what White was trying to provoke by playing 24 P–K4. Offhand, the sacrifice looks promising, but after close scrutiny, one must conclude that it is unsound.

25 P×N   **B×KP**
26 Q–N2   ....

26 ....   **B–KB3**

26 ... N–B5 is relatively better but also ineffective. There would have followed: 27 B×N, P×B; 28 R×P,

B×KNP; 29 B–R6!, P×B; 30 Q×Bch and White should have no difficulty in winning the end game.

27 B–QB3!   ....

Bisguier must have overlooked the effectiveness of this move.

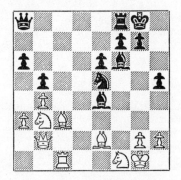

27 ....   **B×P**

Desperation—but what else is there? If 27 ... Q–N1; 28 N–N3. If 27 ... N–N5; 28 B×N, B×B; 29 R×B, P×B; 30 N–B5 and Black has two Pawns for the piece but no attack. If 27 ... N–Q2; 28 B×RP and everything is protected.

28 B×N   **B–R6**

Although White is two pieces ahead, he must still proceed cautiously. Mate is threatened on the move—... Q–N7. This can be met in several ways. One is 29 B×RP, B×B; 30 Q–KB2 but

Black is left with two strong Bishops. Another way is 29 B–KB3, Q×B; 30 B×B, P×B followed by ... K–R1 and ... R–N1ch. On 29 N–K3? comes 29 ... Q–K5!

29 K–B2!   ....

Retaining the two pieces and bringing the King to a safer square—K1.

29	Q–N7ch
30 K–K1	B–R5ch
31 B–N3	B–B3

Hoping White would continue with 21 B–K5, B–R5ch with a repetition of moves. White had no such intentions, however.

32 Q–Q2	R–Q1
33 Q–B4	....

Threatening to force an exchange of Queens with 34 Q–B3, Q–N8; 35 Q–B2 (or even 35 B–B2), Q–R8; 36 B–B3.

33 ....   **Q–Q4**

There is nothing better. If 33 ... B–N7; 34 R–B7, P–B3 (34 ... B–B4; 35 B×RP, P–N3; 36 B–B3, Q–N8; 37 B–B2); 35 B×RP, B×P; 36 B–B7ch, K–B1 (36 ... K–R2; 37

Q–R4 mate); 37 Q–Q6ch, R×Q; 38 B×R mate.

34 B–R4   ....

Forcing the exchange of the KB after which Black's chances fade completely.

34 ....   **B×N**

On 34 ... P–K4, White replies 35 Q–N3.

35 B×B(B6)	B×B
36 B×R	B–N5
37 B–B6	....

White is playing for a pretty finish, hoping Black would oblige by playing 37 ... Q×N. There would have followed 38 R–B8ch, K–R2; 39 R–R8ch. K×R (39 ... K–N3; 40 Q–N5 mate); 40 Q–R6ch, K–N1; 41 Q×P mate.

37	P×B
38 Q×P	P–K4
39 N–B5	Q–R8ch
40 K–Q2	Q–Q4ch
41 K–B3	Q–Q5ch
	Resigns

White easily avoids the perpetual check with 42 K–B2, Q–B5ch; 43 K–N1.

Missing an Opportunity

The type of game I prefer is positional. Being conservative by nature, I feel more secure in positions which do not require giving up material. Occasionally, however, a position will compel one to undertake an attack involving risk. Strangely enough, I get great satisfaction from winning a game through an attack, especially when a sacrifice results in a handsome finish.

In the following game I made two sacrifices. On the 28th move I gave up a Pawn for a promising attack. On the 30th turn I had a golden opportunity to clinch the point but chose the wrong move because of a miscalculation. This blunder almost cost the game, for it required ingenious strategy and continuous threats to avoid a lost ending. My opponent's King-position was precarious, requiring accurate defense which Black put up masterfully. However, with 37 R × N, sacrificing the exchange, I was able to drive the Black King to an unfavorable spot. Careful play by both sides finally brought about a repetition of moves.

NIMZO-INDIAN DEFENSE

International Tournament
Dallas, 1957

S. RESHEVSKY   B. LARSEN

1 P–Q4	N–KB3
2 P–QB4	P–K3
3 N–QB3	B–N5
4 P–K3	P–B4
5 B–Q3	....

More solid is 5 N–K2 as in my game against Najdorf in the same tournament (See Page 39.)

5	P–Q4
6 N–B3	O–O
7 O–O	N–B3
8 P–QR3	B × N
9 P × B	QP × P

A good alternative is 9 ... P–QN3; 10 BP × P, KP × P; 11 B–N2, B–N5.

10 B × BP	Q–B2
11 B–R2	....

The newest attempt in this thoroughly analyzed variation. More frequently seen are B–Q3 or B–K2.

11	P–K4
12 P–KR3	....

Obviously to prevent ... B–N5 but also to provide the square KR2 for the Knight. From this square the Knight might go to KN4 or to KN3 via KB1.

12	P–K5

Black's plan is to blockade the center in order to reduce the scope and power of White's Bishops. White's task will be to liquidate Black's KP with an eventual P–KB3 while Black will endeavor to prevent this.

13 N–R2	B–B4

| 14 B–N2 | QR–Q1 |
| 15 Q–K2 | R–Q3! |

Intending to double Rooks on the Queen-file and leaving himself the opportunity to swing the Rook over to the King-side for attacking purposes.

16 P–QR4   ....

Threatening to win a Pawn with B–R3. 16 P×P was inadvisable because of 16 ... R(Q3)–Q1 followed by N–K4–Q6. Black would have regained the Pawn with ease while his Knight at Q6 would have choked White's pieces.

16	P–QN3
17 KR–Q1	KR–Q1
18 N–B1	Q–Q2

Stopping P×P and perhaps providing the opportunity of sacrificing the Bishop for two Pawns at KR6. Wiser, however, was 18 ... N–QR4 or N–K2.

19 N–N3   **B–K3**

The sacrifice of the Bishop would have been unsound: 19 ... B×P; 20 P×B, Q×P; 21 Q–B1 and Black has no visible compensation for the piece.

20 B–N1   ....

White must retain the two Bishops if he is to hope for any advantage.

20 ....   **B–N6**

21 R–QB1   ....

White must get rid of Black's KP. In order to accomplish this, P–B3 is necessary. After 21 R–KB1, Q–K3, White has to meet the threat of ... B–B5. If 21 R–K1, R–K1; 22 P–B3 is impossible because of 22 ... KP×P; 23 Q×P, P×P; 24 BP×P, N×P; 25 B×N, R×B winding up a Pawn ahead. Therefore the text-move was selected.

21	Q–K3
22 P–B3	B–B5
23 Q–KB2	B–Q6

Wiser was 23 ... KP×P; 24 Q×P, P–N3 and Black's position is quite tenable. Apparently my opponent has a leaning toward complications.

| 24 B×B | P×B |
| 25 R–Q1 | Q–N6 |

Under the circumstances, this is the best. If 25 ... P–B5; 26 P–K4 wins a piece, for the dual threat of P–Q5 and P–K5 cannot be met successfully.

26 P–K4   ....

Capturing the unprotected Pawn would have been rash. For instance: 26 R×P, N–K4; 27 R(Q3)–Q1 (if 27 P×N?, R×R; 28 P×N, R–Q7 winding up the exchange ahead), N–B5, 28 R(Q1)–N1 (the only way to avoid the loss of a Pawn), P×P; 29 KP×P, R–K3 with more than sufficient compensation for the Pawn because White's pieces would have been badly misplaced.

26	**R(Q3)–Q2**
27 P–Q5	**N–K4**
28 P–QB4	....

The sacrifice of a Pawn which should have won by force.

28 ....   **N×QBP**

Black is compelled to accept the offer

of the Pawn. If Black declines by playing 28 ... R–K1, White wins the QP after 29 B×N, R×B; 30 Q–R2, Q–B6; 31 QR–B1, Q–Q5ch, 32 Q–B2.

29 B×N	**P×B**

30 N–R5?   ....

White misses his golden opportunity He could have won with 30 N–B5, K–R1 (30 ... K–B1; 31 Q–N3 and the threat of Q–N7–8 is conclusive); 31 Q–R4, Q–B6 (on 31 ... R–Q3 White is not content with winning merely the exchange, but wins a Rook with 32 Q–R6, R–KN1; 33 N×R, N×N; 34 Q×BPch followed by Q×N); 32 QR–B1, Q–K4; 33 P–B4 (this move I overlooked!), Q–N7; 34 R–N1, Q–B6; 35 R(Q1)–QB1 and the Queen cannot go to a square from which it can protect the KBP.

30	**R–Q3**
31 Q–N3ch	**K–B1**

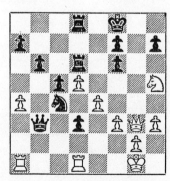

Black's King is now in a comparatively safe position. White is in danger of drifting into a lost ending. Only ingenious strategy can save White now.

32 P–B4   ....

Black was threatening, among other things, 32 ... P–Q7 from where it would have been menacing. 32 Q–N7ch would have been a loss of time, as the following indicates: 32 ... K–K1; 33 N–N3, N–K6; 34 R–Q2 (34 R–K1, P–Q7 wins), Q–B6 with the upper hand.

32 ....   **Q–B6**
33 K–R2   ....

Black was threatening to consolidate his position with ... Q–Q5ch followed by ... P–Q7. If 33 Q×P, Q×Q; 34 R×Q, P–B4 and the ending is greatly in Black's favor. White's only chances are in creating complications in the position.

33 ....   **Q–Q5**
34 Q–N7ch   **K–K1**

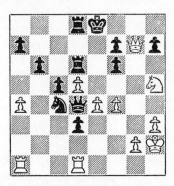

Much better than 34 ... K–K2; 35 N–N3, N–K6; 36 R–K1 with the embarrassing threat of R×N followed by N–B5ch winning the Queen. With his King at K1, Black does not have to worry about the nasty check at KB5.

35 N–N3   ....

Being behind in material, White must continually threaten something.

Black's QP is a bone in White's throat, and counteraction is imperative.

35 ....   **N–K6**
36 R–K1   **P–Q7**
37 R×N   ....

The only chance.

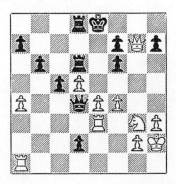

37 ....   **Q×R(K6)**

37 ... Q×R(R8) leads to some wild variations:

(a) 38 N–B5?, P–Q8(Q); 39 Q–N8ch, K–Q2; 40 Q×Pch, K–B1; 41 N–K7ch, K–N2; 42 N–B6ch, R(1)–Q2 and Black wins.

(b) 38 P–K5, P–Q8(Q)? (or 38 ... R×P; 39 P–K6!); 39 P×Rch, K–Q2; 40 Q×Pch, K×P; 41 N–K4 mate.

(c) 38 P–K5, P×P; 39 R×Pch, K–Q2 (39 ... Q×R?; 40 Q×Qch, K–Q2; 41 N–B5 wins); 40 R–K7ch? (40 N–B5 is best; see below), K×R; 41 Q×Q, R×P is in Black's favor.

(d) 38 P–K5, P×P; 39 R×Pch (39 P×P, R×P; 40 R–KB3 is also a possibility), K–Q2 (best); 40 N–B5, P–Q8(Q); 41 Q×Pch, K–B1; 42 N×Rch, R×N; 43 R–K8ch, R–Q1; 44 Q–K6ch, K–N2; 45 Q–B6ch, K–R3; 46 Q–N5ch with perpetual check.

38 Q–N8ch   **K–Q2**
39 Q×Pch   **K–B1**
40 Q×QRP   ....

40 N–B5 fails because of ... Q×BPch.

| 40 .... | Q×BP |

If 40 ... Q–K8 or Q–QN6; 41 N–B5 threatening N–K7 mate is embarrassing.

41 P–R5 ....

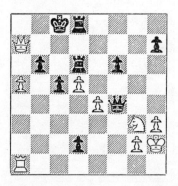

A most unusual position! Although ahead in material, Black must be content with a draw. White is threatening to bring his Rook into play with P×P.

| 41 .... | P–N4 |

Well played. 41 ... P×P; 42 R–QN1 and Black is finished.

| 42 P–R6 | R(3)–Q2 |
| 43 Q–R8ch | Q–N1 |

43 ... K–B2?; 44 Q–B6ch, K–N1; 45 P–R7ch, R×P; 46 Q–N6ch wins.

44 Q–B6ch ....

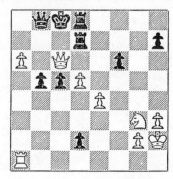

| 44 .... | Q–B2 |

If 44 ... R–B2; 45 Q–K6ch, R(1)–Q2; 46 P–Q6 with White having all the chances.

45 Q–R8ch **Draw**

White must take the draw. 45 P–R7 loses because of 45 ... Q×Q; 46 P×Q R×P. If 45 Q×NP, R–N1 is unpleasant for White. On 45 Q×KBP comes 45 ... K–N1. With the black King safe from attack, White could not have held out much longer.

A Superficial Sacrifice

Arnold Denker is one of our leading veteran chess masters. His style is refreshing, his personality pleasant. He loves to be in lively positions; sacrifices are his specialty. He seems to play with the greatest of ease, never giving the impression that he has an inferior game. He has a lot of talent, but is sometimes carried away by his overoptimism. He could have gone much further in chess but, like many other American masters, he is plagued by a pathetic lack of competition.

In the following game, Denker chose the same line against the Reti Opening that I used several times against Donald Byrne. On his sixth turn, however, he varied and found himself in an inferior position. Realizing that he would be committed to defensive tactics for a long time, he decided to take risks. On his 14th move he undertook a combination which involved the sacrifice of a piece for two Pawns. In addition, my King's security would be slightly impaired.

The sacrifice proved unsound. After the game I asked Denker why he sacrificed. His answer was "It looked good."

RETI OPENING

Rosenwald Tournament
New York, 1957–58

S. RESHEVSKY   A. DENKER

1 N–KB3	N–KB3
2 P–KN3	P–QN3

More usual is 2 ... P–KN3 or ... P–Q4. The purpose of the text-move is to steer into the Queen's Indian Defense if possible.

3 B–N2	B–N2
4 O–O	P–K3
5 P–Q3	....

White is avoiding the usual and well-trodden lines arising from 5 P–Q4, B–K2; 6 P–B4, etc. Instead, the move chosen leads into less familiar patterns. The primary purpose of this move is to help promote P–K4–5.

5	P–Q4

Probably best. In my match against Donald Byrne I tried ... P–QB4 followed by ... P–Q3, but had considerable difficulty in equalizing.

6 P–B4	QN–Q2

I played 6 ... B–K2 against Byrne with good results. The QN should be posted at QB3, after ... P–QB4.

7 P×P	N×P

This loses an important tempo. After 7 ... P×P, however, White replies with 8 N–Q4 with the constant annoying threat of anchoring this Knight at KB5.

8 P–K4	N(4)–B3

8 ... N–N5 is inferior on account of 9 P–QR3, N–QB3; 10 P–Q4, N–B3; 11 N–B3 with the pleasant choice of P–K5 or P–Q5.

9 N–B3	B–K2

If 9 ... N–B4; 10 P–K5, N–Q4; 11 P–Q4, N×N; 12 NP×N, N–K5; 13 Q–B2 with the nasty threat of R–K1.

10 R–K1	O–O

10 ... P–B4 was better, but after 11 P–K5, N–Q4 (11 ... N–N5; 12 P–KR3, B×N; 13 Q×B, N(N5)×P; 14 Q×R); 12 N–K4, White has the better of it.

11 P–Q4	....

White has emerged from the opening with a distinct advantage. Not only is Black's mobility constricted but White has control of the center.

11 ....   B–N5

Decides to give up the Bishop to get breathing space. Perhaps a wiser course was 11 ... R–K1 followed by ... N–B1–N3.

12 Q–B2   ....

Here the Queen protects the QP and also threatens P–K5 followed by N–KN5.

12 ....   P–KR3

Preventing B–KN5 or N–KN5.

13 P–QR3   B×N
14 P×B   P–K4

Denker does not feel comfortable in cramped positions. He decided, therefore, to sacrifice a piece for some attacking chances. I saw this possibility coming but thought the sacrifice to be completely unsound. A conservative and patient player would have continued with 14 ... Q–K2 followed by ... KR–Q1 and ... P–B4.

15 N×P   ....

Not 15 P×P, N–N5; 16 B–B4, Q–K2 and Black recovers the Pawn with a decent position.

15 ....   N×N
16 P×N   N–N5
17 P–KB4   Q–K2

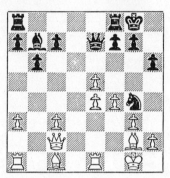

18 P–R3   ....

The only way to play for a distinct advantage. 18 B–K3, N×B; 19 R×N, Q–B4; 20 Q–B2, KR–Q1 gives Black good fighting chances. His control of the Q-file, plus White's inferior Pawn position, would have been sufficient compensation for the Pawn.

18 ....   Q–B4ch
19 K–R1   Q–B7

If 19 ... N–B7ch; 20 K–R2 and the threat of B–K3 cannot be met.

20 R–K2   ....

If 20 Q×Q, N×Qch; 21 K–N1, N–Q6; 22 R–Q1, KR–Q1; 23 B–K3, N–N7 with a playable game. If in this 24 R–Q4, P–QB4; 25 R–Q6, N–B5.

20 ....   Q×NP

21 P×N   **QR–Q1**

His King being exposed, White must proceed with caution. Should Black succeed in doubling his Rooks on the Q-file, White's position might become critical.

22 B–K3   **Q×NP**

If 22 ... R–Q2; 23 R–Q2, KR–Q1; 24 QR–Q1 and Black is forced to exchange both Rooks. This would have simplified White's task.

23 R(K2)–K1   ....

23 R–Q1 looks like the obvious move but after 23 ... Q–N6 White has no satisfactory method of getting his pieces on the King-side. If 23 K–N1?, B×P!

23 ....   **P–KB4**

The only plausible continuation. If 23 ... R–Q2; 24 QR–Q1, KR–Q1; 25 R×R, R×R; 26 Q–K2, Q–R5ch;

9

27 K–N1, and Black's attack has lost its force.

24 Q–K2   ....

The correct move. 24 P×P is unsatisfactory. There follows: 24 ... R×P; 25 Q–B2 (25 B×B, R–R4ch), R–R4ch; 26 K–N1, R–R6 threatening ... R–N6 and if 27 K–B1, B×Bch; 28 Q×B, R–N6, etc.

Nor is 24 P×P e.p. playable on account of 24 ... R×P; 25 P–B5 (25 P–K5, R–B4 again), R(B3)–Q3 followed by ... R–Q6 and if 26 P–K5?, R–Q7!

24 ....   **Q–R5ch**
25 K–N1   **P×P**
26 R–KB1   ....

Better than 26 QR–Q1, R–Q6; 27 R×R, P×R; 28 Q–KB2, Q–N5 with the possibilities of ... P–KN4 or ... R–B4.

26 ....   **R–B4**

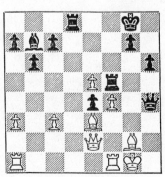

With the serious threat of ... R–R4
but I was anticipating this when I made
my 26th move.

27 B–B2   ....

Parries the threat effectively.

27 ....   **Q×P**

There is nothing better. 27 ...
Q–K2; 28 B×P(K4) ends all hope for
Black.

28 B–R4   ....

Winning material by force, but Black
still has some fight left.

28 ....   **Q×B**
29 R×R   **P–K6**

Setting a trap. If 30 B×B, R–Q7;
31 Q×P (31 B–Q5ch, K–R2), Q–N5ch,
32 K–B1 (32 K–R1, Q–R5ch), Q×Rch;
33 K–K1, R–Q6 with fairly good
chances of surviving.

30 R–Q1   ....

Simplifying by forcing the exchange
of Rooks.

30 ....   **R×Rch**

Otherwise, White plays 31 B×B.

31 Q×R   **B×B**
32 K×B   **Q–K5ch**

(See top of next column.)

33 Q–B3   ....

Position after 32 ... Q–K5ch

Also sufficient would have been 33
R–B3. There might have followed 33
... P–K7; 34 Q–K1, Q×P (34 ...
P–KN4; 35 K–B2, P–N5; 36 R–K3);
35 K–B2, Q–B4ch (Black has no per-
petual check with 35 ... Q–R7ch; 36
K–K3, Q–K4ch; 37 K–Q2, Q–Q4ch;
38 K×P); 36 K×P, Q×RP; 37
K–B1 and White would have had no
real difficulty in winning although
Black would have had four Pawns for
the Rook.

33 ....   **Q–B7ch**
34 K–N1   ....

Equally good was 34 K–N3 and if 37
... P–K7; 35 K–B2 stops the Pawn.

34 ....   **Q–B8ch**

White was threatening 35 R–B8ch,
K–R2; 36 Q–B5ch. 34 ... P–K7 is of
no avail on account of 35 K–B2.

35 Q–B1   **Q×RP**

Preventing R–B8ch.

(See diagram on next page.)

36 Q–B4ch   ....

White still must not relax. 36 P–K6
would be more risky. Black would have
continued 36 ... Q–Q3!; 37 Q–QB4,

Position after 35 ... Q×RP

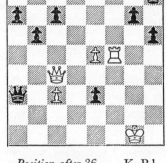

Position after 36 ... K–R1

Q–N6ch;   38 K–B1, Q–R6ch;   39
K–K1? (39 K–K2 would have been
correct), Q×R; 40 P–K7ch, K–R2;
41 P–K8(Q), Q–B7ch; 42 K–Q1,
Q–Q7 mate.

36 ....   K–R1

(See top of next column.)

37 R–B3   ....

Winning the passed Pawn by force.
37 P–K6 was, however, good enough,
for if 37 ... Q–Q3; 38 Q–K4, Q–N6ch
(38 ... Q–Q8ch; 39 K–N2, Q–Q7ch;
40 K–R3 and there are no more checks
left); 39 K–B1, Q–R6ch; 40 K–K2,
etc. Nor would 37 ... Q–B8ch have

accomplished anything because of 38
Q–B1, Q×P; 39 R–B8ch, K–R2; 40
Q–B5ch, P–N3; 41 Q–B7ch, Q–N2;
42 P–K7.

37 ....   P–QN4
38 Q–B1   ....

Threatening R–B8ch and mate in
three moves.

38 ....   K–N1
39 R×P   Q–B4
40 Q–B2   P–QR4
41 P–K6   Q–K2
42 Q–B5   P–B3
43 R–B3   Resigns

The threat of 44 Q–B7ch convinces
my opponent of the hopelessness of
continued resistance.

The Sacrifice of a Mere Pawn

Alexander of England is a veteran who is a very hard man to beat. He
is resourceful and most dangerous when attacking. In the following game
all went quietly during the first seventeen moves and the position seemed
to offer nothing to either side. Then the fireworks started—all as a result
of my choosing a continuation which involved the sacrifice of a Pawn.
Against the resulting attack, my opponent defended brilliantly. He
seemed to have solved all his problems. On my 24th turn, however, I

made a subtle retreat of the Bishop. This surprise move decided the issue. Alexander was forced to give up a Bishop for three Pawns—ordinarily about an even exchange—but the resulting position was lost for Black.

ENGLISH OPENING

Chess Olympics
Munich, 1958

S. RESHEVSKY   C. H. O'D. ALEXANDER

1 P-QB4 ....

This move has become fashionable recently. The reason for its popularity is the belief among leading players that it is less committing than 1 P-Q4. This is true to a certain extent. The main drawback to 1 P-QB4 is that it gives Black a large choice of equalizing variations. This is only true, however, if Black knows all the latest wrinkles in those variations.

1 .... **P-KN3**

This move practically limits Black to adopting either the King's Indian Defense or the Dutch Defense. 1 ... N-KB3 is, of course, less committing.

2 P-KN3 **B-N2**
3 B-N2 **P-K4**

Black's intentions become clear. He wants to play an early ... P-KB4. This setup is a favorite of Alexander. The purpose of this maneuver is to obtain quick control of Black's K5 square. If White plays P-K4 belatedly,

Black is able to build up an attack by replying with ... P-KB5.

4 N-QB3 **P-Q3**
5 P-Q3 ....

If 5 N-B3, P-KB4; 6 P-Q4, P-K5 with a fine position for Black.

5 .... **P-KB4**
6 P-K4 **N-K2**

Black wants to recapture with the Knight when White plays P×P. However, 6 ... N-KB3 seems better.

7 KN-K2 ....

7 P-B4, KP×P; 8 B×P was to be considered seriously.

7 .... **O-O**
8 O-O **QN-B3**
9 P-B4 ....

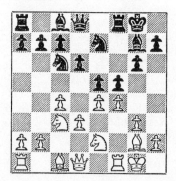

The position is almost symmetrical, the only difference being that White has a Pawn at QB4. That difference does not give any particular advantage. The position is approximately equal.

9 .... **P×KP**
10 QP×P ....

On 10 N×P, Black replies 10 ... P-KR3 (to prevent N or B-KN5); 11 P×P, R×Rch; 12 Q×R, P×P and White's isolated QP is weaker than

Black's KP. 13 N–B6ch does not mean anything. Black simply plays 13 ... K–R1 followed by ... N–B4.

10 ....   B–K3

11 N–Q5   ....

I was considering 11 P–N3 but decided against it. White would have been compelled to make a series of defensive moves. And my opponent could have simplified the position by a few exchanges: 11 P–N3, P×P; 12 P×P (12 B×P or R×P would have isolated White's KP unnecessarily), B–N5 (threatening ... B×QN); 13 B–N2(13 B–B3, B×B; 14 R×B would have overexposed White's King), N–Q5 and now Black has the choice of exchanging some minor pieces after 14 Q–Q2, or playing 14 .... KN–B3 or even ... P–B4 followed by ... KN–B3 with an excellent game.

The primary purpose of the text-move is to get this Knight to K3 where it would prevent Black from playing ... B–KN5.

11 ....   Q–Q2

A natural looking move. Apparently it is made to enable Black to play ... B–R6.

12 R–N1   ....

Preparing for P–QN4 in case Black continues with 12 ... B–R6 as expected.

12 ....   B–N5

My opponent must have decided that White's Bishop was weak anyhow and planned to give up his Bishop for a Knight instead of playing ... B–R6. This proved to be a wrong decision. Later in the game, White's KB became very much alive.

13 N–K3   B×N

I prefer 13 ... B–R4. My opponent probably feared that the Bishop at KR4 might get into trouble. There is, however, no way of endangering the Bishop. White's best would have been 14 B–B3.

14 Q×B   N–Q5

The position is approximately even now. White has the two Bishops; Black has a well-posted Knight at his Q5. White's problem is to find an avenue of activity for his KB.

15 Q–Q3   P×P

To give his Bishop greater scope.

| 16 P×P | P–QR4 |

Preventing P–QN4.

| 17 B–Q2 | P–B4 |
| 18 P–B5 | .... |

I decided that the time for aggressive action had come.

| 18 .... | N(K2)–B3 |

Best. For if 18 ... P×P; 19 P×P, N(Q5)×P (19 ... KN×P; 20 B–R3 wins a piece); 20 N×N, R×N (20 ... N×N; 21 B–K4, B–Q5ch; 22 K–R1 and Black's KRP must fall); 21 B–R3, with sufficient compensation for the Pawn. In this variation White also has 21 R×R, Q×R; 22 Q×Q, N×Q; 23 B×NP.

| 19 N–Q5 | .... |

Threatening P–B6.

19	N–K4
20 Q–KR3	N×QBP
21 B–N5	....

(*See top of next column.*)

Black is confronted with a serious threat: 22 N–K7ch, K–R1; 23 N×Pch or P–B6.

| 21 .... | QR–K1 |

Meets that threat nicely.

Position after 21 B–N5

| 22 P–B6 | Q×Q |
| 23 B×Q | .... |

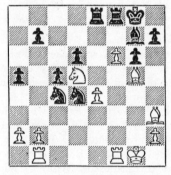

Here I expected 23 ... B–R1 and I had decided to continue with 24 N–K7ch, K–B2; 25 B–R6 winning the exchange, but I was aware of the fact that it still would have been a herculean task to win the game.

| 23 .... | R–K4! |

A terrific rejoinder which I had not counted on! The point is that after 24 N–K7ch, K–B2; 25 P×Bch, K×P, Black regains his piece by force, for if 26 R×R, R×Bch followed by ... K×R, and if 26 B–R4, P–KN4 again regaining a piece with a won position.

| 24 B–B1 | .... |

One good move deserves another in reply! This retreat of the Bishop meets the crucial situation surprisingly well. The point is that after Black retreats his Bishop, 24 ... B–R1, White wins material with 25 P–N3 when the Black Knight is trapped.

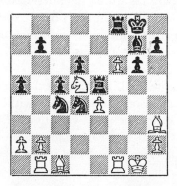

24	N–K7ch
25 K–R1	R×KP

Best under the circumstances. If 25 ... N×B; 26 QR×N and Black loses a piece with a worse position than after the text-move.

26 P×B	R×Rch
27 B×R	K×P

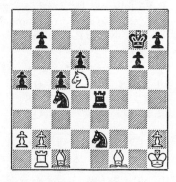

Black has three Pawns for the piece—usually sufficient compensation. But White's two Bishops are too powerful, and Black's Knights are miserably

placed. It is clear that Black's prospects are very dim.

28 B–N5	P–R3
29 B–Q8	N–Q7
30 B–N2	....

30 R–Q1, N×B; 31 R×N is also sufficient, but retaining the Bishops makes the task easier.

30	R–QR5

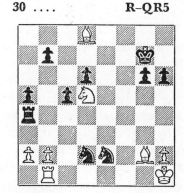

31 R–R1	....

31 R–Q1 was tempting but bad: 31 R–Q1, R×P; 32 R×N, R–R8ch; 33 B–B1, R×Bch; 34 K–N2, R–B4! and Black remains with four Pawns for the piece.

However, 31 R–K1 was to be considered, for after 31 ... R×P; 32 R×N, R–R8ch; 33 B–B1, N×B (33 ... R×B; 34 K–N2, R–Q8; 35 N–B3 winning a piece); 34 K–N2, R–Q8; 35 N–B3, R–R8; 36 B–K7 and White should have little difficulty in winning.

31	K–B2
32 P–QR3	....

Threatening R–Q1 or R–K1.

32	R–R5?

Black was in terrific time trouble but his position was hopeless anyhow.

33 B×R	Resigns

A Surprise Sacrifice

The Dutch player Van den Berg is not recognized as an outstanding master. He is, however, well known as a great theoretician. Dr. Max Euwe and I were once discussing an opening variation. Dr. Euwe finally suggested that we consult Mr. Van den Berg regarding the latest analysis of this variation. I was told by Dr. Euwe that Mr. Van den Berg remembers hundreds of games by heart, including the tournaments in which they were played. He has been a collaborator of the famous "Archives" for years.

I was pitted against Mr. Van den Berg in the 12th round of the Israeli International Tournament. I had to win in order to keep up with the leader, Laslo Szabo. The opening was one of the latest variations of the King's Indian Defense. I managed to get a passed Pawn. This, instead of being an advantage, turned out to be a disadvantage. I had to use all my resources to find adequate measures to defend this Pawn.

My opponent played the mid-game superbly. I was beginning to get worried. On my 27th move I suddenly saw a combination which looked extremely promising. It involved sacrificing my Queen for a Rook and Bishop plus positional superiority. My opponent being in time trouble, I decided to plunge into this sacrifice. This turned out to be sound and my opponent's resistance collapsed quickly.

KING'S INDIAN DEFENSE

Israeli International Tournament

Tel Aviv, 1958

S. RESHEVSKY   VAN DEN BERG

1	P–QB4	N–KB3
2	N–KB3	P–KN3
3	P–KN3	B–N2
4	B–N2	O–O
5	O–O	P–Q3
6	P–Q4	N–B3

Here Black chooses one of the newest setups in the King's Indian Defense. The purpose is to prepare for ... P–QN4, exerting pressure against White's QBP. The other two alternatives are 6 ... QN–Q2 followed by ... P–K4, etc., or 6 ... P–B4 followed by ... N–B3. At the present time the text-move gives White more difficulty in obtaining an opening advantage.

7	N–B3	P–QR3
8	P–KR3	....

8 B–B4 followed by R–B1 is a good alternative. Also to be recommended is 8 P–N3, R–N1; 9 B–N2, P–QN4; 10 P×P, P×P; 11 R–B1.

8	....	R–N1
9	B–K3	P–QN4
10	P×P	P×P
11	N–Q2	B–Q2

12 R–B1   ....

Here I was considering 12 N–N3 (to take away the square QR4 from Black's Knight) but after 12 ... P–N5; 13 N–N1 (if 13 N–R4, N–R2 and the Knight is under serious attack), putting the Knight out of play.

12 ....   **N–QR4**

Also playable was 12 ... P–N5; 13 N–R4, N–QR4.

13 P–QN4   **N–B5**
14 N×N   **P×N**

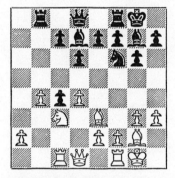

I achieved what I started out to do— get a passed Pawn and give Black a doubled Pawn. These theoretical advantages remain theoretical only because of the following facts: (1) My passed Pawn cannot advance with ease. (2) Black's doubled Pawns are not a disadvantage to him since one of them is a passed Pawn far in the enemy's territory.

15 P–R3   **P–B3**

Obviously, to support his QBP with ... P–Q4.

16 Q–Q2   **P–Q4**
17 B–N5   ....

With the logical intention of preparing P–K4.

17 ....   **R–K1**

Well played. Black is preparing to play ... P–K4 himself.

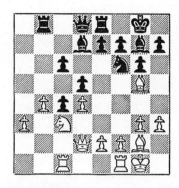

18 KR–K1   ....

The immediate 18 P–K4 produces nothing: 18 P–K4, P×P; 19 N×P, N×N; 20 B×N, B×RP; 21 KR–Q1, B–N5; 22 P–B3, B–Q2; 23 R×P, Q–N3 with even chances.

18 ....   **R–R1**

Of course not 18 ... P–K4 because of 19 P×P, R×KP, 20 B–B4 winning the exchange.

19 P–QR4   ....

19 ....   **Q–N3**

Interesting was 19 ... P–K4; 20 P×P (20 P–K4, P×QP; 21 Q×P, P–R3!), R×KP; 21 B–K3 (not 21 P–K4?, P–Q5!; 22 B×N, P×N and wins), followed by B–Q4 with slightly the better of it.

20 P–N5   ....

Stronger was 20 R–N1 followed by P–R5 and N–R4–B5. The result of the text-move was that White was left with a weakened passed QRP.

| 20 .... | P–K3 |

20 ... P×P would have been bad because of 21 B×N, P×B (21 ... B×B; 22 N×QP followed by N×Bch winning the exchange); 22 N×QP, Q–Q3; 23 P×P, B×NP; 24 N–B3, B–B3; 25 P–Q5, B–N2; 26 N–K4 and Black is in trouble.

21 P×P	B×P
22 R–N1	Q–R4
23 R–KB1	N–Q2
24 B–B4	B–B1

White's passed Pawn is not an asset; it is, rather, weak and feebly protected. Black's pieces seem to be well posted. If Black could gain control of the QN-file White would be in real trouble.

| 25 Q–N2 | .... |

Intending to play B–Q2.

| 25 .... | R–R2 |
| 26 B–Q2 | R–N2 |

Correct was 26 ... Q–R3.

| 27 Q×R! | .... |

There is very little doubt that my opponent did not see this sacrifice. Ordinarily, of course, a Rook and Bishop are not sufficient material for a Queen. In this case, however, there are the additional important considerations of White's passed Pawn and the control of the seventh rank.

| 27 .... | B×Q |
| 28 R×B | .... |

| 28 .... | Q–Q1 |

There is nothing better. For instance, if 28 ... N–N3; 29 N–K4, Q–R3; 30 N–B6ch, K–R1; 31 R×P and wins. If

28 ... N–B3; 29 N–K4, Q–Q1; 30
B–R5!

29 R(B1)–N1   B–N2

Black's pieces are almost completely
out of play.

30 N–N5   K–R1

30 ... N–N3 loses on account of 31
B–R5 winning the Knight.

31 P–R5   ....

White's passed Pawn is now something to be really concerned about.

31 ....   N–N1
32 N–B7   R–B1
33 P–K3   ....

Protecting the QP. White need not
be in any hurry. Black is not going
anywhere.

33 ....   N–B3
34 P–R6   N×P

Obviously a desperate attempt to get
some counterplay; but if Black sits
back and does nothing he is going to be
strangled slowly but surely.

35 P×N   B×P
36 P–R7   Q–B3
37 R–N8   ....

37 B–K3 was also sufficient to win
but after 37 ... B×B; 38 P×B,
Q–QB6; 39 R–N8, Q×Pch, 40 K–R2,
Q×RP; 41 R×Rch, K–N2; 42 R–B8,
Q–R7 and Black would have been able
to put up longer resistance.

37 ....   Q×Pch
38 K–R2   B×P
39 R×Rch   K–N2
40 N×Pch   K–B3
41 R–KB1   ....

This is the move that White had in
mind when he made his 37th move.

41 ....   Resigns

Temporary Immobility and a Temporary Sacrifice

Occasionally one gets into a cramped position, voluntarily or otherwise. In the following game against Mr. Sherwin I intentionally permitted my opponent to immobilize my pieces temporarily. My strategy involved sacrificing a Pawn on my 17th move. This suddenly opened up the position to my advantage.

After regaining my Pawn on the 23rd move, the tables were turned decisively. My opponent now had great difficulty in developing his pieces. Perfect defense was necessary to save White's game. Sherwin failed to find the correct continuation. I won the exchange on the 29th move and the rest was easy.

KING'S INDIAN DEFENSE

Rosenwald Tournament
New York, 1958–59

J. SHERWIN   S. RESHEVSKY

1 P–Q4	N–KB3
2 P–QB4	P–KN3
3 N–QB3	B–N2
4 P–K4	P–Q3
5 P–B3	....

The Saemisch Variation. This setup by White against the King's Indian Defense was at one time considered extremely dangerous for Black. But adequate defenses have been found gradually and the King's Indian is again considered to be one of Black's best defenses.

| 5 .... | O–O |
| 6 B–K3 | QN–Q2 |

Another popular line leading to equality is 6 ... P–K4; 7 KN–K2, P–B3; 8 Q–Q2, P×P; 9 N×P, P–Q4, etc.

| 7 Q–Q2 | P–B4 |

This continuation tends to keep Black's KB in the game, while 7 ... P–K4 decreases this Bishop's activity, at least temporarily. Either line is playable but the text-move is not as well analyzed.

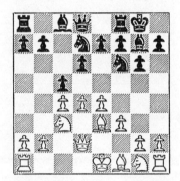

| 8 KN–K2 | P–QR3 |

Intending an early ... Q–B2.

| 9 N–B1 | P×P |
| 10 B×P | N–K4 |

| 11 B–K2 | .... |

White could have given Black a doubled Pawn by playing 11 B×N but at the expense of handing over control of his important Q4 square to Black.

11	....	Q–B2
12	P–QN3	N–B3
13	N–Q5	....

My opponent made this move with a bang, trying to convey the message that he has almost a winning position. The move looks good, but not that good.

| 13 | .... | Q–Q1 |

If 13 ... N×N; 14 B×B, K×B; 15 BP×N, N–K4; 16 O–O with more freedom for White's pieces. It appears as if the text-move seriously cramps Black's position—but Black has a plan in mind.

14 B–N6   ....

If 14 B×N, P×B; 15 R–QN1, P–B4 and Black has the better of it.

14	....	Q–Q2
15	R–QN1	P–K3
16	N×Nch	B×N
17	O–O	P–Q4
18	BP×P	P×P

(See top of next column.)

This was the plan I had in mind when I made my 13th move. This temporary sacrifice of a Pawn secures complete equality, at least.

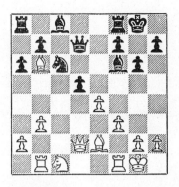

19 P×P   ....

Neither is 19 Q×P any more promising. There would have followed: 19 ... Q×Q; 20 P×Q, N–N5; 21 B–B5 (if 21 P–Q6, B–B4. If 21 R–Q1, B–B4; 22 N–Q3, N×QP with the better chances). B–B4!; 22 B×N (if 22 B×R, K×B winning material), B×R; 23 B×R, K×B with more than sufficient compensation for the Pawn.

| 19 | .... | N–K2 |
| 20 | P–Q6 | .... |

20 R–Q1 looks slightly better. There would follow: 20 ... Q–Q3; 21 Q–R5 (21 B–B2, R–Q1), B–B4; 22 N–Q3, Q×QP with the better prospects.

| 20 | .... | Q–B3 |

21 B–B2   ....

If 21 P×N, Q×Bch; 22 K–R1, B×P with two powerful Bishops.

21	....	R–Q1
22	R–Q1	B–B4
23	N–Q3	R×P
24	QR–B1	....

White could have put up greater resistance with 24 Q–K1. This would have made it possible for him to get out of the nasty pins.

24	....	Q–Q2
25	B–B5	R–Q4
26	Q–K3	R–QB1

This position is full of interesting possibilities. The immediate threat is 27 ... B×N; 28 R×B (28 B×B, N–B4 winning material), N–B4; 29 R×R, Q×R; 30 Q–B2, B–Q5; 31 B×B, R×Rch. This threat is not met satisfactorily by 27 K–R1. The winning continuation would be: 27 ... B×N; 28 R×B (28 B×B, N–B4), N–B4; 29 R×R (insufficient is 29 Q–K4, B–Q5; 30 P–KN4, N–R5; 31 B–R3, R–K1. If in this 30 B–R3, N–N6ch; 31 P×N, R–R4ch, etc.), Q×R; 30 Q–N1, Q–Q7!; 31 B–B4, N–N6ch; 32 P×N, Q–R3ch; 33 Q–R2, Q×Rch, etc.

27 N–B2   ....

27 N–N4 fails on account of 27 ... R(B1)×B; 28 either R×R, R×Rch.

27 ....   **B–N7**

The winning continuation.

28 R–B4   ....

28 Q×N is met by 28 ... Q×Q; 29 B×Q, R(B1)×R.

28 ....   **P–QN4**

29 Q×N   ....

If 29 R–KR4, R(B1)×B; 30 Q×R, R×Q; 31 R×Q, B×R.

29	....	P×R
30	R×R	Q×R
31	B–N4	P–B6
32	B–B4	....

32 ....   **Q–Q2**

Black is playing it simply. A neat finish could have been brought about by the following: 32 ... P–B7; 33 B×Q, P–B8(Q)ch; 33 B–K1 (33 Q–K1, Q×Qch; 34 B×Q, R–B8; 35 K–B1, B–B6), B–K3; 34 N–Q3, Q–K6ch; 35 B–B2, R–B8ch; 36 N×R, Q×Nch; 37 B–K1, Q×B mate.

33 Q×Q   ....

33 B×Pch, K–N2 does not improve
White's chances.

33	B×Q
34 N–Q3	B–B4
35 B×RP	R–R1
36 B–B4	P–B7
37 B–Q2	R–Q1

White is forfeited on time. However,
his position is hopeless.

5

THE ART OF DEFENSE

To meet the onslaught of an attacking player it is necessary to find the best moves to meet the threats. Sometimes it is possible to counterattack immediately, but defensive tactics are more customary. When the assault has simmered down you may be able to take advantage of the weak pawn structure or other weaknesses created by the attack, or you may play for an immediate win if your opponent sacrificed material.

A great many attacks are unsound, especially premature assaults made without sufficient preparation in the opening of a game, but they may still be dangerous. The defender must be able to demonstrate that a faulty attack can be resisted successfully.

A premature attack can often be met by moves which defend the immediate threats and at the same time promote the development of pieces. When correctly opposed, such attacks usually meet swift retribution. However, attacks later in the game, after development has been completed, may be more difficult to withstand. Of course, a faulty attack, perhaps due to desperation, is relatively easy to ward off, but it may be impossible to oppose a sound attack based on positional superiority. However, the resources of a defender are remarkable. Often in seemingly hopeless positions, a move is found that answers the threats and may even turn the tables.

In this chapter we present some games in which the art of defense against powerful attacks is exemplified. The last game of the chapter shows how tenacious defense in a difficult situation can save an apparently lost game.

Trying Too Hard

Sometimes a player is too aggressive. It may be a natural style of play, or it may be assumed on special occasions. It is commonly but erroneously believed that the best way to beat a conservative opponent is to unleash an attack as quickly as possible and throw everything at him, including the proverbial kitchen sink. Unless the attack is completely sound (which is unlikely at an early stage of the game), this is the worst possible strategy to adopt. A conservative player is at his best when defending and can usually meet a premature attack successfully.

In the following game, Robert Byrne sat down with the intention of crushing me with an irresistible attack. This became evident when he played the aggressive 12 . . . P–KN4. The assault proved to be an abortive enterprise. I met the onslaught with a few defensive moves, then crashed through on the Queen-wing, winning a Pawn. My opponent's attack never had sufficient momentum to make any headway.

DUTCH DEFENSE

Wertheim Memorial Tournament
New York, 1951

S. RESHEVSKY   R. BYRNE

1 P–Q4   P–KB4

The Dutch Defense is rarely seen nowadays. Botvinnik occasionally uses it. With accurate opening play White can obtain the upper hand. Black's serious problem is the development of his Queen-Bishop.

2 P–QB4   N–KB3
3 P–KN3   P–K3

3 . . . P–KN3, the Yugoslav Variation, is an attempt to get away from the well-trodden path but promises no better fate.

4 B–N2   B–K2
5 N–KB3   O–O
6 O–O   P–Q4
7 Q–B2   P–B3
8 QN–Q2   . . . .

Much better than 8 N–B3. This Knight is headed for K5 and the King-Knight for Q3. This setup for the

Knights is ideal, as will be seen later in the game.

8 . . . .   Q–K1

Headed for KR4. With the aid of other pieces, the Queen will be utilized here in the planned attack.

9 N–K5   Q–R4
10 R–N1   . . . .

Both sides have declared their intentions. White is going to proceed on the Queen-wing, Black on the King-side.

10 . . . .   P–QR4

If 10 . . . Q×KP; 11 B–B3 wins the Queen.

10

11 P-QN3 ....

White must strive for P-QN4-5 in order to weaken Black's QP formation. 11 P-QR3, with the intention of playing 12 P-QN4, would be met by 11 ... P-R5!

11 .... **QN-Q2**
12 N-Q3 ....

An excellent square for the Knight. From here it can be played to KB4, driving the Queen away, when necessary to do so.

12 .... **P-KN4**
13 P-QR3 **B-Q3**

Obviously, Black's QB is out of action. This will greatly contribute to my opponent's downfall.

14 N-B3 **N-K5**
15 N(B3)-K5 ....

Blocking Black's KB and also enabling White to drive Black's KN with P-B3 if necessary.

15 .... **R-B3**

My opponent is throwing all available pieces into the fray.

16 B-B3 **Q-R6**
17 B-N2 **Q-R4**
18 P-QN4 **RP×P**
19 RP×P **R-KR3**
20 P-R3 **N×N**
21 P×N **B-B1**
22 P-B5 **R-N3**

With the intention of playing ... P-B5.

23 K-R2 ....

With the serious threat of winning the Knight with P-B3.

23 .... **P-B5**

Black is compelled to resort to drastic measures. 23 ... P-Q5, enabling 24 ... N-B6, is met by 24 B-N2, winning a Pawn.

24 B-B3 ....

24 .... **P×Pch**

If 24 ... Q-R3 (which is better than the text-move); 25 B-N4 (to prevent ... P-N5), P×Pch; 26 P×P followed by 27 B-K3 or N-B2 with excellent prospects. After 24 ... Q-R3, White must not play 25 P×P, P-N5; 26 B-N2, P×P and if 27 B×P, Q-R5,

threatening ... R–KR3, and if 27
B–B3, R–N7ch is sufficient to draw.

25 P×P Q–R3

25 ... P–N5 fails on account of 26
N–B4, Q–R3; 27 B×N, P×B; 28
Q×P with a clearly won position. In
this, White must not play 27 N×R,
Q×Pch; 28 K–N1, P×B; 29 P×P,
N×NP, etc.

26 B×N P×B
27 N–B2 ....

Winning the King-Pawn by force.

27 .... Q–N2
28 Q×P B–Q2

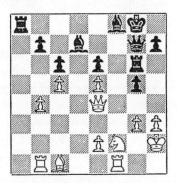

Black finally develops his Queen-
Bishop. There is no semblance of an
attack left and Black has no compensation for the Pawn he lost.

29 B–N2 B–K1

30 R–QR1 ....

Getting control of the Rook-file.

30 .... R–Q1
31 Q–K3 ....

To get the Knight to Q6 via K4.

31 .... Q–QB2
32 N–K4 B–K2
33 N–Q6 R–N2
34 Q–N3 R–N3

The only way to defend the KP. 34
... B–Q2 fails because of 35 N–B5,
R–B2; 36 N–R6ch.

35 R–R7 R–N1
36 K–N2 ....

A waiting move.

36 .... Q–Q2
37 R(1)–QR1 P–R4
38 R–R8 R×R

38 ... Q–Q1 is bad because of 39
N×P and 38 ... Q–B2 loses to 39
N×B.

39 R×R	B×N
40 KP×B	K–R2
41 Q–QB3	R–N1
42 Q–B6	....

(See diagram at right.)

42	P–N5

There is no defense against the threat
of R–Q8. If 42 ... B–B2; 43 R×R
followed by Q–R8ch. If 42 ... B–N3;
43 Q–R8ch, R×Q; 44 R×R mate.

43 R–Q8	P×Pch

Position after 42 Q–B6

44 K–R2	Resigns

44 ... Q–B2 loses to 45 Q×Qch,
B×Q; 46 R×R followed by P–Q7.

A Colorful Grandmaster

Miguel Najdorf is one of the most colorful grandmasters in chess. His
temperament and nervous actions are well known to chess followers. His
style resembles that of Alekhine. He is an outstanding student of the
game, and he is especially known for his great knowledge of the latest
analyses of the openings. He loves attacking positions. He is resourceful,
fearless, and always dangerous. His record against minor masters is
fantastic.

When my first match against Najdorf was arranged, I knew that I was
going to have a real fight on my hands. I spent a considerable time in
preparing for the match. In addition to brushing up on my openings, I
devoted a lot of attention to my opponent's preferences for different
variations.

Fortunately, I was able to make a good showing during the first half
of the match. Being discouraged by his poor start, my opponent's confidence was greatly shaken. I was able to win the match by a comfortable
margin.

In the first game, which appears on these pages, Najdorf apparently
decided to throw caution to the winds and launch an immediate attack.
White started his assault on the 12th move, before completing development. The attack was successfully met. Then White decisively weakened
his position by his aggressive 24th move. Black then restricted the

mobility of White's pieces. With all the steam gone from his attack, White overstepped the time limit in a lost position.

NIMZO-INDIAN DEFENSE

Najdorf–Reshevsky Match
New York, 1952

M. NAJDORF   S. RESHEVSKY

1	P–Q4	N–KB3
2	P–QB4	P–K3
3	N–QB3	B–N5
4	Q–B2	....

In recent years this move has come into disfavor. It has been replaced by the more flexible 4 P–K3. That is not to say that the text-move is inferior. It might come into vogue again in the future.

4 ....   P–B4

My other favorite is 4 ... N–B3, the Milner-Barry variation.

5	P×P	O–O
6	P–QR3	B×BP
7	N–B3	N–B3
8	P–QN4	....

The aggressive method of handling this variation. 8 B–N5, P–QN3; 9 P–K3, B–N2; 10 O–O, R–B1, etc., does not promise much for either side.

8	....	B–K2
9	P–K3	P–Q3
10	B–N2	P–QR4

Provoking the attack of White's QNP in order to get Black's QB4 square accessible for his Knights. Although Black is losing time by having to retreat his Knight, he is sufficiently compensated by the increase in the mobility of his pieces.

11	P–N5	N–N1
12	N–N5	....

Typical of Najdorf—going in for the attack. Correct and conservative was 12 B–K2 followed by O–O.

12 ....   QN–Q2

There are no immediate threats, so Black calmly proceeds to develop his pieces.

13 B–K2   ....

Better than 13 B–Q3, where the Bishop would have been subject to attack by N–K4 or B4.

13	....	P–R3
14	P–KR4	....

A clear declaration of aggressive intentions. Najdorf certainly had this continuation in mind when he made his 12th move. That he chose such a dangerous plan in the first game is difficult to understand. Positionally correct was 14 KN–K4.

14	**Q–B2**

Obviously, 14 ... P×N; 15 P×P,
Q–B2 (15 ... N–K1??; 16 Q–R7
mate) is bad for Black, since White
would regain the piece and open the
Rook file for a devastating attack.

15 QN–K4	**P–K4**

Reducing the effectiveness of White's
QB. This was essential, even at the
expense of weakening Black's Q4
square.

16 N–N3	**....**

Aiming at KB5.

16	**R–Q1**

The freeing move of 16 ... P–Q4
tempted me, but after 17 N–B5, R–K1;
18 N×Bch, R×N; 19 N–B3, P×P; 20
Q×P with the better position because
of the two Bishops. White can also
reply to 16 ... P–Q4 with 17 QR–B1
to advantage.

17 R–QB1	**....**

Preventing ... P–Q4.

17 R–QB1	**....**
18 N(5)–K4	**B–K3**

Black has gradually developed his
pieces favorably with no visible attacking dangers forthcoming.

19 N–KB5	**QR–B1**

19 ... B×N; 20 N×Nch, B×N;

21 Q×B would have been unwise for
Black because he would have given
away his most active Bishop.

20 N×Bch	**....**

My opponent had no way of
continuing to bring more pressure
against my King. In addition, Black
was seriously threatening to demolish
White's position with 20 ... P–Q4.

20	**Q×N**
21 N×Nch	**Q×N**
22 Q–K4	**....**

Stopping P–Q4.

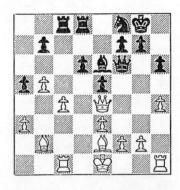

22	**P–QN3**

If 22 ... P–Q4; 23 Q×KP, Q×Q;
24 B×Q, P×P; 25 B–Q4 and White
has slightly better prospects.

23 P–R5	**N–Q2**

24 P–B4? ....

Unnecessarily weakening himself. Better was 24 O–O, and after 24 ... N–B4; 25 Q–B3 it would still have been difficult for me to have made immediate progress.

24	B–B4
25 Q–B3	N–B4

With unpleasant threats of 26 ... B–K5 or N–Q6ch. White is unable to continue with 26 O–O because of 26 ... P–K5!; 27 B×Q (otherwise Black plays Q×B), P×Q; 28 B×R, P×B, winning two pieces for a Rook.

26 P×P	P×P
27 O–O	....

Better was 27 Q–N3, N–K5 (Black can also simply continue with 27 ... R–K1; 28 O–O, Q–K3); 28 Q×KP, Q–N4 with many complications.

27	B–Q6

28 KR–Q1 ....

28 Q–N3 is met by 28 ... Q–N4. Equally unpleasant for White is 28 Q×Q, P×Q; 29 B×B, N×B; 30 R–QB2, K–N2; 31 B–R1, N–B4! followed by either R–Q6 or N–K5 with a big edge in the end game.

It is clear that White has little hope of survival if an end game is reached. The main reasons for this are Black's greater control of space, especially the QR–file, and White's poor Pawn structure.

28	Q–K3

The purpose of Black's moves from now on is to further restrict the mobility of White's pieces.

29 R–Q2	....

29 B×B, N×B; 30 R–B2, N×B loses a Pawn.

29	P–B3
30 Q–B1	....

White is slowly being strangled and is running out of constructive moves.

30	P–K5

The noose is being tightened.

31 Q–Q1	P–R5
32 B–Q4	N–N6

Forfeited on time. The position was hopelessly lost for White.

Meeting the Attack

This third game of my match against Najdorf was quite similar to the first. For eight moves the openings were identical. Although I was successful in the initial encounter, I decided to vary somewhat on my ninth move. In the first game my opponent vigorously endeavored to start an attack. Calm and calculated defensive measures met this threat successfully.

In the third game I obtained equality in the opening. On his 16th turn Najdorf chose a continuation which gave me an isolated Pawn, but the greater mobility of my pieces provided sufficient compensation. There followed a strategic rearrangement of pieces on both sides. No visible progress could be claimed by either player.

On his 30th turn Najdorf again decided to play aggressively. I found the correct defensive setup, and, in addition, obtained two Bishops and the much better Pawn position. When any semblance of an attack had vanished, my opponent found himself in a hopelessly lost end game.

NIMZO-INDIAN DEFENSE

Najdorf–Reshevsky Match
New York, 1952

M. NAJDORF	S. RESHEVSKY
1 P–Q4	N–KB3
2 P–QB4	P–K3
3 N–QB3	B–N5
4 Q–B2	P–B4
5 P×P	O–O
6 P–QR3	B×BP
7 N–B3	N–B3
8 P–QN4	B–K2

9 P–K3   ....

The natural P–K4 is inferior because it cuts off the diagonal QN1–KR7. In addition, it makes White's Q4 and KB4 squares accessible to Black's pieces. There could have followed: 9 ... P–Q3; 10 B–N2, P–K4!; 11 P–R3 (preventing ... B–N5), N–KR4 threatening the freeing P–B4, and if White prevents this with 12 B–Q3, then 12 ... N–B5 is cumbersome for White.

9	P–QN3

An improvement on 9 ... P–Q3 played in the first game. The text-move tends to bring speedier pressure on White's QBP by getting the QR to QB1.

| 10 B–N2 | B–N2 |
| 11 B–Q3 | .... |

This Bishop belongs at K2 where it would be less subject to attack, but Najdorf has a different idea in mind; he intends to get his Queen located on K2.

| 11 .... | R–B1 |
| 12 O–O | .... |

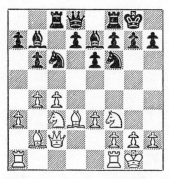

12 ....   **P–KR3**

A precautionary move. The immediate 12 ... Q–B2 costs a Pawn: 13 N–QN5, Q–N1; 14 B×N, B×B; 15 B×Pch, K–R1; 16 QR–Q1, P–N3; 17 B×P, P×B; 18 R×P with ample compensation for the piece. I considered 12 ... P–Q4 but after 13 P×P, P×P; 14 Q–K2 or KR–Q1 Black is left with an isolated Queen-Pawn.

13 KR–Q1   **P–R3**

Preparing for ... Q–B2. The Queen must be developed so that the KR can get into play.

14 Q–K2   **Q–B2**
15 QR–B1   **P–Q3**

15 ... KR–Q1 is the obvious move here and perhaps the correct one, but I wanted my opponent to continue the way he did. The text-move makes the temporary sacrifice more attractive.

16 N–QN5!?   **....**

Looks like a brilliant stroke but actually leads to nothing for White. Simply 16 N–K4 or N–QR4 was more promising.

16 ....   **P×N**

Refusing to capture the Knight would have been fatal: 16 ... Q–N1; 17 B×N, B×B (17 ... P×B dangerously exposes the King to attack); 18 N×P!, R–B2; 19 B–N1 with a terrific grip on the position.

17 P×P   **Q–N1**
18 P×N   **R×P**
19 R×R   **B×R**

White has a majority of Pawns on the Q-side, Black a majority in the center. Black's QNP, although isolated, is not subject to immediate pressure. The position is approximately even.

20 N–Q4   **B–N2**
21 P–K4   **....**

Preventing ... P–Q4 but giving Black a temporary target.

21 ....   **Q–R1**

21 ... P–Q4; 22 P–K5, N–Q2; 23 P–B4 would enhance White's chances.

22 P–B3   **N–Q2**

Both sides are beginning to jockey for position.

23 B–B4	N–K4
24 B–N3	B–R3

Provoking White's next move.

25 P–N5	B–N2
26 P–QR4	....

The advance of this Pawn enables Black's Queen to get into play via QR4.

26	K–R1

Black wants to place his Rook on QB1 but if 26 ... R–B1, with Black's King still at KN1, White has the possibility of playing N × P, etc., obtaining a Rook and two Pawns for Bishop and Knight. Avoidance of this possibility was the reason for Black's move.

27 Q–K3	....

The position is approximately even at this point. Najdorf, however, is not convinced of that. He is beginning to follow an aggressive and dangerous

course which quickly gets him into trouble. The correct continuation was 27 R–QB1, R–B1; 28 Q–Q2 with an even end game resulting.

27	R–B1
28 N–K2	K–R2

With the King at R1 Black's Knight cannot move because of Q × RPch.

29 N–N3	....

Is Black's QNP immune? If White captures the Pawn he gets much the worst of it: 29 Q × NP, N–B5; 30 B × N, R × B; 31 N–B3 (31 P–R5, P–Q4 with similar results. If 31 R–Q4, R–B7!), P–Q4; 32 Q–B2, P–Q5!; 33 N–K2 (33 R × P?, B–B4), P–K4 with a winning position.

29	Q–R4

29 ... N–B5 was also good.

30 P–B4	....

Further weakening his Pawn position. 30 R–QB1 was the logical continuation and would have given my opponent fair chances of holding his own.

30	N–B5
31 B×N	R×B
32 Q–Q3	....

This is the point of White's strategy. He is going to get his KP to Q6. It soon becomes clear, however, that White must pay a heavy price for this accomplishment.

32	Q×RP
33 P–K5ch	K–N1
34 P×P	B–Q1

(See diagram at right.)

White's passed Pawn is no serious threat. On the other hand, White's King position is seriously threatened by the coordinated action of Black's Queen, Rook, and Queen-Bishop. In addition, White's isolated Pawns are extremely vulnerable.

| 35 N–R5 | R–B7 |
| 36 R–Q2 | R×R |

Position after 34 ... B–Q1

37 Q×R	P–B3
38 Q–K2	Q–K5
39 Q×Q	....

White cannot avoid the exchange of Queens without giving material. If 39 Q–Q2, Q–Q4, etc.

39	B×Q
40 P–N4	K–B2
41 K–B2	
Resigns	

After 41 ... B–Q6 the QNP is lost. Eventually, the QP would also have fallen.

Defending with Confidence

Meeting a vicious assault against one's King often requires precise defense. Strong nerves are indispensable in such situations. In addition, complete self-confidence is necessary.

In the first game of our second match Mr. Najdorf chose his favorite King's Indian Defense. The particular variation played was of theoretical value. On my ninth move I decided to give the impression of losing a few tempi with my Queen-Bishop in order to cause an almost imperceptible weakness in my opponent's Pawn formation. This apparent loss of time induced Najdorf to attack.

I focused my attention on the Queen-side while my opponent concentrated on the King-side. He lined up all his available forces for the assault against my King. Being ready to meet the attack I calmly proceeded to capture Najdorf's QRP. Then Black's onslaught got under way and was met by defensive moves. To continue with the attack, Najdorf was compelled to sacrifice a Knight on his 32nd turn. This turned out to be faulty. Within a few moves Black's position was lost.

KING'S INDIAN DEFENSE

Najdorf–Reshevsky Match
Buenos Aires, 1953

S. RESHEVSKY	M. NAJDORF
1 P–Q4	N–KB3
2 P–QB4	P–KN3
3 N–QB3	B–N2
4 P–K4	P–Q3
5 B–K2	O–O
6 N–B3	P–K4
7 O–O	N–B3

This is the popular continuation at present. It certainly is more aggressive than the quiet 7 ... QN–Q2; 8 R–K1, P–B3; 9 B–B1, etc.

8 B–K3   ....

Avoiding all the complications arising from 8 P–Q5, N–K2; 9 N–K1, N–Q2; 10 N–Q3, P–KB4; 11 P–B3, P–B5, when Black's attack has been proven to be quite dangerous.

8	N–KN5
9 B–N5	....

White is willing to lose some time to provoke 9 ... P–B3. I felt intuitively that I would be sufficiently compensated by the following three considerations: (1) Black's Pawn solidity on the King-

side would be somewhat weakened; (2) his King would be partly exposed: (3) his King-Bishop would be out of play, at least temporarily.

9 ....   **P–B3**

9 ... B–B3 gives White an advantage as follows: 10 B×B, Q×B (10 ... N×B; 11 Q–Q2); 11 P–KR3, N–R3 (11 ... P×P?; 12 N–Q5 wins a piece); 12 P–Q5, N–Q1 (12 ... N–K2 loses a Pawn after 13 N–QN5); 13 P–QN4 with a considerable edge.

10 B–B1   **N–R3**

The alternative 10 ... P×P; 11 N×P, N×N; 12 Q×N, P–KB4; 13 Q–Q5ch, K–R1; 14 B×N, P×B; 15 B–K3 is in White's favor.

11 P×P   **BP×P**

If 11 ... QP×P; 12 N–Q5, B–K3; 13 B–K3 with positional advantage. White's Knight at Q5 could not be easily dislodged.

12 B–N5   **Q–Q2**

The Queen is badly posted here, but 12 ... Q–K1; 13 N–Q5, Q–B2; 14 P–KR3, threatening to win a piece with 15 Q–Q2, is uncomfortable for Black.

13 N–Q5	K–R1
14 P–QN4	....

Beginning action on the Queen-wing.

14	N–B2
15 B–K3	N(B3)–Q1

To bring this Knight over to KB5.

16 Q–Q2	N–K3
17 KR–Q1	P–B3
18 N–B3	....

Black has succeeded in driving this Knight away but at the cost of weakening his Pawn position.

18	Q–K2
19 QR–N1	P–KN4

It is quite obvious at this point that White's efforts will be on the Queen-side, Black's on the opposite wing.

20 P–KR3	....

Necessary, to prevent ... P–N5, or ... N–B5 followed by ... B–N5.

20	Q–B3
21 R–N3	R–KN1
22 R–R3	N–B5
23 N–R2	....

White must not be impetuous and grab the Pawn. For instance, if 23 R×P, R×R; 24 B×R, P–N5; 25 P×P, B×P; 26 B–K3, B–R3 and Black has a dangerous attack.

23	Q–N3

If Black tried to save the Pawn it would have seriously damaged his Queen-side Pawn structure: 23 ... P–QR3; 24 P–N5, Q–N3; 25 P×BP, P×P; 26 P–B5.

24 R×P	R×R
25 B×R	P–R4

Black is now going all out for the assault. It is up to White to meet the coming attack with calm, solid defense. I felt that I could do just that.

26 B–K3	....

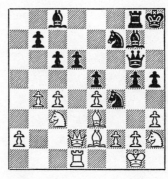

26	B–R3

Here Black missed his most promising continuation: 26 ... P–N5. This would have seriously threatened to open the KN-file with 27 ... P–N6. White's best would have been 27 P×P, P×P; 28 P–N3 (if 28 N–B1, B–R3; 29 N–N3, K–N2 with various threats, for

instance 30 ... R–R1 followed by ...
B–KN4 and ... Q–R2), N–R6ch (28
... N–N4 is very interesting and com-
plicated); 29 K–N2, B–B1 followed by
... K–N2 and ... R–R1 with better
chances than in the game.

27 P–B3   ....

Making it much more difficult for
Black to play ... P–N5.

27 ....   B–K3
28 P–QR4   ....

If Black does not undertake vigorous
action on the King-side, White is
simply going to take advantage of his
extra Pawn on the other wing.

28 ....   Q–B3
29 P–R5   P–N5

Desperate as this move turned out to
be, it was unavoidable.

30 BP×P   P×P
31 B×P   Q–R5

31 ... B×P was better.

32 Q–KB2   ....

In anticipation of my opponent's
next move.

32 ....   N×Pch?

This unsound sacrifice can be ex-
plained by the fact that Najdorf was in
terrific time trouble. However, Black's
chances were dim. If 32 ... Q×Qch;
33 K×Q, B×P, I would have had
little trouble in winning the end game
with a Pawn ahead. Retreating the
Queen, instead of the text-move, would
have been an admission of loss of time.

33 P×N   Q×P

The position looks promising for
Black, but only superficially.

34 Q–B6ch   ....

The reason for White's 32nd move,
Q–KB2, now becomes clear.

34 ....   K–R2

If 34 ... R–N2?; 35 Q×Rch
followed by B×Q. If 34 ... B–N2; 35
Q×QB (or 35 B×Q, B×Qch; 36
B–N2, B–R6; 37 R–Q2), Q×QBch;
36 K–R1, N–N4; 37 Q–N6.

35 Q×QB   Q×QBch
36 K–R1   R–N2
37 B–B5ch   K–R1
38 Q–K8ch   R–N1
39 Q×N   R–N2
40 Q–B8ch   R–N1
41 Q–B7   B–N2
42 Q–R5ch   Resigns

Premature Attack

Against sound opening moves the staging of an early attack, before completing development, is a violation of opening principles. Such an attack may be dangerous and must be met carefully, but it eventually fails when the attacker runs out of ammunition and becomes vulnerable to a counterattack.

In the following game, an inferior opening plus a premature attack led to a quick collapse of my opponent's position.

ENGLISH OPENING

Manhattan–Marshall Match
New York, 1958

S. RESHEVSKY   S. BERNSTEIN

1 P–QB4   N–QB3

An attempt to steer away from well-known lines.

2 N–QB3   P–K4
3 N–B3   P–Q3
4 P–KN3   B–K3

This might be an indication that Black has intentions of castling on the Queen-side.

5 P–Q3   B–K2
6 B–N2   Q–Q2
7 O–O   B–R6

To try to get rid of White's KB is a good idea, but not at the expense of time. Preferable was 7 ... N–B3 followed by castling on the King-side.

8 P–Q4   P–KR4!?

Ambitious, courageous, but unwise, Safer was 8 ... B×B; 9 K×B, P×P; 10 N×P, N–B3 in which Black has the worst of it, but is not lost.

9 P×P   B×B
10 K×B   P–R5
11 P×QP   ....

(See top of next column.)

11 ....   RP×P

Position after 11 P×QP.

Black sacrifices a piece in an attempt to sustain his attack. If 11 ... B×P; 12 N–K4. If 11 ... BP×P; 12 N–Q5. In either case Black has no visible compensation for the Pawn.

12 P×B   Q–R6ch
13 K–N1   ....

13 ....   P–N7

Relatively best was 13 ... N–K4;

14 BP×P, N×Nch; 15 R×N,
Q×RPch; 16 K–B1, N×P (16 ...
Q–R8ch; 17 K–B2, R–R7ch; 18
K–K3, Q–N7; 19 N–Q5 and wins);
17 B–K3, N–B4 with some fighting
chances.

14 R–K1   **KN×P**

14 ... N–K4 is met by 15 B–B4.

15 B–B4   ....

Black's attacking chances have suddenly disappeared.

15 ....   **R–Q1**
16 N–Q5   **N–N3**

(*See diagram at right.*)

17 B–N3   ....

If 17 B×P, N(N3)–K4! If 17
N×Pch, K–B1; 18 B–Q6ch, K–N1
and the threat of ... N–K4 could have
caused annoyance.

17 ....   **K–B1**

Position after 16 ... N–N3

18 Q–N3	**P–B3**
19 QR–Q1	**N(N3)–K4**
20 N×N	**P×N**
21 Q×P	**R–Q3**
22 R–Q3	....

Also good was 22 Q×BP, R–N3; 23
B×P.

22	**R(Q3)–R3**
23 Q–R8ch	**K–B2**
24 R–B3ch	**Resigns**

Provoking an Attack

Deliberate provocation of an opponent's attack requires iron nerves and
an enormous amount of self-confidence. Before allowing an onslaught
against the King, one must be reasonably sure that his analysis is
faultless. Merely relying on the opponent's weakness and errors is folly.
The underrating of opponents has cost many players many points.

Some players, including some well-known grandmasters, intensely
dislike being on the defensive. They avoid being attacked at all cost.
Attacking is their aim. This attitude is obviously a fault which can be
costly on occasion. There are few great players in the world who play
equally well when attacking or defending.

In my game against one of the leading Argentine players I had to decide
whether to subject myself to an attack. On my 13th move I allowed Mr.
Foguelman to prevent me from castling. This kept my King-Rook out of
play for quite a while. My position was temporarily cramped. Before
deciding to go on the defensive I spent a good deal of time assuring myself

that defensive measures would be adequate. I felt that after the storm was over I was going to emerge with the superior position.

SICILIAN DEFENSE

International Tournament
Buenos Aires, 1960

ALBERTO FOGUELMAN   S. RESHEVSKY

1 P–K4	P–QB4
2 N–KB3	P–Q3
3 P–Q4	P×P
4 N×P	N–KB3
5 P–KB3	....

This move is seldom seen in serious competition. The only thing that can be said in its favor is the element of surprise. This variation should give Black no difficulty in equalizing.

5	P–K4

The sharpest continuation. Also sufficient for equality is 5 ... N–B3; 6 P–QB4, P–K3; 7 N–B3, B–K2; 8 B–K3, O–O; 9 B–K2, P–Q4.

6 B–N5ch	QN–Q2

Better than 6 ... B–Q2; 7 B×Bch, QN×B; 8 N–B5, N–N3; 9 O–O, P–Q4; 10 B–N5 and Black faces a serious problem in completing his development.

7 N–B5	P–Q4

Black temporarily gives up a Pawn in order to free himself.

8 P×P	P–QR3
9 B–R4	....

No better is 9 B×Nch, Q×B; 10 N–K3, P–QN4; 11 P–QB4, B–B4; 12 N–B3, O–O where Black has excellent play for the Pawn sacrificed.

9	P–QN4
10 B–N3	N–N3
11 N–K3	B–QB4
12 N–B3	....

On 12 O–O Black regains his Pawn with 12 ... KN×P and with the much superior position.

12	B–N2

Before making this move I consumed a considerable amount of time. I discarded 12 ... O–O because of 13 O–O, P–N5 (13 ... B–N2 is met by 14 N–K4); 14 N–K4, N×N; 15 P×N, P–B4; 16 P×P, B×P; 17 K–R1 and Black would have difficulty in regaining his Pawn favorably. The text provokes White to undertake aggressive action or give the Pawn immediately, obtaining the slightly inferior position.

13 N–B5	....

White accepts the challenge. I was reasonably certain he would. 13 O–O, QN×P; 14 N×N, N×N; 15 R–K1, O–O is certainly not too promising for White. Worse was 13 N–K4, N×N; 14 P×N, Q–R5ch; 15 P–N3, Q×KP.

13	P–N3

13 ... O–O is refuted by 14 N–K4, N×N; 15 P×N and White remains a clear Pawn ahead. 14 P–Q6 also gives Black the problem of regaining the Pawn.

14 N–N7ch	K–B1

15 B–R6   K–N1

When I played 12 ... B–N2 I had to consider the possible consequences of the present position. The question was whether I would be able to extricate myself from the cramped position and emerge with some advantage. I decided that I would be able to do so.

16 Q–Q2   P–N5

An immediate effort to regain the Pawn.

17 N–K2   ....

Incorrect was 17 N–K4, N×N; 18 P×N, Q–R5ch followed by ... Q×KP with the upper hand.

17 ....   P–R4

Threatening to win a piece with ... P–R5.

18 P–Q6!   ....

A clever way of meeting the threat!

Now if 18 ... P–R5; 19 N–K6, Q×P (19 ... P×N; 20 B×KP mate); 20 Q–N5! (futile would have been 20 N×B, Q×N; 21 B–K3, Q–N4 with a fine position), KN–Q4; 21 N×B, Q×N; 22 Q×KP, etc.

18 ....   KN–Q4

18 ... Q×P was bad on account of 19 Q–N5 with the unpleasant threat of 19 N–B5 or 19 R–Q1. Neither was 18 ... B×QP any good because of 19 O–O–O with White's QR assisting in the attack.

19 N–N3   B×P

Finally regaining the Pawn! Black is now threatening to win a piece with 20 ... B–KB1. Can White do anything about it?

20 N(N7)–B5   ....

There is no way to save the Knight. If 20 N–K4, B–KB1; 21 B–N5, Q–B2, etc.

20 ....   P×N
21 N×P   ....

(*See diagram on next page.*)

21 ....   Q–B3

Not 21 ... B–KB1? because of 22 B×B, K×B (22 ... Q×B; 23 Q–N5ch); 23 Q–R6ch and Black is lost, for if 23 ... K–K1; 24 N–Q6ch,

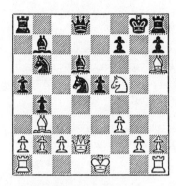

Position after 21 N×P.

K–K2; 25 N×B, Q–B2; 26 B×N,
N×B; 27 O–O–O, Q×N; 28 KR–K1
with a winning attack despite the fact
that Black is a piece ahead!

| 22 P–N4 | B–KB1 |
| 23 B–N5 | .... |

White's hope for an attack is gone.
He could have put up a little more
resistance with 23 B×B, K×B; 24
O–O–O, P–R5; 25 B×N, N×B; 26
KR–K1.

23	Q–N3
24 P–KR4	P–R3
25 B–K3	N×B
26 N×N	....

After 26 Q×N, P–R5 White loses
another piece.

26	P–R5
27 B–B4	N×B
28 N×N	B×P

The rest is elementary.

29 R–KB1	Q–K5ch
30 Q–K3	Q×Qch
31 N×Q	P–K5
32 N–Q5	K–N2
33 K–B2	R–Q1
34 N–B4	B–B4ch
35 K–N3	B–Q3

Winning more material by force.

| 36 QR–B1 | KR–K1 |
| 37 P–B3 | R–K3 |

Threatening ... R–B3.

38 P–N5	P×P
39 P×P	R–N3
Resigns	

Saving a "Lost" Game

Dan Yanofsky is a tough opponent. His style is defensive but quite
accurate. When given the slightest opportunity, he is strong enough to
beat the best.

In the following game I experimented with a new move in a well-known
variation of the King's Indian Defense. Yanofsky played the opening well,
obtaining equality. Mid-game maneuvering finally gave me a slight
advantage in space control. On my 25th turn I missed the right
continuation.

Not being content to split the point, I began to press too much. I blundered on the 29th move, losing a Pawn. Many such mistakes are fatal, as we have seen. At adjournment everyone thought that I was lost, including myself. I remember being up till 3 o'clock in the morning in an effort to find a saving continuation. I have saved many games through reluctance to give up when the chips were down.

KING'S INDIAN DEFENSE

International Tournament
Dallas, 1957

S. RESHEVSKY	D. A. YANOFSKY
1 P–Q4	N–KB3
2 P–QB4	P–KN3
3 N–QB3	B–N2
4 P–K4	P–Q3
5 B–K2	O–O
6 N–B3	P–K4
7 O–O	N–B3

7 ... QN–Q2 or ... P–B3 are other alternatives. The text-move, however, is more aggressive and more difficult for White to meet.

8 P–Q5   ....

The only other continuation, in which White can hope for any advantage, is 8 B–K3. I experimented with this move against Najdorf. There followed 8 ... N–KN5; 9 B–N5, P–B3; 10 B–B1, N–R3; 11 P×P, BP×P; 12 B–N5, Q–Q2; 13 N–Q5 with much the better of it. However, Black could have played better with 10 ... P×P; 11

N×P, N×N; 12 Q×N, P–KB4; 13 Q–Q5ch with a minimal advantage.

8 ....   **N–K2**

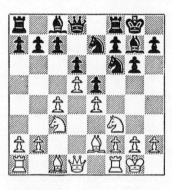

9 P–QN4   ....

Experimenting with a new move which has no future. Better is 9 N–K1, N–Q2; 10 N–Q3, P–KB4; 11 P×P, P×P; 12 P–B4, P–K5; 13 N–B2 with the better position.

9	**P–QR4**
10 B–R3	**P×P**
11 B×P	**....**

The idea behind White's 9th move was to develop the Bishop on this diagonal where it can assist the advance of the QBP. At K3 this Bishop is subject to attack by Black's KBP. The objection is the isolation of White's QR and QB Pawns.

11	**N–Q2**
12 N–K1	**P–KB4**

(See diagram on next page.)

13 B–B3   ....

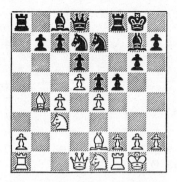

Position after 12 ... P–KB4

More exact was 13 N–Q3, P×P; 14 N×P(K4), N–KB4; 15 P–B5 with pressure on the QP. If 13 ... N–KB3; 14 B–B3 to protect the KP adequately.

13	P×P
14 N×P	N–KB4
15 N–Q3	N–B3

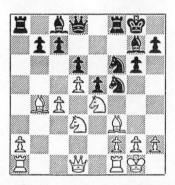

Black must get rid of the Knight too favorably posted at White's K4. A good alternative was 15 ... N–Q5; 16 B–N4, N–KB3; 17 N×Nch, Q×N; 18 B×B, QR×B; 19 P–B3, QR–K1 with equal chances.

16 N×Nch   ....

16 P–B5 fails on account of 16 ... N×P; 17 Q–N3, B–K3; 18 N–N5 (18 N×QP?, N–B5 wins a piece), Q×N; 19 B×N, B×B; 20 Q×Bch, K–R1, 21 Q×NP, P–K5 winning the exchange.

| 16 .... | Q×N |
| 17 B–K4 | .... |

Black was threatening ... P–K5 followed by ... Q×R winning the exchange.

| 17 .... | B–Q2 |
| 18 P–QR4 | .... |

Important, for it prevents either ... R–R5 or ... B–R5.

| 18 .... | N–Q5 |
| 19 P–R5 | .... |

Releasing the Queen and the Queen-Rook.

| 19 .... | B–B4 |
| 20 R–K1 | .... |

White must not relinquish control of his K4 square. If, for instance, 20 B×B, Q×B (... P×B is also strong); 21 P–B3, P–K5; 22 P×P, Q×KP and Black has made considerable progress. In this, 23 R–K1 would cost the exchange after 23 ... N–K7ch; 24 R×N, Q–Q5ch.

20 ....   **Q–N4**

Threatening ... B–N5 followed by ... N–B6ch.

21 K–R1   ....

In order to answer 21 ... B–N5 with 22 P–B3. I considered 21 B–Q2, Q–R5; 22 P–B3, P–KN4; 23 P–N3, Q–R3 (or even 23 ... B×B!; 24 P×Q, N×Pch,

etc.) and White's KB3 square would
have been seriously weakened.

21 ....   B×B
22 R×B   N–B4

Black is unable to make any further
progress on the King-side and decides
to adopt defensive tactics. Bringing
back the Knight is quite necessary so as
to protect the QP which is going to be
subjected to pressure.

   23 B–Q2   ....

Better was 23 P–B5 and if 23 ...
N–R5; 24 Q–KB1.

   23 ....   Q–Q1

The crucial position of the game has
been reached. White has succeeded in
obtaining a slight edge. The correct
continuation, however, is extremely
difficult at this point. Should White
confine his efforts to the King-side, or

the Queen-side? I decided to concentrate on the former. I now believe that
efforts on the Queen-side would have
been more productive. Thus: 24
Q–N3, P–B3 (24 ... N–Q5 would have
been answered by 25 Q–R2 and the
black Knight is misplaced defensively);
25 P–B5 with complications favorable
to White.

   24 R–N1   R–N1
   25 Q–N4   P–B3

To open the QB-file.

   26 P–B4   ....

Although this move looked promising,
it created as many difficulties for me as
for my opponent.

   26 ....   R–K1

Of course, Black must not play 26 ...
KP×P; 27 N×P when Black's K3
would become accessible to White's
Knight.

   27 QR–K1   Q–B2
   28 BP×P   ....

This helps Black by giving a good
square for his Knight at Q3. Better
was 28 Q–Q1, guarding the QB2 square,
followed by Q–N3.

   28 ....   QP×P

(See diagram on next page.)

   29 N–B4?   ....

Position after 23 ... QP×P

Losing material. The position has become quite critical for White. Among other things, Black threatens ... P×P followed by ... Q–B7. If 29 P×P, P×P; 30 B–B3, R–N6!; 31 B×P?, B×B; 32 N×B, R×N; 33 R×R, Q×R; 34 R×Q, R–N8ch.

White's difficulties arose from excessive aggressiveness. Relatively best was 29 B–N4 and if 29 ... N–Q3; 30 B×N, Q×B; 31 N–B4 with approximate equality.

29	**N–Q3!**
30 N–K6	**N×R**
31 Q×N	**....**

If 31 N×Q, N–B7ch; 32 K–N1, N×Q; 33 N×R, R×N.

31	**R×N**

Black cannot very well keep the exchange because White's Knight is too well posted.

32 P×R	**Q–Q3**
33 B–B3	**Q×P**

Black is a Pawn ahead, and White has no visible compensation for it. It is most disheartening to be in such positions, but every player is occasionally driven into these unpleasant situations. Only a fighting spirit and sheer tenacity can save him.

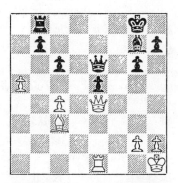

34 P–R3	**R–KB1**
35 R–QN1	**R–B5**
36 Q–K3	**R–B2**

Obviously, it would have been foolhardy for Black to have captured the QBP and allowed the capture of his QNP, giving White a dangerous passed Pawn.

37 Q–K2	**P–R3**

37 ... P–K5 was better, but Black was reluctant to commit himself before adjournment.

38 R–K1	**....**

Preventing ... P–K5.

38 ...	**R–B4**
39 K–R2	**B–B1**
40 K–R1	**B–N2**

The adjourned position.

41 R–QN1	**R–B2**

If 41 ... Q–B2; 42 K–N1, B–B1; 43
Q–Q3 and Black is stymied.

42 R–N6   ....

Intending P–R6 forcing the exchange of Pawns, which would isolate
Black's QBP.

42 ....   **P–K5**

Black's only hope of making headway
is to advance this Pawn.

43 B×B   **R×B**

43 ... K×B?; 44 Q–N2ch wins a
Pawn.

44 P–R6   **P×P**
45 R×RP   **R–N2**

With the serious threat of 46 ...
R–N8ch; 47 K–R2, Q–K4ch; 48
P–N3, R–N7. If 46 R–R1, simply 46
... P–K6 which would pin down
White's Queen in stopping the further
advance of the Pawn.

46 Q–Q1   ....

Preventing ... R–N8ch and at the
same time creating a few threats. For
instance: 46 ... Q×BP; 47 R–R8ch,
K–R2 (47 ... K–B2?; 48 Q–Q6,
Q–B8ch; 49 K–R2 and Black is in
serious trouble); 48 Q–R1!, R–N2; 49
Q–K5 with the threat of Q–K8 and
Black's chances of winning would have
been destroyed. In this, if 48 ...
P–N4? (instead of ... R–N2); 49

Q–R8ch, K–N3; 50 R–N8ch, K–R4;
51 K–R2!, Q–K7; 52 Q–B6, R–N7;
53 Q–N6ch, K–R5; 54 Q×RPch,
Q–R4; 55 R–KR8, Q×Q; 56 R×Q
mate.

If 46 ... P–K6; 47 R–R8ch, K–R2;
48 Q–Q4, R–N2; 49 Q–Q8, Q–N1; 50
Q×Q, R×Q; 51 R×R, K×R; 52
K–N1, K–B2; 53 K–B1, K–K3; 54
K–K2, K–K4; 55 K×P, P–B4; 56
P–N3, P–R4; 57 P–R4 draws.

46 ....   **Q–B3**

Black decides to play it safely.

47 R–R8ch   **K–N2**
48 R–K8   **R–K2**
49 R×R   **Q×R**
50 Q–Q4ch   **K–B2**
51 K–N1   **P–B4**

51 ... P–K6 leads to nothing. White
wins the KP by playing 52 K–B1,
P–K7ch; 52 K–K1 and with the aid
of the Queen can capture the Pawn at
will.

52 Q–Q5ch   **K–N2**

52 ... K–B3 was slightly better.

53 K–B2   **Q–R5ch**
54 K–K2   **Q–B5**
55 Q×BP   **P–K6**
Draw

On 56 Q–K7ch comes 56 ... K–N1;
57 Q–K6ch, K–N2; 58 K–Q3, Q–B8ch;
and Black's Pawn is immune to capture because of ... Q–K8ch.

6

WINNING ATTACKS

A sustained, successful attack is always thrilling to the player and kibitzer alike—especially if lively combinations are used to execute the attack. The weapons are checks, captures, and tactical operations such as pins, forks, discoveries, attacks on a piece or its guard, mating threats, etc.

A check must be answered at once; a capture usually requires an immediate recapture; tactical operations, or the threat of putting them into execution, make it necessary for the opponent to defend himself. During the process of an attack, the opponent's moves are nearly always limited to those which prevent mate, recapture lost material, or meet an important threat. Eventually, a position is reached in which the opponent cannot prevent mate or must lose so much material that further resistance is futile.

As we have seen, an attack can be refuted if it is unsound; but many faulty attacks succeed against imperfect defense. And there are other attacks which succeed against any defense because they are based on full development and superiority in position. The groundwork is laid in the opening and the early stages of the middle game. The player who succeeds in positionally outplaying his opponent may be able to conduct an attack that wins by force.

In this chapter we present some games won as a result of sound attacks, based on positional advantages—attacks which would probably have won against any defense.

Early Fireworks

C. Guimard of Argentina prefers complicated positions. He got his wish in this exciting little game. By the tenth move it was quite evident that the game was not going to end in a draw.

The attack was based on an opening advantage. Black's ninth move made it possible for me to make an aggressive reply, and the fireworks got under way after White's tenth. Thereafter, almost every move by White threatened something or prevented the opponent from defending himself against the next threat. The game ended with a double check on White's 27th move.

QUEEN'S GAMBIT DECLINED

Wertheim Memorial Tournament
New York, 1951

S. RESHEVSKY   C. GUIMARD

1 P–Q4	N–KB3
2 P–QB4	P–K3
3 N–QB3	P–Q4
4 P×P	....

The Exchange Variation, a favorite of mine against the Orthodox Defense of the Queen's Gambit Declined.

4	P×P
5 B–N5	P–B3
6 Q–B2	B–K2
7 N–B3	QN–Q2
8 P–K3	N–R4

The usual move is 8 ... O–O.

9 P–KR4 ....

If 9 B×B, Q×B; 10 B–K2 (10 B–Q3, N–B5!), O–O with even chances. If I had any hope of getting an initiative in the opening I had to resort to the aggressive text-move.

9 .... P–B3

Now the fireworks start.

(See top of next column.)

10 P–KN4 N–B1

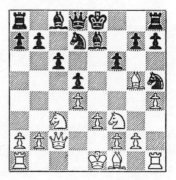

Position after 9 ... P–B3

Best. If 10 ... P×B; 11 P×P, B×P; 12 R×N and White must win a Pawn.

11 P×N	P×B
12 P×P	B×P
13 N–K5	B–B3
14 O–O–O	Q–K2

Black must try to castle.

15 P–B4 B–K3

Preparing to castle on the Queen-side. If 15 ... N–K3 (intending to castle on the King-side); 16 B–Q3.

16 P–K4 ....

Now 16 ... O–O–O is met by 17 P×P, B×P (17 ... B×N; 18 QP×KB); 18 N×B, R×N; 19 B–B4, R–R4; 20 N–B7, R–N1; 21 N–Q6ch winning the exchange.

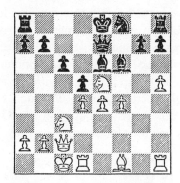

16	P×P

17 P–Q5   **B×N**

There is nothing better, for if 17 ...
P×P; 18 B–N5ch, N–Q2; 19 N×QP
and Black's defense is demolished.

18 BP×B   **B–N5**

If 18 ... P×P; 19 B–N5ch, B–Q2;
20 N×QP, Q×P; 21 N–B7ch.

19 B–K2   **B×B**
20 Q×B   ....

(See top of next column.)

20 ....   **N–Q2**

20 ... Q×P is no better: 21 P×P,
P×P; 22 N×P and the threat of 23
N–Q6ch is disastrous.

21 Q×P   **O–O**
22 P–K6   **P×P**

If 22 ... N–B3; 23 P–Q6!

Position after 20 Q×B

23 N×P   **Q–N4ch**
24 K–N1   **N–B4**

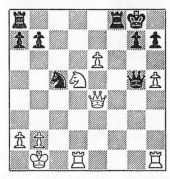

24 ... N–B3 was better but after 25
N×Nch, Q×N; 26 P–K7, KR–K1,
27 KR–K1, Black's chances were nil.

25 Q–QB4   **QR–B1**
26 P–K7   **KR–K1**
27 N–B6 dbl.ch.   **Resigns**

The Bishop vs. The Knight

A Bishop is generally more valuable than a Knight. There are, of
course, exceptions to this rule—but when the opponent's Pawns are on
squares of the same color as the Bishop, the Bishop will prevail. This was
demonstrated in the following game.

Against my Queen-Pawn opening, Mr. Santasiere set up the Nimzo-
Indian Defense. The line chosen is difficult for both sides. I castled on the

King-side, Mr. Santasiere on the Queen-side. The only minor pieces left were a Bishop and a Knight. My Bishop proved superior to my opponent's Knight because it enjoyed greater scope.

I started an attack against the black King. Although my opponent defended himself courageously, I was able to tie up his pieces with the aid of my Queen, two Rooks, and the strongly posted Bishop. Through the continuous application of pressure I was able to win a Pawn on my 33rd move. Immediate penetration of Black's defenses followed.

NIMZO-INDIAN DEFENSE

U.S. Championship Tournament
New York, 1951

S. RESHEVSKY   A. E. SANTASIERE

1	P–Q4	N–KB3
2	P–QB4	P–K3
3	N–QB3	B–N5
4	P–K3	P–QN3
5	N–K2	B–R3
6	N–N3	....

The other good alternative is 6 P–QR3, B–K2; 7 N–B4, P–Q4; 8 P×P, B×B; 9 K×B, P×P; 10 P–KN4 with some positional pressure.

6 ....   **B×Nch**

Premature. Better was 6 ... O–O; 7 P–K4, P–Q3; 8 B–Q2, P–B4; 9 P–QR3, B–R4 as Keres played against me in the Candidates' Tournament of 1953.

7 P×B   **P–Q4**

Better was 7 ... P–Q3 or 7 ... O–O.

8 B–R3   ....

Now Black finds it difficult to castle on the King-side.

8 ....   **Q–B1**

It would not have been advisable for Black to play 8 ... P×P. For one thing, he would be capturing a doubled Pawn. For another, White would gain too much space after 9 P–K4, QN–Q2; 10 P–B4.

9	N–R5	N×N
10	Q×N	....

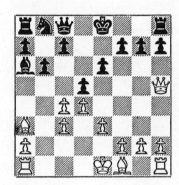

10 ....   **Q–Q2**

If 10 ... P×P?; 11 Q–KN5 threatening 12 Q–K7 mate and 12 Q×P.

11 P×P   ....

To be considered was 11 Q–N5, P–KB3; 12 Q–R5ch, Q–B2; 13 Q–B3 and Black's Pawn position would have been slightly weakened.

11 ....   **Q×P**

Of course, 11 ... B×B would be bad because of 12 P×P. Equally bad would be 11 ... P×P on account of 12 Q–K5ch winning a Pawn.

12 Q–N4   **P–N3**

12 ... R–N1?; 13 Q–R4 winning the Rook-Pawn.

13	B×B	N×B
14	O–O	O–O–O
15	Q–K2	K–N2

16 B–K7   ....

White's aim is to get the Bishop to a more favorable post where it will exert maximum pressure.

16 ....   **R–Q2**
17 B–B6   **R–QB1**
18 P–QR4   ....

The beginning of an attempt to break up the strong Pawn formation near the King.

18 ....   **Q–QR4**

Temporarily stopping the advance successfully.

19 R–R3   ....

19 ....   **P–B3**

Black is beginning to realize that he must not undertake aggressive action. Rather, he is compelled to defend himself, for if 19 ... P–B4; 20 R–N1

(threatening R–N5 winning the Queen), N–B2; 21 Q–B3ch, K–N1; 22 B–K5 and Black is badly tied up.

20 B–K5   **N–B2**

The Knight is trying desperately to get into the game.

21 P–QB4   ....

To keep the Knight out of Black's Q4.

21 ....   **N–K1**
22 P–B5   **P–B3**
23 B–N3   ....

23 ....   **P–K4**

Black does not dare play 23 ... P×P on account of 24 R–N1ch, K–R1; 25 R(R3)–N3, N–B2; 26 R–N7, P×P; 27 Q–N2 and wins.

24 BP×P   **RP×P**
25 P×P   **P×P**
26 R–N1   ....

White's pressure against the weakened and more vulnerable King is steadily being increased.

26 ....   **R–R1**
27 Q–N4   **N–B3**
28 Q–B3   ....

Against 28 Q–K6 Black replies 28 ... Q–Q4 and if 29 Q×N?, Q–Q8ch.

28 ....   **Q–Q4**
29 Q–K2   **Q–R4**

White was threatening to play 30
Q–N2 attacking two Pawns.

30 R(R3)–N3   R–R3

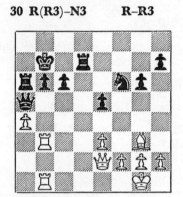

Black seems to have met all threats
satisfactorily, but his defense must break
down sooner or later.

31 P–R3   ....

Making room for the King—always
a good idea when there is no particular
hurry. White has plenty of time to
make preparatory moves. Black is
going nowhere.

31 ....   N–K5
32 Q–N4   N–B4

33 B×P   P–R4

34 Q×NP!   ....

This must have come as a surprise to
my opponent. Now Black cannot play
34 ... N×R on account of 35 Q–K8!
with the double threat of Q×Rch and
Q–N8 mate.

34 ....   Q×P
35 Q–K8   ....

The threat of Q–N8 mate is decisive.

35 ....   R–QB2
36 B×R   K×B
37 Q–K7ch   Resigns

A Wild Game

My opponent in this game, Mr. Simonson, was known for his enterprising play. He was full of ideas. I am using the past tense because he
has been away from chess for about ten years. This is unfortunate
because he was indeed a colorful player with an interesting and appealing
personality. His fault was unsteadiness. Nevertheless, he was a very
dangerous opponent, apt to come up at any time with a winning
combination.

Here he played a risky variation of the Queen's Gambit Declined. On
his ninth turn he chose a move which deprived him of castling on the
King-side. On his 15th he played P–QN4, giving up the idea of
attempting to castle on the other wing. I castled on the Queen-side.

Both the KR and the QB files were opened. The black King was
subjected to attack. On the 30th move I won the King-Pawn. After that
the outcome was not in doubt.

QUEEN'S GAMBIT DECLINED

U.S. Championship Tournament
New York, 1951

S. RESHEVSKY   A. SIMONSON

1 P–Q4	P–Q4
2 P–QB4	P–K3
3 N–QB3	N–KB3
4 P×P	....

The Exchange Variation, which has enjoyed great popularity among the experts in recent years. It is a solid and positional line. Black must defend exceptionally well to hold his own. Judging from tournament experience, White has had excellent results with this line.

4	P×P
5 B–N5	....

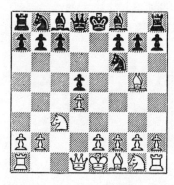

5	QN–Q2

The latest improvement is 5 ... P–B3; 6 Q–B2 (to prevent ... B–KB4), N–R3; 7 P–K3, N–QN5; 8 Q–Q2, P–QR4; 9 P–QR3, N–R3; or, in this, 8 ... B–KB4 first; 9 R–B1, P–QR4 with a satisfactory position in both cases.

If White plays 6 P–K3 (after 5 ... P–B3), then 6 ... B–KB4 solves the problem of how to develop the QB satisfactorily, for Black can exchange Bishops when White plays 7 B–Q3.

6 P–K3	P–B3
7 B–Q3	B–Q3

More usual here is 7 ... B–K2; 8 Q–B2, O–O; 9 N–B3, R–K1; 10 O–O, N–B1, etc. However, Simonson does not like to follow the trodden path. He prefers to inject a new twist into any opening variation. Being bored by analyzed variations, he always seeks new ideas, even though dangerous and perhaps unsound.

8 KN–K2	P–KR3
9 B–R4	P–KN4?

9 ... O–O; 10 Q–B2, R–K1 was wiser but too quiet and conservative for my opponent.

10 B–N3	B–K2
11 P–KR4	....

Beginning action on the King-wing and making it imprudent for Black to castle there.

11	R–KN1

11 ... P×P isolates Black's KRP. 11 ... P–N5; 12 P–R5 isolates Black's KNP.

12 P×P	P×P
13 Q–B2	N–B1
14 O–O–O	B–K3
15 P–B3	....

Preparing to strike at the center with P–K4. This is the fastest way for White to make headway. This is true because of the black King's position.

15	P–N4?

Hoping to work up an attack against the King, but the move is too energetic. Better was 15 ... Q–R4 followed by ... O–O–O, getting the black King away from the center. The text-move irrevocably gives up the idea of castling.

16 K–N1   ....

Contemplating immediate action on the QB-file.

16 ....   **Q–N3**
17 R–QB1   **P–R4**

Undaunted, Simonson continues with the attack.

18 P–K4   ....

White is way ahead in development. All his minor pieces are strategically posted for coordinated action. On the other hand, Black has no minor pieces on the Queen-wing to bolster his attack.

18 ....   **N–N3**
19 P×P   ....

19 P–K5, N–Q2; 20 N–Q1, N–N1; 21 N–K3, K–Q2 followed by ... N–R3 was not promising for White.

19 ....   **N×P**
20 N×N   ....

(See top of next column.)

20 ....   **P×N**

Position after 20 N×N

Forced, for if 20 ... B×N; 21 N–B3, B–K3 (if 21 ... Q×P; 22 N×B, Q×N; 23 B–K4 followed by B×Pch); 22 B×N, P×B (if 22 ... R×B; 23 R–R8ch, B–B1; 24 B–Q6); 23 Q–K2, B–B4ch; 24 K–R1, K–B1; 25 R–R7 and Black is in a bad way.

21 N–B3   **P–QN5**
22 N–N5   ....

Black's situation has become acute. White has many possibilities. Black has no counterplay at all.

22 ....   **K–B1**

There is nothing better. If 22 ... R–QB1; 23 Q×Rch (also 23N –B7ch, K–Q2; 24 Q–R4ch, K–Q1; 25 R–B6 suffices), B×Q; 24 R×Bch, B–Q1; 25 B–B7, Q–K3; 26 R×Bch, K–K2; 27 R×R and wins.

23 N–B7	R–Q1
24 QR–K1	....

Black's next move is forced, for White is threatening to win a piece with N × Bch.

24	N–B5

The only try. If 24 ... N–R5 (to keep the Rook out); 25 N × Bch, P × N; 26 B–B7.

25 B × N	P × B
26 N × Bch	P × N
27 R–R6	....

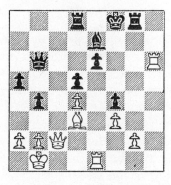

Threatening to capture the King-Pawn, thereby exposing the black King to a quick assault.

27	R–Q3

If 27 ... Q × P; 28 R(R6) × P, B–B3; 29 R–Q1! and the threat of B–R7 cannot be met satisfactorily.

28 Q–B8ch	....

28	Q–Q1

Insufficient was 28 ... K–B2; (if 28 ... K–N2; 29 R–R7ch) on account of 29 B–N6ch!, R × B; 30 R × R, K × R; 31 Q–N8ch, K–B3; 32 R–R1!, B–Q1 (if 32 ... Q × P; 33 Q–R8ch wins the Queen); 33 R–R6ch, K–K2; 34 Q–N7ch, K–K1; 35 R–R8 mate.

29 Q–B1	....

White must win a Pawn by force—and the game.

29	B–N4

29 ... R × P fails on account of 30 Q × Pch, K–N1; 31 R(K1)–R1, and the threat of R–R8ch followed by R–R7 mate cannot be met.

30 R(R6) × P	R × R
31 R × R	K–B2
32 R–K5	R–K1

33 R–B5ch   ....

I decided not to play for an end game. Careful play would have been required to win after 33 R × P, R–K8; 34 Q × R, Q × R, and Black would have had drawing chances after 33 R × P, R–K8; 34 R × Q, R × Qch; 35 K × R, B × R.

33 ....   **K–N2**

34 Q–B6   R–K8ch
35 K–B2   Q–K2
36 R × P   R–K7ch
37 K–N3   Resigns

The final position. The threat of 38 Q–N6ch is decisive. For example: 37 .... R–K6; 38 Q–N6ch, K–R1 (if 38 ... K–B1; 39 R–B5ch); 39 R–Q8ch, Q × R; 40 Q–R7 mate.

Waiting Tactics

Gligorich, the best Yugoslav player, is indeed a tough opponent. He is both an aggressive and a defensive player. He is most dangerous in combinational, attacking positions. Given a slight edge, he will seldom let his opponent out. In my match with him I had to be at my best to win by a score of 5½ to 4½.

In this first game of our match, Gligorich set up his favorite King's Indian Defense against my Queen-Pawn opening. His 14th and 16th moves clearly indicated that he refused to undertake any positive action. He was waiting for me to take action first. Although waiting tactics are sometimes necessary, or even imperative, they are usually quite costly. In this game, the loss of time incurred by my opponent gave me the necessary time to break through on the Queen-side. This did not become apparent until my 25th move.

Black having defended himself satisfactorily on the Queen-wing, I suddenly shifted to the King-side, assailing the King with all my forces. By sacrificing the Knight on my 38th move, the outcome became obvious.

KING'S INDIAN DEFENSE

Gligorich–Reshevsky Match
New York, 1952

S. RESHEVSKY	S. GLIGORICH
1 P–Q4	N–KB3
2 P–QB4	P–KN3
3 N–QB3	B–N2
4 P–K4	P–Q3
5 N–B3	O–O
6 B–K2	P–K4
7 O–O	....

At the present time, 7 P–Q5 is believed to give White the best chance for any kind of an opening advantage, but I consider castling just as good a move.

7	QN–Q2

7 ... N–B3; 8 P–Q5, N–K2, etc., leads to more problems for both sides.

8 R–K1	P–B3
9 B–B1	R–K1

9 ... P–QR4 or 9 ... N–K1 are to be seriously considered.

10 P–Q5	....

10 R–N1 with the idea of continuing with P–QN4 is more flexible and gives Black more trouble.

10	P–B4

If 10 ... P×P; 11 BP×P, P–QR4; 12 B–KN5, P–R3; 13 B–Q2 and White

will benefit much more from the opening of the QB-file because he controls the vital squares—his QN5 and QB4. In addition, Black would have great difficulty in developing his Queen-Bishop and Queen-Knight.

11 P–QR3	....

Preparing for P–QN4.

11	R–B1

Preparing for ... N–K1 and ... P–B4.

12 P–KN3	....

In anticipation of ... P–B4.

12	N–K1
13 P–QN4	.....

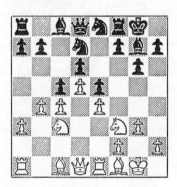

13	Q–K2

Interesting and involved was 13 ... P–B4. There might have followed: 14 N–KN5, N(Q2)–B3 (if 14 ... N–B2; 15 KP×P, NP×P; 16 N–K6, N×N; 17 P×N, N–B3; 18 Q–B3 and White is on top); 15 KP×P, NP×P; 16 B–R3 with the annoying threat of N–K6.

14 R–R2	....

To get out of a possible pin after Black has moved his King-Pawn.

14	N–B2
15 B–K3	P–N3

15 ... P–B4 loses to 16 NP×P, N×BP; 17 B×N, P×B; 18 P–Q6.

16 N–KR4   ....

16 ....   **N–K1**

My opponent obviously adopted a sit-and-wait policy, to see what I was going to do. I believe it would have been wiser to continue with 16 ... P–B4, Black's main objective in the King's Indian Defense. After 17 KP×P, NP×P; 18 P–B4, P–K5 (not 18 ... KP×P; 19 B×P which gives White a big plus) both sides have chances. Gligorich probably did not like the idea of isolating his KB-Pawn.

17 Q–B1   **N–B2**

Come and get me!

18 B–N5   ....

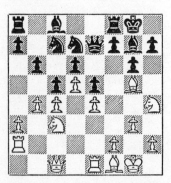

18 ....   **B–B3**

18 ... P–B3; 19 B–R6 is difficult for

Black. He is unable to continue with 19 ... P–B4 on account of 20 KP×P, NP×P; 21 B×B, Q×B; 22 B–R3, P–B5; 23 N–B5 and wins the Queen-Pawn. The inability to play ... P–B4 would cause his position to remain unpleasantly cramped.

19 B–R6   **B–N2**

My opponent was apparently content to draw, but I was not.

20 B–R3   **R–K1**

Now ... P–B4 is definitely out. Hereafter, Black's course must of necessity be defensive. White's problem is where to attempt a breakthrough—on the Queen-side or on the King-side. Black will face great difficulty in either case.

21 B×B   **K×B**
22 Q–Q2   ....

The purpose of this move is to make it impossible for Black to recapture with the Queen-Pawn after White plays P×P (... QP×P would permit P–Q6). Consequently, White is in a position to open up the QN-file. My immediate objective was to start operations on the Queen-wing.

22 ....   **N–B1**
23 B×B   **KR×B**
24 P×P   **NP×P**

See note to White's 22nd move.

25 R–N2   N–Q2

26 N–R4   . . . .

To prevent ... N–N3. Fruitless would have been 26 R–N7 on account of 26 ... N–N3; 27 Q–R2, KR–QN1; 28 R×R, R×R; 29 R–QN1, Q–Q1 followed by ... N–Q2 and Black would have gained control of the important QN-file.

26 . . . .   R(B1)–QN1
27 R(K1)–N1   Q–Q1

Bad would have been 27 ... R×R; 28 R×R, R–QN1; 29 Q–R5 winning a Pawn.

28 K–N2   . . . .

An important waiting move. The importance lies in the fact that Black is somewhat in "zugzwang."

28 . . . .   P–KR3

On 28 ... R×R comes 29 R×R, R–N1; 30 N–KB3–K1–Q3 with promising chances for White.

29 Q–R5   N–N3
30 N×N   P×N
31 Q–B3   . . . .

With the serious threat of 32 P–B4.

31 . . . .   K–N1

(See top of next column.)

32 Q–Q2   . . . .

If 32 R×P?, R×R; 33 R×R, N×P winning the exchange.

Position after 31 ... K–N1

32 . . . .   R×P

Relatively best was 32 ... K–N2; 33 R×P, R×R; 34 R×R, R×P; 35 Q–N2, R–R1 (otherwise 36 R–N8); 36 R–N7 with some pressure.

33 Q×P   . . . .

The capture of this Pawn enables White to undertake aggressive action on the King-wing.

33 . . . .   N–K1
34 P–B4   P×P
35 R–KB2   . . . .

35 . . . .   Q–K2

If 35 ... P×P; 36 R×BP!, K×R; 37 Q×Pch, K–K2; 38 Q–K6ch, K–B1; 39 R–B1ch, K–N2; 40 Q–N6ch, K–R1; 41 R–B8 mate.

If 35 ... Q–B3 (relatively best); 36 R×BP, Q–N2 (if 36 ... Q–B6; 37

N×P!); 37 Q–N5 threatening 38
Q–K7.

| 36 Q×BP | R–R5 |
| 37 R(N1)–KB1 | .... |

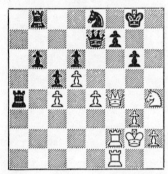

37 ....   R–N2

Insufficient is 37 ... R×P on account
of 38 N×P!, P×N; 39 Q–B8ch,
Q×Q; 40 R×Qch, K–R2; 41
R(B1)–B7ch, K–R3; 42 R–R8ch,
K–N4; 43 P–R4ch, K–N5; 44 R–B4
mate.

| 38 N×P | P×N |
| 39 Q–R6 | .... |

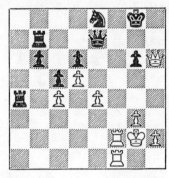

39 ....   Q×Pch

There is no adequate defense. R–
B8ch is threatened. If 39 ... N–N2;
40 Q×P, R–R1; 41 R–B7, Q×R; 42
R×Q, R×R; 43 Q×P and White
should win because of the passed Pawns
and Black's exposed King-position. In
addition, White had a good alternative
here in 41 R–B4–R4, threatening mate
with Q–R7.

40 K–N1	Q–Q5
41 K–N2	Q–K5ch
42 K–R3	Q–B4ch
	Resigns.

Turning the Tables

Grandmaster Miguel Najdorf is always on the lookout for the opportunity to attack. He is not particularly comfortable when he has to defend.
For my own part, I do not mind being on the defensive, but occasionally
I will turn to the attack when the prospects of aggressive action are good,
or when I have no alternative.

Conducting the black pieces in the eleventh game of our match, Mr.
Najdorf played the well-analyzed Queen's Gambit Accepted. My 14th
move, P–QR3, was an improvement. My 16th must have come as a
complete surprise since it allowed Black to capture the King-Bishop.

Najdorf's 17 ... Q–K4 was a clear indication that he contemplated
aggressive action on the King-side. I decided to throw caution to the
wind and went over to the attack myself by playing 21 P–KN4. Najdorf
was visibly disturbed and surprised by this sudden change of strategy.
Black's Queen being forced out of play, I was able to build up the attack
with rapidity.

QUEEN'S GAMBIT ACCEPTED

Najdorf–Reshevsky Match
Buenos Aires, 1953

S. RESHEVSKY   M. NAJDORF

1 P–Q4	P–Q4
2 P–QB4	P–QB3
3 N–KB3	N–B3
4 N–B3	P–K3
5 P–K3	P–QR3
6 B–Q3	P×P
7 B×BP	P–QN4
8 B–N3	....

The alternative 8 B–Q3 can lead to the Meran Variation: 8 ... QN–Q2; 9 P–K4, P–B4; or 8 ... P–B4; 9 O–O, QN–Q2; 10 Q–K2, B–N2; 11 R–Q1, Q–B2; 12 B–Q2, B–K2, in either case with approximate equality. According to latest analysis, White has better chances of obtaining an opening advantage with the text-move.

8	P–B4
9 O–O	B–N2
10 Q–K2	....

10 P×P, Q×Q; 11 R×Q, B×P leads to simplification. 10 P–QR4 is adequately met by 10 ... P–N5.

10	QN–Q2

To recapture the BP with the Knight, after 11 P×P.

11 R–Q1	B–K2
12 P–K4	....

12	P×P

Black must proceed cautiously. If he decides to win a Pawn with 12 ... P–N5 he can get himself into inextricable trouble. For instance, 13 P–K5, P×N; 14 P×N, B×P (14 ... N×P; 15 B–R4ch, K–B1; 16 QP×P, Q–B2; 17 N–K5, Q×P; 18 P×P with a distinct advantage); 15 P–Q5, P×P (15 ... P–K4; 16 P×P, O–O; 17 N–Q2); 16 B×P, B×B; 17 P×P, B×R; 18 P×Nch, K–B1; 19 Q–B4, Q–K2; 20 P–Q8(Q)ch, R×Q; 21 R×Rch, Q×R; 22 Q×P mate.

13 N×QP	Q–B2
14 P–QR3	....

Simply to prevent 14 ... P–N5. The more aggressive 14 B–N5 can be handled by Black as follows: 14 ... P–N5; 15 N–R4, Q–K4; 16 B×N, N×B; 17 N–N6, R–Q1; 18 B–R4ch, K–B1 and Black is well off.

14	O–O
15 B–N5	N–B4

If 15 ... Q–K4; 16 P–B4, Q–QB4; 17 QR–B1 and White has gained valuable tempi.

16 QR–B1	....

Ordinarily, it is bad policy to give up a Bishop for a Knight, especially when it might be used for the attack. This case, however, is the exception. If 16 ... N×B; 17 N×N (threatening 18

N–Q5!), Q–N1 (the only half-decent move); 18 P–K5, N–Q4; 19 B×B, N×B; 20 N–B5, B–B3; 21 N(3)–K4 or R–Q6 with much the better of it.

In this, if 17 ... Q–N3 (instead of ... Q–N1); 18 P–K5, N–Q4; 19 N×N, B×N; 20 B×B, B×N; 21 R–Q6 and wins. Or if 17 ... Q–QB5; 18 Q×Q, P×Q; 19 N–R5 winning a Pawn.

16 ....　　　　　　　P–R3

17 B–R4　　　　　　　Q–K4

Swinging his Queen over to the Kingside with evil intentions.

18 B–B2　　　　　　　QR–B1
19 N–B3　　　　　　　....

Inviting Black's next move.

19 ....　　　　　　　Q–R4

Offhand, this looks like a pretty good square for the Queen, but it turned out quite differently.

20 P–KR3　　　　　　P–N4

Black's plan: if White replies 21 B–KN3, P–KN5; 22 P×P, Q×P with a fairly good position.

21 P–KN4　　　　　　....

I had decided on this aggressive continuation on my 19th turn.

21 ....　　　　　　　Q–N3

The sacrifice of the Knight fails, as

follows: 21 ... N×NP; 22 P×N, Q×Pch; 23 B–N3, P–KR4; 24 N–Q2, Q–R6; 25 Q–B1, Q–N5; 26 Q–N2 and White successfully wards off any possible attack.

22 N–K5　　　　　　　....

White could easily have gone wrong here by playing 22 P–K5?—a tempting move. There would have followed: 22 ... N(B3)–K5!; 23 B–KN3 (if 23 P–N4, N×N; or if 23 N×N, N×N: 24 B–KN3, N×B; 25 P×N, R×B or B×N and wins), N×B; 24 P×N, Q–N2 with a slightly better position.

22 ....　　　　　　　Q–N2

Not too promising a square for a Queen!

23 B–KN3　　　　　　KR–Q1
24 Q–K3　　　　　　　....

Preparing to get the Queen to QR7 after Black's Knight is dislodged from his QB4.

24 ....　　　　　　　P–QR4?

Daring, but making it easier for White. Najdorf's temperament is not well suited to such positions. Calmness and patience are required in a position such as this. Black must defend carefully and wait for the opportunity for counterplay. Correct was 24 ... Q–B1; 25 R×R, Q×R; 27 R–Q1, Q–K1 and it is difficult for White to make rapid progress.

25 R×Rch   B×R

25 ... R×R; 26 P–N4, P×P; 27 P×P, N–R5; 28 N×NP is just as bad for Black.

26 P–N4   P×P
27 P×P   ....

27 ....   N–R5

If 27 ... N–R3; 28 Q–R7, R×N (if 28 ... R–N1; 29 N–Q3 wins); 29 Q×B, N×QNP; 30 R–Q1!, Q–B1 (if 30 ... B–B2; 31 B–N1 and Black's Knights are clumsily posted. If 30 ... N×B; 31 R×Bch, K–R2; 32 N×P, threatening R–R8ch followed by N–K5 mate); 31 R×B, Q×R; 32 Q×Pch, K–R1; 33 N–N6 mate.

28 N×NP   B–N3
29 Q–R3   ....

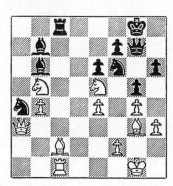

29 ....   N×KP

Interesting and complicated is 29 ... R×B; 30 R×R, N×KP, and now White must be careful. If 31 Q×N, N×B; 32 N–Q7, Q–N3; and then if 33 N×B, Q–K5; 34 P×N?, Q–K8ch; 35 K–R2, Q–R8 mate. Safest for White would have been 31 N–Q6, N×N (31 ... N×B; 32 Q×N and White has nothing to worry about); 32 Q×N and should win easily.

30 B×N (K4)   R×Rch
31 Q×R   B×B

It appears as though Black has weathered the storm, but actually his real troubles are just about to begin.

32 N–Q6   B–Q4
33 N–K8   Q–B1

33 ... Q–R1 is no better, because of 34 Q–B8.

34 Q–B8   ....

34	Q×P

There is no escape. If 34 ... P–B3; 35 N–Q7, Q×P (35 ... Q–B2; 36 N–Q6ch. If 35 ... Q–K2; 36 N(K8)× Pch, K–B2; 37 Q–N8 mate); 36 N(K8)×Pch, K–B2; 37 Q–N8ch,

K–K2; 38 Q–K8 mate.

35 N–B6ch	K–N2
36 Q–N8ch	Resigns

For if 36 ... K×N; 37 N–Q7ch, K–K2; 38 Q–B8ch etc.

A Mating Attack

This game clearly indicates how effective the Reti Opening can be, especially when slightly mishandled by Black. As a result of his opponent's opening inaccuracies, White sets up a strong attacking position on the King-side. Meantime, Black concentrates his pieces for an attack on the Queen-side, leaving insufficient protection for his King. After the 19th move, White's crushing attack cannot be met.

RETI OPENING

Rosenwald Tournament
New York, 1956–57

S. RESHEVSKY   M. PAVEY

1 N–KB3	P–Q4
2 P–KN3	N–KB3
3 B–N2	P–B4
4 O–O	N–B3
5 P–Q3	P–K3

The setup with 5 ... P–KN3, etc., is preferable.

The pattern is set. White is going to operate on the King-wing, Black on the Queen-side.

6 QN–Q2	B–K2
7 P–K4	O–O
8 R–K1	P×P

Unnecessarily opening lines for White. Sounder was 8 ... P–QN3 followed by ... B–N2 or ... B–R3.

14 P–QR4	P×P
15 R×P	B–R3
16 P–R4	QR–N1
17 P–R5	KR–Q1
18 B–B1	B–N2

9 P×P	Q–B2
10 P–K5	N–Q4
11 P–B3	P–QN3

11 ... P–QN4 would have saved a tempo.

Unwilling to part with his Bishop, but this decision is soon proven unwise. White's KB will now assume a tremendous role in accelerating the attack.

12 Q–K2	P–QR4
13 Q–K4	P–QN4

19 B–Q3	P–N3
20 P×P	RP×P
21 Q–KN4	....

21 ....   N–B5

Why not 21 ... N×BP? The reason: there follows 22 B×P!, N×R; 23 B–R7ch, K–R1 (if 23 ... K–B1; 24 Q–N8 mate. If 23 ... K×B; 24 K–N2 and the threat of R–R1 is fatal); 24 Q–R5 (threatening B–N6ch followed by Q–R7ch and Q×P mate), K–N2; 25 N–K4, threatening Q–R6ch with mate to follow.

22 B–K4	N–R4
23 B×P	P×B
24 Q×NPch	N–N2

25 R–KN4   K–B1

25 ... B–B1 is of no avail because of 26 N–N5 threatening Q–R7 mate.

26 N–K4   Resigns

White has too many threats: (1) 27 B–R6 followed by B×Nch and mate to follow; (2) 27 N(4)–N5 with the threat of N–R7ch and Q×N mate. Black's relative best is 26 ... N×P (26 ... B–R5; 27 R×B, Q–B2; 28 R–R8ch, K–K2; 29 B–N5ch, etc.) 27 Q×Nch, K–K1; 28 N×N with the crushing threat of Q–B7 mate.

A Delightful Game

Before this ninth game of my match against Donald Byrne I was leading by 5–3 and needed only one-half point of the two remaining games to win the match. With such a psychological edge I was naturally able to play with great ease and confidence. The game turned out to be the most interesting of the match.

Up to the eighth move, a well-known variation of the English Opening was adopted. On his eighth turn Byrne played ... P–KR4 before castling, with the intention of launching an attack. He withheld castling until his 13th move.

White began action on the Queen-side by playing 13 P–QN4. By playing 16 ... P–B3 my opponent's King-side was slightly weakened. Thereafter, Black's position gradually began to deteriorate. White conducted a sustained attack as one threat followed another. Black's KNP was brought under pressure. After the 26th move Black had his King on K1 and his KR on KR1, having been forced to "uncastle." On the 32nd move White won the KNP. On the 33rd move White offered the sacrifice of the Queen or the exchange. Black accepted the latter. Four moves later, Black's flag dropped in a completely lost position.

ENGLISH OPENING
(MCO, Page 336, Col. 30, Note N)
D. Byrne–Reshevsky Match
New York, 1957

S. RESHEVSKY   D. BYRNE

1 N–KB3	P–QB4
2 P–B4	N–QB3
3 P–KN3	....

3 P–Q4, P×P; 4 N×P, N–B3; 5 N–QB3, P–K3; 6 P–KN3, Q–N3, as in the game D. Byrne against Geller in the USA–Russia match, is slightly in Black's favor.

3	P–KN3
4 B–N2	B–N2
5 O–O	P–Q3
6 N–B3	N–R3

I experimented with this move in the 1956–57 Rosenwald Tournament against Larry Evans. The purpose is to get this Knight to KB4 where it will exert pressure on White's Q4 square.

7 P–Q3	N–B4
8 B–Q2	P–KR4

A bold move intending ... P–R5 to open up the KR-file. For this threat, which White meets easily, Black gave White's pieces free access to Black's KN4 square.

9 P–KR4	....

Perhaps better is 9 P–KR3, and if 9 ... P–R5, 10 P–KN4.

9	B–Q2
10 R–N1	....

White's best plan is to initiate vigorous action on the Q-side.

10	R–QN1
11 P–R3	N(B4)–Q5
12 N–KR2	....

Exchanging Knights at this point would accomplish nothing. White's Knight is needed for both aggressive and defensive purposes.

12	Q–B1

Castling would have been wiser.

13 P–QN4	O–O

13 ... P×P; 14 P×P, P–QN4; 15 P–K3 wins a Pawn for White.

14 P–N5	....

Opening up the QN-file by playing 14 P×P was fruitless. The text-move tends to restrict the mobility of Black's pieces.

14	N–K4
15 N–Q5	....

Black is slowly being faced with some problems. The KP requires protection.

| 15 .... | R–K1 |
| 16 B–N5 | P–B3 |

Creating a serious weakness which eventually proves disastrous. Comparatively best was 16 ... Q–Q1 followed by ... N–K3, driving White's Bishop away.

17 B–Q2	N–N5
18 P–K3	N×N
19 K×N	N–B4

Black could have put up stronger resistance with 19 N–K3–B1 where the Knight would have protected the KNP.

20 N–B4 ....

| 20 .... | K–B2 |

There is nothing better. If 20 ... K–R2; 21 B–K4 and Black is unable to drive away the Knight by 21 ... P–K4 on account of 22 N×RP, P×N; 23 Q×Pch, K–N1 (if 23 ... B–R3; 24 P–N4); 24 B–Q5ch, B–K3 (24 ... K–B1; 25 Q–B7 mate); 25 Q×N and wins.

21 B–K4 ....

Tying up the Black Knight.

21 .... R–KR1

To get to KR3 and protect the KNP. 21 ... P–K4 is impossible because of 22 B–Q5ch.

22 Q–B3 R–R3

Black seems to have consolidated his position but new threats are imminent.

23 P–Q4 ....

Threatening P–Q5 which, if permitted, would give White effective control of Black's K3 square.

23 .... P–K4

Going after the Pawn loses for Black as follows: 23 ... P×P; 24 P×P, N×QP; 25 B×Pch, R×B; 26 Q×RP B–B4; 27 N×R, B×N; 28 Q–Q5ch, N–K3; 29 QR–K1 and Black is helpless against White's doubling Rooks on the K-file.

24 P×KP QP×P

Worse was 24 ... BP×P. There would have followed: 25 B–Q5ch, K–K2; 26 N×Pch, R×N; 27 P–K4,

N–R3; 28 B×N, R×B; 29 Q–B7ch
and wins easily.

25 N–Q3   ....

25 N–Q5 was also good.

25 ....   **R–KR1**

Better was 25 ... K–N1, but after 26
B–Q5ch, K–R1; 27 P–K4, N–Q5; 28
Q–N2, R–R2; 29 P–B4, Black's posi-
tion remains unpleasant.

26 B–Q5ch   **K–K1**

It is interesting to observe that after
having castled, Black has returned to
the uncastled position.

26 ... K–B1 or K–K2 was bad
because of 27 N×BP followed by B–N4.

27 Q–N2   ....

Making possible White's next move
in order to open either the King or
Bishop file.

27 ....   **N–R3**
28 P–B4   **N–N5ch**
29 K–R1   **P×P**

Against 29 ... P–B4 the reply would
have been 30 P–K4 when both the King
and Bishop files would have been forced
open.

30 KP×P   ....

30 ....   **P–N3**

This loses, but other moves are also
bad. For instance, 30 ... P–B4; 31
QR–K1ch, K–Q1; 32 B–B7, R–R3;
33 N–K5!

31 Q–K4ch   **K–B1**
32 Q×P   **N–R3**
33 P–B5!   ....

Offering the sacrifice of the Queen
which Black does not accept. The
soundness of this sacrifice is proven by
the following: if 33 ... B–K1; 34
N–B4, B×Q; 35 N×Bch, K–K1; 36
QR–K1ch, K–Q1; 37 N×R, B×N;
38 B–B6 and the threat of R–K8ch
cannot be met.

33 ....   **B×P**
34 R×B   **Q×R**
35 N–B4   **R–N1**
36 R–K1   **R–Q1**
37 Q×Q   **Forfeit**

A Quick Attack

R. Persitz of Israel is the best prospect among the young chess players of that country. He is calm, cool, and collected. He is capable of initiating and carrying through an attack with precision. When the situation calls for it, he is just as able to defend himself in tight spots. The enviable combination of his chess ability and fine personal qualities should carry him far in the chess field.

Fortunately for me, Mr. Persitz had an off day when we met in the second round of the first Israeli International Chess Tournament. In an unusual form of the English Opening, my opponent developed his pieces slowly and permitted me to gain a strong center. As a result, I was able to launch a King-side attack on the tenth move, advancing my KN and KB Pawns to the fifth rank. Black failed to put up the best resistance in a difficult situation and his position became unbearably cramped. On my 16th turn I posted my Queen strategically so that a mating threat could be set up. The offer of a Knight on the 23rd move brought the game to a sudden end.

Although it is unusual to start a King-side assault so early in the game, this was by no means a premature attack. It was made possible by White's lead in development and control of the center in the first nine moves.

ENGLISH OPENING

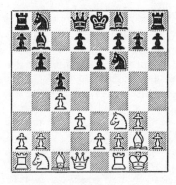

Position after 6 P–Q3

Israeli International Tournament
Haifa, 1958

S. RESHEVSKY	R. PERSITZ
1 N–KB3	N–KB3
2 P–B4	P–K3
3 P–KN3	P–QN3
4 B–N2	B–N2
5 O–O	P–B4
6 P–Q3	....

6 P–Q4, P×P; 7 N×P or Q×P leads into familiar lines of the Queen's Indian Defense. The text-move leads into less-known ground in which Black has to play very accurately to obtain equality. White's immediate objective is to build up a wonderful center with P–K4, etc.

(See next column.)

6	B–K2?

6 ... P–Q4 is indicated, in order to prevent 7 P–K4. The intended reply to 6 ... P–Q4 was 7 P×P, P×P; 8 N–R4 to be followed by N–KB5. Here, if 7 ... N×P (instead of ... P×P); 8 Q–R4ch, Q–Q2; 9 Q–KN4 with good attacking chances.

| 7 P–K4 | .... |

White has now achieved his objective. The freeing move of 7 ... P–Q4 is no longer available to Black, on account of 8 BP×P, P×P; 9 P–K5, KN–Q2; 10 P–Q4!, O–O; 11 N–B3 with much the better of it.

7	O–O
8 N–B3	N–B3
9 N–K1	....

Announcing an immediate Pawn-push with P–KB4 and P–KN4. This aggressive threat, although at an early stage, is difficult to meet.

9 ....   Q–B2?

My opponent apparently decided to ignore the threat. 9 ... P–Q4 would have been ineffective because of 10 BP×P, P×P; 11 P×P, N–QR4 (11 ... N–Q5; 12 P–Q6 wins material); 12 Q–B3, Q–Q2; 13 N–B2, QR–Q1; 14 N–K3, White remaining a Pawn ahead with an excellent position.

Relatively best was 9 ... N–K1; 10 P–B4, P–B4.

10 P–B4	QR–Q1
11 P–KN4	....

The onrush of the Pawns is a serious matter for Black; his position will become steadily more cramped.

(See top of next column.)

11 ....   N–Q5

Position after 11 P–KN4

More prudent was 11 ... N–K1 in order to meet 12 P–N5 with ... P–B3, at least attempting to break up White's formidable Pawn formation. My opponent's complacency causes a rapid deterioration of his game.

12 P–N5	N–K1
13 P–B5	P–N3

Black's position is already untenable. Ineffective is 13 ... P×P; 14 P×P, B×B; 15 N×B, when the threat of N–Q5 is hardly pleasant. Neither is 13 ... P–B3 playable, on account of 14 P–N6, P–KR3; 15 Q–R5 followed by the sacrifice of a piece with B×RP.

14 B–B4   ....

14 ....   Q–B1

14 ... B–Q3 is impossible because of 15 P–K5, B–K2; 16 P–B6 winning a

piece. If 14 ... P–Q3, 15 P–B6 also wins a piece. And 14 ... P–K4 dangerously hands over control of Black's Q4 square.

| 15 P–B6 | B–Q3 |
| 16 B×B | .... |

16 P–K5, B–N1 followed by ... P–Q3 would have freed Black's pieces unnecessarily.

| 16 .... | N×B |
| 17 Q–N4 | N–K1 |

Black's timidity in the opening has completely immobilized his forces.

18 Q–R4 ....

18 .... **P–K4**

Relatively best was 18 ... P–KR4, but after 19 P×P e.p., K–R2; 20 N–B3 and White is a clear Pawn ahead plus the superior position. Also decisive would have been 19 R–B2 followed by N–B3 with concentration on Black's KRP.

19 Q–R6 .....

Black's position is now hopeless. White can bide his time in building up a mating net at KN7 or KR7.

19 .... **N–K3**

| 20 N–K2 | Q–B3 |
| 21 R–B3 | B–B1 |

22 N–B2 ....

I could have won a piece with 22 R–R3 but Black would have captured two Pawns for the piece after 22 ... N×NP; 23 Q×N, Q×P. The text-move is more decisive.

22	P–Q3
23 N–K3	N(K3)–B2
24 N–B5	**Resigns**

The final position. The white Knight at B5 blocks the black Queen-Bishop. Consequently, the threat of 25 R–R3, with mate to follow, cannot be successfully met.

Counterattack

I always prefer playing a match as compared to a tournament. In the latter there is quite often the element of luck. An inferior player may have a good day. If you have the misfortune of opposing him at that time, you are out of luck. The element of luck is undoubtedly reduced to a minimum in a match.

In my ten-game match with Paul Benko there were several hard-fought and interesting games. The following game turned the tide in my favor. Mr. Benko chose a variation of the Queen's Indian Defense which he had played successfully against Steinmeyer prior to our match. In both games, Benko castled on the Queen-side, indicating his aggressive intentions. Steinmeyer decided to defend, and lost. I counterattacked immediately, putting my opponent on the defensive. He never had a chance to carry out his intended attack.

In sacrificing a Pawn on my 16th move I was able to throw all my forces against the King's defenses. White put up stout resistance but the fierce attack could not be met successfully.

QUEEN'S INDIAN DEFENSE

Benko–Reshevsky Match
New York, 1960

P. BENKO   S. RESHEVSKY

1	P–Q4	N–KB3
2	P–QB4	P–K3
3	N–KB3	P–QN3
4	N–B3	B–N2
5	B–N5	B–K2
6	Q–B2	P–KR3
7	B–R4	....

White gains nothing by 7 B×N, B×B; 8 P–K4, P–Q3 followed by an eventual ... P–QB4.

7	....	P–Q4
8	B×N	....

An obvious loss of tempo, but White has something in mind.

8	....	B×B
9	P×P	P×P
10	P–K3	O–O
11	O–O–O	....

White's plan becomes clear. He intends to continue with P–KN4 and P–KR4 with apparently good attacking prospects. Black has the two Bishops but his QB is inactivated.

11	....	P–B4
12	K–N1	N–B3

Here Mr. Steinmeyer erred in playing ... N–Q2 where the Knight cannot be used in the called-for counterattack.

13	P×P	N–N5
14	Q–N3	P×P
15	P–QR3	B×N
16	Q×B	....

White has nothing better. If 16 P×B, N–B3; 17 R×P, Q–K2 and Black has more than ample compensation for the Pawn. The exposed position of White's King would have proved fatal.

16 ....   P–Q5

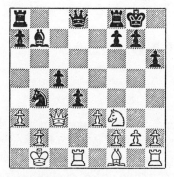

By sacrificing a Pawn, Black's pieces suddenly become alive. The white King is subjected to a fierce attack.

17 P×P   B–K5ch
18 K–R1   ....

If 18 K–B1, N–R7ch wins the Queen.

18 ....   N–B7ch
19 K–R2   P×P
20 N×P   R–B1
21 Q–Q2   ....

21 B–B4?, R×B; 22 Q×R, B–Q4.

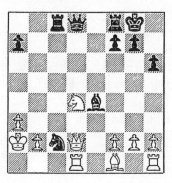

21 ....   Q–N3

Although Black has a promising position he still must find the correct continuation. The obvious 12 ... Q–Q4ch nets nothing on account of 22 N–N3, Q–K3; 23 Q–Q6 and White escapes. The text wins by force.

22 P–B3   ....

Interesting is 22 N×N. There follows 22 ... R×N; 23 Q–N4, R–N1! ;24 Q×Q, R×Q; 25 R–QN1, B–Q4ch; 26 K–R1, R–N6; 27 B–R6, R×Pch; 28 P×R, R–R7 mate.

22 ....   B–Q4ch
23 K–N1   N×Pch
24 K–R1   KR–Q1

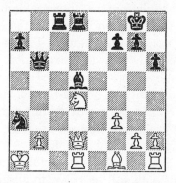

The quickest way to win. Also sufficient was 24 ... N–B5; 25 B×N, B×B, etc.

25 P×N   B–N6
26 R–QN1   ....

26 B–K2 is answered by 26 ... B×R; 27 R×B, R–B4 and the threat of ... R(B4)–Q4 cannot be parried.

26 ....   R×N
27 Q–N2   Q–KB3
28 B–R6   R–B7
29 Q×B   R–QN5ch
Resigns

7

WINNING THE END GAME

The average chess player dislikes the end game. It has been said that the reason for this is because most of his games do not get that far, and it is probably true that the usual home or club game between amateurs ends in the middle game. Another reason for the common dislike of endings is not so easy to understand. They are considered boring. Once the Queens are off the board the excitement is supposed to be over; there are no more combinations or sacrifices of pieces, so why bother playing on? Granted, the beauty of a well-played ending is more delicate than the flagrant fireworks of a rowdy middle game, but both are artistic. There is usually an exactitude and precision in end-game play which is lacking in many mid-game combinations.

Even if a player does not appreciate end-game play, he should learn it. Not only will he begin to admire the artistry of a skillful player in this phase of the game, he will also win more chess games. It is difficult to impress on most learners that the end game should be studied before taking up the openings and the complications of the middle game. In the ending there is relative simplicity and it is possible to learn the powers of the pieces without confusion. Furthermore, the basic winning positions of the end game—particularly Pawn structure—can be understood so that these positions can be reached, if possible, by conscious effort in the earlier parts of the game.

In tournament play many games are adjourned when the ending has been reached. Conforming to unwritten law, the players then analyze the positions, often with the help of other players or "seconds." Sometimes this requires hours of study. In this chapter there are some games which were adjourned in fairly even positions but which I was able to win as a result of analysis or because my opponent faltered during the play-off.

A Long Struggle

This eighth game of my match with Donald Byrne was unique in every phase. The opening, an irregular variation of the Reti Opening, was handled energetically by White. By playing 7 N–R4 and 8 P–KB4, threatening P–K5, he presented Black with the serious problem of castling with impunity. Instead, Black chose to win a Pawn, overlooking the fact that White could regain the Pawn with the superior position. Black's poor position necessitated the fiercest resistance. White sacrificed a piece on his 27th move. Black brought his King to the middle of the board, sacrificing his Queen for two Rooks.

The ending was extremely interesting. The result should have been a draw, but when White played 45 Q×Pch, he gave up his last chance of splitting the point. This, however, was not obvious, since even after the 72nd move, some of the experts at the club declared their inability to see a win for Black—but White resigned after Black's 88th move.

RETI OPENING

D. Byrne–Reshevsky Match
New York, 1957

D. BYRNE	S. RESHEVSKY
1 N–KB3	N–KB3
2 P–KN3	P–QN3
3 B–N2	B–N2
4 O–O	P–B4
5 P–Q3	....

Intending to build up a strong center with P–K4–5. 5 P–Q4 leads into familiar lines of the Queen's Indian.

5	P–N3

To be recommended is 5 ... P–Q4; 6 P–B4, P–K3 and if 7 P×P, N×P; 8 Q–R4ch, N–Q2; 9 N–K5, B–Q3 with a good game.

6 P–K4	....

(See next column.)

6	P–Q3

Necessary to prevent P–K5. If 6 ... B–N2; 7 P–K5, N–Q4 (7 ... N–N5; 8 R–K1, N–QB3; 9 P–KR3 and White's KP cannot be captured); 8 N–N5

Position after 6 P–K4.

(threatening to win a piece with P–QB4), Q–B1; 9 Q–B3 with the twin threat of Q×Pch and P–QB4.

7 N–R4	....

Preventing ... B–N2 which would cost Black a piece after P–K5.

7	N–B3
8 P–KB4	P–K3

Preventing 9 P–KN4 to which Black would now reply 9 ... N×KP and if 10 P×N, Q×N.

9 N–QB3	....

9 ....   N–Q2

9 ... B–N2 is not playable. There would follow: 10 P–K5, P×P; 11 P×P, N–Q2; 12 N–K4, N(Q2)×P; 13 B–N5, Q–Q5ch; 14 K–R1, O–O; 15 P–B3, Q–Q2; 16 N–B6ch with sufficient attacking chances for the Pawn.

10 N–B3   P–QR3
11 P–Q4   B–N2
12 P×P   ....

12 P–Q5 is met satisfactorily with 12 ... N–Q5; 13 N×N, P×N; 14 N–K2, P×P; 15 P×P, Q–B3.

12 ....   N×P

13 B–K3   ....

13 P–B5 is stronger and if 13 ... O–O; 14 B–N5 in which 14 ... B–B3 fails because of 15 B×B, Q×B; 16 Q×P. After 13 P–B5 Black would have

had to play 13 ... P–K4, giving up control of the square Q4.

13 ....   B×N

In making this move I thought that it won a Pawn by force but found out differently. 13 ... O–O was indicated.

14 P×B   N×P
15 N–Q4!   N–K2?

Correct was 15 ... P–Q4 and if 16 N×N, B×N; 17 Q–Q4, P–B3 (not 17 ... O–O; 18 P–B5 threatening B–R6 winning the exchange) with even chances. 15 ... N×BP loses material after 16 B×Nch, B×B; 17 Q–Q3.

16 N×P!   ....

Winning back the Pawn with the superior position. This I overlooked when I played 13 ... B×N.

16 ....   P×N
17 B×N   B×B
18 Q–Q4   K–B2

Forced. After 18 ... O–O; 19 Q×B, Black cannot defend both the KP and the QNP.

19 Q×B   Q–B2
20 B–Q4   KR–K1
21 P–N4   Q–D5
22 P–B5   NP×P
23 P×P   ....

(See diagram on next page.)

23 ....   R–N1ch

Position after 23 P × P

If 23 ... N × P; 24 R × Nch, P × R; 25 Q × Pch, K–K2 (25 ... K–N1; 26 Q–N5ch, K–B2; 27 Q–B6ch, K–N1; 28 Q–N7 mate); 26 R–K1ch, K–Q1; 27 B × Pch wins.

| 24 K–R1 | P–K4 |
| 25 P–B6 | .... |

It looks bad for Black, but this is no time to think about that. Fierce resistance is called for.

25	N–N3
26 Q–N7ch	K–K3
27 B × KP	....

White is compelled to continue aggressively because the position has become dangerous for him too.

| 27 .... | QR–N1 |

27 ... K × B loses immediately on account of 28 QR–K1ch. 27 ... N × B

also loses as follows: 28 Q–K7ch, K–Q4; 29 QR–Q1ch, K–B3 (29 ... K–K5; 30 R–Q4ch); 30 R × Pch, K–N4; 31 Q × Nch winning the Queen. Black could have drawn, however, with 27 ... P × B, for if 28 QR–Q1, KR–Q1 and White can make no progress; and if 28 P–B7, KR–QB1 threatening to exchange Queens. White would have been forced to take the draw by perpetual check with 28 Q × Pch, K–K2; 29 Q–N7ch, K–K3; 30 Q–N6ch, etc.

28 P–B7	KR–KB1
29 R–B6ch	K × B
30 Q–B3	N–B5

If 30 ... Q–K5; 31 R–K6ch

31 R × N	Q × R
32 R–K1ch	K–B4
33 Q–Q3ch	....

| 33 .... | K–B3 |

If 33 ... K–N4; 34 R–N1ch, K–B3; 35 R–KB1 as in the game. Here, if 34 ... K–R5; 35 Q × Pch. Or if 34 ... K–R3; 35 Q–R3ch. Or if 34 ... K–R4; 35 Q × Pch, Q–R3; 36 Q–B5ch, K–R5; 37 Q–N4 mate.

34 R–KB1	Q × Rch
35 Q × Qch	K–N2
36 Q–N2ch	....

White is under the delusion that he has winning chances; otherwise he would have captured the QRP which would have led to an easy draw.

36	K×P
37 Q–Q5ch	K–K2
38 Q–K4ch	K–Q2
39 Q×Pch	K–B3
40 Q–K4ch	K–B2
41 Q–B4ch	K–N2
42 Q–Q5ch	K–B2?

Allowing White the chance to draw. 42 ... K–R2 was correct, as happened later in the game.

43 Q–B4ch	K–N2
44 Q–K4ch	....

Here I was offered a draw and declined.

44	P–Q4

The only try for a win. If 44 ... K–R2; 45 Q–K7ch, K–R1; 46 Q–K2 and Black is forced to play 46 ... P–N4 if he wants to try for a win, but then the Black King would have been too exposed against the constant threat of perpetual check.

45 Q×Pch	....

Missing the correct continuation to draw. Correct was 45 Q–K7ch, K–R1; 46 Q–K2, P–N4; 47 P–QR4, drawing easily.

45	K–R2

The ending is now lost for White. Black's method of winning is as follows:

1. Place the Rooks on the QB-file and capture both QB-Pawns.

2. Attack and win White's KRP with the two Rooks.

3. Force the white King into a first rank where the two Rooks will be in a position to threaten mate.

All this has to be accomplished without permitting White a perpetual check.

46 P–B4	R(B1)–B1
47 Q–Q7ch	K–R1
48 K–N1	R–B4
49 K–B1	R(N1)–QB1
50 P–KR4	R×P
51 P–R5	R×P

Operation No. 1 has been completed. White's QB-Pawns have been captured.

52 P–R6	R(B1)–B2
53 Q–R4	K–R2
54 Q–KB4	R(7)–B3
55 K–K2	R–K2ch
56 K–Q3	R–Q2ch
57 K–K3	R–K3ch

| 58 K–B3 | R–R2 |
| 59 Q–B8 | R(K3) × P |

The second operation is finished. White's KRP has been captured.

60 K–K4	R–R7
61 Q–KN8	R–Q2
62 K–K3	P–R4
63 Q–K6	R(R7)–R2
64 Q–N8	R(R2)–K2ch
65 K–B3	R–Q6ch
66 K–B4	R–Q8

Black is maneuvering the White King to the side of the board.

67 Q–B4	R–B8ch
68 K–N5	R–N2ch
69 K–R6	R(B8)–KN8
70 Q–Q4	R(N8)–N5
71 Q–Q8	R(N5)–N3ch
72 K–R5	R–N7
73 K–R6	....

If White is to be mated, Black must get one of his Rooks off the second rank,

but in that case White is permitted perpetual check. Therefore, Black proceeds to force the white King to Black's first rank. Then Black will be able to threaten mate and at the same time keep one of the Rooks on the second rank to avoid perpetual check.

| 73 .... | R–QN2 |
| 74 Q–Q5 | R–QB7 |

Preventing K–N5.

75 Q–N3	R–B4
76 Q–K3	R–Q2
77 Q–K6	R(Q2)–QB2
78 Q–K4	R(B2)–B3ch
79 K–N7	K–N2

To free the Rook at QB4.

80 K–B7	R–R4
81 K–N7	R(R4)–R3
82 K–B8	....

Mission accomplished. The white King is on Black's first rank.

82	R–R1ch
83 K–K7	R–R2ch
84 K–Q8	R–QB2
85 Q–Q5	K–R2
86 Q–K5	R–QN2
87 Q–KN5	R(B3)–B2
88 Q–K5	R–R2
Resigns	

The final position. White cannot meet the threat of 89 ... R–R1ch; 90 Q×R, R–N1ch winning the Queen.

The King Takes a Hand

E. Olafsson of Iceland is a young but resourceful player. He does not make blunders often. To beat him, one has to outplay him.

The following game was a tough struggle from the opening on. Adopting the Gruenfeld Indian Defense, Olafsson gave me some anxiety when he played N–N3 on his 6th move. I found it difficult to obtain an opening advantage.

We reached a mid-game replete with many possibilities for both sides. The action was centered on the Queen-side. After the exchange of Queens, an interesting end game followed. Although I had two Bishops against my opponent's Bishop and Knight, it was still difficult to make progress. Fortunately, I was able to bring my King deep into my adversary's territory. The combined action of the King and the Bishops brought fruitful pressure upon my opponent's Pawns on both wings.

GRUENFELD INDIAN DEFENSE

International Tournament
Dallas, 1957

S. RESHEVSKY   E. OLAFSSON

1 P–Q4	N–KB3
2 P–QB4	P–KN3
3 P–KN3	B–N2
4 B–N2	P–Q4

The Gruenfeld Indian Defense, which had been in disfavor for several years, has been revived recently by some masters. With this defense, Olafsson scored an impressive win against Szabo.

5 P×P	N×P
6 N–KB3	....

6 P–K4, N–N5; 7 P–Q5, P–QB3; 8 P–QR3, Q–R4 leads to complications favoring Black.

| 6 .... | N–N3 |

Exerting immediate pressure on White's QP.

(See diagram on next page.)

| 7 O–O | .... |

7 P–K4 is perhaps a more forceful method of attempting to get an opening

Position after 6 ... N–N3

---

advantage, but after 7 ... P–QB4; 8 P–Q5, P–K3, exact and enterprising play is required. For instance, White may have to sacrifice a Pawn by playing 9 O–O, O–O; 10 N–B3, B×N; 11 P×B, P×P.

7 ....   N–B3
8 P–K3   ....

The only way to protect the QP. 8 B–K3 fails because of 8 ... N–B5.

8 ....   O–O

8 ... P–K4 was an alternative.

9 N–B3   P–QR4

Forestalling P–QR3 followed by P–QN4.

10 P–Q5   N–N5
11 P–K4   P–QB3
12 P–QR3   N–R3
13 P×P   P×P

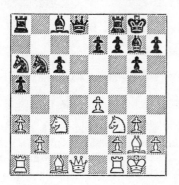

White has succeeded in isolating two of Black's Pawns. Black's compensation is more freedom of pieces. The chances are about even.

14 Q–B2   ....

The exchange of Queens would have brought Black's Rook into play. The Queen at K2 would have been a target for Black's QB at QR3.

14 ....   Q–B2
15 N–QR4   ....

To get rid of Black's Knight which is too well posted.

15 ....   N×N
16 Q×N   R–N1
17 Q–B2   ....

If 17 R–N1, N–B4; 18 Q–B2, N–N6 with a strongly posted Knight.

17 ....   R–N4

Intending to pile up on White's QNP.

18 R–Q1   Q–N3
19 P–K5   ....

Protecting the QNP and at the same time blocking Black's KB.

19 ....   B–B4

White's KP is immune to capture. If 19 ... B×P; 20 B–K3, Q–B2 (20 ... Q–N2; 21 N×B, R×N; 22 B–R6, R–K1; 23 Q×BP); 21 N×B, Q×N; 22 B–R6, R–K1; 23 Q×BP and wins. Best was 19 ... B–N5 threatening ...

B×N followed by ... B×KP. White's
best reply would have been 20 Q–B4,
B×N; 21 B×B, B×P; 22 R–Q7
threatening R×P and R–N7 with
chances for both sides.

20 Q–B4   P–KR4

Black was afraid of 21 Q–KR4
followed by B–R6 and N–N5.

21 B–K3   P–B4

Best, for if 21 ... Q–B2 or N2; 22
N–Q4 is overpowering.

22 B–KB1   N–B2

23 P–QR4   ....

Interesting is 23 P–QN4, RP×P; 24
P×P, R×P; 25 Q×P (25 B×P,
R×Q; 26 B×Q, R–B3 and White's
advantage has been dissipated), Q–N1
(25 ... Q×Q; 26 B×Q wins the KP);
26 Q×P, B–N5; 27 B–N2, R–K1
winning back the Pawn with equality.

23 ....   R×P
24 B×P   Q–N2
25 N–Q4   ....

(See top of next column.)

25 ....   B–K3

Better was 25 ... B–K5, but White
could have retained some initiative
with 26 B×P, R–B1 (26 ... R–K1; 27
B–B6, retaining the Pawn at least

Position after 25 N–Q4

temporarily); 27 QR–B1 (27 B–R3,
N–K3!), B×P; 28 N–N5.

26 N×B   ....

White now has two Bishops but it is
still difficult to make headway.

26 ....   N×N
27 B–QR3   R–N3
28 Q–Q5   Q–R2

The exchange of Queens would have
cost Black a Pawn.

29 Q–K4   Q–B2
30 QR–B1   ....

30 P–B4 would have weakened
White's King-position unnecessarily.

30 ....   Q×P
31 Q×Q   B×Q
32 B×P   R–K1
33 R–Q7   R–N7

Threatening ... B–Q5.

34 B–B4   ....

(See diagram on next page.)

34 ....   R–QB1

34 ... B–Q5 would have been a
blunder because 35 B–R3, B×Pch
(35 ... R×P; 36 R×B winning a
piece); 36 K–B1 wins material.

Position after 34 B–B4

some chances to make progress but was not overoptimistic. However, after a half-hour of strenuous analysis, I came to the conclusion that I had a won position.

35 B–R3 ....

The move that not only gets White out of the nasty pin, but enables him to make some progress.

42	B–QB4	K–B1
43	P–B4	B–B3
44	K–B2	K–K1

35	....	R–N3
36	B–N5	R×R
37	B×R	R–Q3

44 ... K–K2 would, of course, bring the black King toward the center more quickly but would block the black Bishop. White would have won a Pawn with 45 B–Q2, N–B3; 46 B–N5.

45	B–Q2	B–Q1
46	K–K3	....

38 K–B1 ....

38 B–Q2 is met by 38 ... R×R; 39 B×R, N–B4; 40 B–QN5, N–N6.

38	....	R×R
39	B×R	N–B4
40	B–QN5	N–N6
41	B–K3	N–Q5

Here we adjourned. After a fierce struggle in the middle game, a close end game has been reached. At the time of adjournment I felt I had

To make any headway, White must bring his King toward the center.

46	....	N–B4ch
47	K–K4	K–Q2

If 47 ... N–Q3ch; 48 K–Q5, N×B; 49 K×N, K–Q2; 50 K–N5 and White wins easily.

48 K–Q5	B–N3
49 B–N5ch	K–B2
50 P–R3	N×P
51 B–K8	....

51 ....   N–B8

Black's King-side Pawns are doomed. For instance, 51 ... N–B4; 52 B×BP, N–K2ch; 53 K–K6, K–Q1; 54 K–B6, B–Q5ch; 55 K–N5.

| 52 B–K1 | N–K6ch |
| 53 K–K5 | .... |

If 53 K–K4?, N–B4 and White cannot play 54 B×BP because of 54 ... N–Q3ch winning the Bishop.

53 ....   N–B5ch

A better try was 53 ... B–Q5ch, for if 54 K×B, N–B7ch; 55 K–K5, N×B; 56 B×P, N–Q6ch and although the ending is eventually lost, Black can put up some resistance.

| 54 K–B6 | B–Q5ch |

Better was 54 ... B–K6, but after 55 B×BP, N–Q7; 56 B×P, B×P; 57 B×P, White should win with careful play.

55 K×P	N–Q3ch
56 K–B8	N×B
57 K×N	....

57 ....   B–K6

If 57 ... K–N3; 58 B–Q2 followed by K–B7.

58 B×Pch	K–B3
59 K–B7	B×P
60 K×P	P–R5
61 K–R5	....

Black resigns. For if 61 ... B–N6; 62 B–Q8, K–B4; 63 B×P, B–Q3; 64 B–K1 and both Pawns cannot be stopped.

The Experts Can be Wrong

Herbert Seidman is a resourceful and dangerous opponent. He likes to avoid well-known variations in the openings. He prefers to play quiet and noncommittal openings. In the following game I managed to obtain a small advantage in the middle game. It took a long time before any progress was noticeable.

On the 36th move an unusual incident occurred. Being under the illusion that my Bishop would be protected at KN3, I lifted the Bishop to play it there. Fortunately, I noticed my error before releasing the Bishop, and luckily there was just one other square left where the piece could go safely.

At the time of adjournment the position was in my favor. Even the experts admitted that I had an edge, but none thought it was enough to win. The experts were wrong. After 13 moves of the play-off the Queens were exchanged and White resigned after Black's 67th move.

SICILIAN DEFENSE

Rosenwald Tournament
New York, 1957–58

H. SEIDMAN	S. RESHEVSKY
1 P–K4	**P–QB4**
2 N–KB3	**P–K3**
3 P–Q3	....

P–Q4 is the usual move here. Seidman prefers to choose a more conservative and less explored line.

3	**N–QB3**
4 P–KN3	**P–KN3**
5 B–N2	**B–N2**
6 O–O	**KN–K2**

Better than 6 ... N–B3 where the Knight could be attacked by P–K5.

7 P–B3	**P–Q4**
8 QN–Q2	**O–O**
9 N–N3	....

Of questionable merit. The Knight is somewhat out of play here. Wiser was 9 R–K1 followed by N–B1.

9	**P–N3**
10 P×P	**P×P**

10 ... N×P is a good alternative.

11 B–B4	**B–B4**
12 R–K1	**Q–Q2**

The position is approximately equal. Both sides have developed their pieces, and neither has any particular weakness.

13 N–K5	....

White is too anxious to simplify the position through several exchanges of pieces. Better was 13 Q–Q2 followed by R–K2 and QR–K1.

13	**N×N**
14 B×N	**P–B3**

Avoiding any further exchanges which would have oversimplified.

15 B–B4   ....

15 ....   **QR–K1**

15 ... P–KN4 immediately would have cost Black a Pawn: 16 R×N, Q×R; 17 B×Pch, K–R1; 18 B×R, R×B; 19 B–K3 and Black would have had insufficient compensation for the Pawn, even with the two Bishops.

16 P–Q4   **P–B5**
17 N–Q2   **P–KN4**
18 B–K3   **B–N5**

Provoking White's next move.

19 P–B3   ....

Further weakening his position, but there was nothing better. If 19 B–B3, B–K3 followed by ... N–B4, and if 19 Q–B2, N–B4 followed by ... N×B.

19 ....   **B–K3**
20 N–B1   **N–B4**
21 B–B2   **N–Q3**
22 Q–Q2   **P–KR3**

Obviously to enable ... P–B4–5 to be played.

23 R–K2?   ....

Apparently underestimating the strength of Black's ... P–B4–5. 23 P–KR4 was indicated. Although this would have weakened White's King-side Pawn position, it would have made it more difficult for Black to have made rapid progress.

23 ....   **P–B4**
24 QR–K1   **P–B5**
25 P–KN4   ....

As good as any other move. 25 P×P, P×P would open the KN-file to Black's pieces. White is reduced to passive resistance only.

25 ....   **P–QR4**

Black's best chances are on the Queen-side.

26 P–KR3   **P–N4**
27 N–R2   ....

A waste of time. The Knight belong on the Queen-side for defensive purposes

27 ....   **R–K2**

Intending to double Rooks on the King-file and eventually effect an exchange of major pieces. I was convinced that if I could accomplish this I would easily break through on the Queen-side.

| 28 Q–B2 | P–N5 |
| 29 P–KR4 | K–B2 |

Preventing 30 RP×P, RP×P; 31 Q–N6 winning the KNP.

Position after 34 R×R

| 30 B–R3 | .... |

If 30 RP×P, RP×P; 31 Q–R7, R–KR1; 32 Q–B2, KR–K1; 33 Q–R7, K–B3 followed by ... B–N1.

| 30 .... | R(B1)–K1 |
| 31 K–N2 | .... |

White is marking time, having nothing else to do.

31	K–N1
32 RP×P	RP×P
33 Q–N6	B–B2
34 R×R	....

(See top of next column.)

| 34 .... | Q×R |

The move I had in mind when I

made my 31st move. Judging from my opponent's expression, he seemed surprised by this move. Obviously, 34 ... R×R; 35 Q×P loses a Pawn.

| 35 Q–B2 | Q–Q2 |

Not permitting White's Queen to occupy his QR4 square from where it could become active on the Queen-side.

| 36 N–B1 | .... |

| 36 .... | B–K3 |

Here I almost made the fatal error of playing ... B–N3. One of the few instances where luck played a great part. Correct was 36 ... R×R.

37 Q–N6	Q–K2
38 N–Q2	B–B2
39 Q–B2	Q–Q2
40 R×R	Q×R

P×RP; 45 P×P, N–N4 winning a
Pawn.

43	P×P
44 P×P	**Q–R5**

Threatening ... Q–B7 followed by
... N–N4.

| **45 Q–N2** | **Q–B7** |

If White exchanges Queens the game
is hopelessly lost. For instance: 46
Q×Q, B×Q; 47 B–K1, N–N4; 48
N–B1, P–R5 followed by ... B–N8 and
the RP is lost.

| **46 Q–N6** | .... |

The only hope for White is to seek
complications.

| **46 ....** | **B–B1** |

Necessary. 46 ... Q×N; 47 Q×N,
B–B2; 48 Q–Q8ch followed by Q×NP
gives White excellent chances for a
perpetual check.

Black finally achieved his objective—
the placing of his Bishop on the diagonal
KR2–QN8 on his next move. The
strength of this becomes more and more
apparent as the game progresses.

At this point (at adjournment) most
experts, including my opponent, con-
ceded that I had a definite edge, but
none thought that it was sufficient for
the point.

41 K–N1	**B–N3**
42 Q–Q1	**Q–N4**

Threatening ... P×P followed by
... Q–N7. A good alternative was 42
... N–N4; 43 Q–QB1, P–R5 with the
serious threat of ... P–R6. If, after 42
... N–N4, White plays 43 Q–R4, then
43 ... N×BP!; 44 Q×Qch, B×Q;
45 P×N, P×P; 46 B–K1, P–B7!.

| **43 Q–R1** | .... |

Against 43 Q–QB1 Black replies
effectively 43 ... Q–R5; 44 P–R3,

47 Q×P   ....

Again the only try, for if 47 N–B1 or B–K1, Q×BP is fatal.

47	**Q×N**
48 Q×Pch	**N–B2**

After 48 ... K–R2; 49 Q×NP, Q×BP; 50 Q×P, White has too much counterplay.

49 Q×BP   ....

Usually, three Pawns are sufficient for a minor piece—but Black is going to win a Pawn by force.

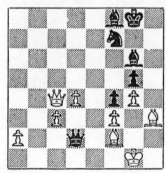

49	**B–Q6**
50 Q–N3	**Q–K7**
51 B–N2	**B–B5**
52 Q–N1	**Q×RP**

53 Q×Q   ....

Best. If 53 Q–N6ch, B–N2; 54 P–Q5, Q–R8ch; 55 K–R2, Q×P; 56 P–Q6, Q–B3, etc.

53	**B×Q**
54 B–B1	**N–Q3**

Were White able to get P–B4 in, it might have been very difficult for Black to win.

55 B–K2	**N–B5**
56 K–B1	**N–Q7ch**

57 K–N2   ....

Forced, for if 57 K–K1, N–N8!; 58 P–B4, B–N5ch; 59 K–Q1 (59 K–B1, N–Q7ch followed by ... N×QBP), N–B6ch; 60 K–K1, N×Bch; 61 K×N, B×Pch.

57	**B–R6**
58 B–K1	**B–B8**
59 B–R6	**....**

There is nothing better. 59 B×N, B×B; 60 P–B4, B–K6; 61 P–Q5, K–B2 and the black King gets to QB4 and White's Pawns are doomed.

59	**N–B5**
60 K–B1	**N–K6ch**
61 K–K2	**B–N6**

(See diagram on next page.)

62 P–B4   ....

There is no adequate defense. If 62 K–Q3, B–B7ch; 63 K–K2, B–Q8ch; 64 K–B2, B–N6. Black can repeat this maneuver, preventing White from playing P–B4. At the same time, Black

Position after 61 ... B–N6

would be able to bring his own King into active play.

62 B–Q2 loses a Pawn: 62 ... B–Q8ch; 63 K–K1, B×Bch; 64 K×B, B×P.

| 62 .... | N×BP |
| 63 K–Q3 | N–K6 |

64 B–N7	K–B2
65 B–R5	B–R6
66 K–K4	....

This loses a piece, but the position was hopeless anyhow.

66	B–B7ch
67 K–K5	N–B5ch
Resigns	

An End-Game Error

At the Israeli International Tournament of 1958 it was fairly obvious from the beginning that first place was going to be won by either Szabo of Hungary or myself. Our individual game would probably decide the issue, and by chance this game was scheduled for the last round.

In the meantime, the two of us had to chalk up points in order to keep up with each other. We had to be careful not to drop a point, or even half a point. All this was a considerable strain on the nerves. Most of the other participants were not easy to beat.

In my game with Mr. Wade of England, he fought like a tiger. He held his own until after adjournment. Fortunately for me, he got into terrific time trouble and made a slip in the end game which cost him the opportunity to draw. This contest is a good illustration of end-game technique.

KING'S INDIAN DEFENSE

Israeli International Tournament
Tel Aviv, 1958

| R. WADE | S. RESHEVSKY |
| 1 P–Q4 | N–KB3 |

2 P–QB4	P–KN3
3 N–QB3	B–N2
4 P–K4	P–Q3
5 P–B4	....

It would appear that this four-Pawn attack gives White complete control of the center—but this is an illusion. Black can break up this control without difficulty. Immediate counterattack on the Pawn formation is necessary.

5	O–O
6 N–B3	P–B4

The best method of dissolving the Pawn structure. Another adequate way is 6 ... P–K4.

7 P–Q5	....

Interesting is 7 B–K2, P×P; 8 N×P, N–B3; 9 B–K3, N–KN5 or B–N5, etc.

7	P–K3
8 B–K2	R–K1
9 O–O	P×P
10 KP×P	N–N5

Threatening ... N–K6. Black is willing to lose a few tempi in order to effect an exchange of White's QB for Black's Knight.

11 B–Q3	N–K6
12 B×N	R×B
13 Q–Q2	R–K1

13 ... Q–K2; 14 QR–K1, R×R; 15 R×R, Queen moves, and Black would lose an important tempo.

14 QR–K1	R×R
15 R×R	N–Q2

16 P–KN4	....

An aggressive continuation. There is no way for White to take advantage of Black's retarded development. For instance: 16 Q-K3, N–B3; 17 Q–K7, Q×Q; 18 R×Q, K–B1 and White's Rook must retreat, for if 19 R–QB7, N–K1 wins the exchange.

If 16 N–K4, N–B3; 17 N×Nch, B×N; 18 Q–K2, B–Q2 and White has made no progress.

White's text-move is designed to restrict the movement of Black's Knight. It also enables White to start an attack with either P–KB5 or P–KN5.

16	N–B3
17 P–KR3	P–KR3

To be able to answer P–B5 with ... P–KN4.

18 K–R2	B–Q2
19 P–N5	P×P

20 P×P	....

If 20 N×P, N–R4 (threatening ... Q–B3); 21 QN–K4, N×P; 22 Q×N?, B–K4.

20	N–R4
21 N–K4	B–B4
22 P–N3	Q–Q2
23 N–B2	....

Protecting the KRP and at the same time forcing the exchange of Bishops.

23	B×B
24 Q×B	R–K1
25 R×R	Q×R
26 Q–K4	....

White is rightly going in for the exchange of Queens, since his King is badly exposed.

26 ....   **K–B1**

The immediate exchange of Queens would have been unfavorable for me: 26 ... Q×Q; 27 N×Q, B–B1 and the black King would have come to the Queen-side too slowly.

27 Q×Q   **K×Q**
28 N–Q3   **....**

To keep the black Knight out of White's KB4. The ending is approximately even. There are, however, some chances on the Queen-side for Black.

28 ....   **B–B6**

To prevent N–Q2–K4, when Black's King would be compelled to defend his QP. I wanted my King to be free for action.

29 K–N2   **P–R3**
30 P–QR4   **K–Q2**
31 N–R2   **....**

Intending N–N4–R6.

31 ....   **N–N2**

To meet N–N4 with ... N–B4, preventing N–R6.

32 K–B2   **N–B4**

White is now unable to play 33 K–K2 because 33 ... N–Q5ch would win a Pawn.

33 N–B3   **....**

An admission that his 31st move was a waste of time.

33 ....   **K–B2**
34 K–K2   **P–N4**
35 RP×P   **P×P**
36 N–B2   **K–N3**
37 N–K4   **B–N2**
38 K–Q3   **P×Pch**

Black would have had better winning chances with 38 ... K–R4 followed by ... K–N5. White's task of defense would have been much more difficult. The best move after 38 ... K–R4 would have been 39 N–B3.

39 P×P ....

If 39 K × P, B–B1 (threatening to win a Pawn with ... N–K6ch); 40 K–Q3, K–N4; 41 N(3)–Q2, K–N5 and White is practically in "zugzwang."

39 ....   **K–R4**
40 N–K1   **B–K4**

In order to free the Knight for possible action.

This was the adjourned position. Although Black has some pressure, it was still extremely difficult to make substantial progress. To keep up with my rival, Szabo, I had to find some way of winning this ending. I spent many hours analyzing this adjourned position.

41 N–QB2   **B–B5**

With the dual purpose of tying down the Knight at K4 and preventing N–K3.

41 ... K–R5 looks like a natural, but is unproductive. White replies 42 N–K3, N×N; 43 K×N, K–N5; 44 K–Q3, B–B5; 45 P–R4, B–K4; 46 N–Q2, B–N6; 47 N–K4, B×P; 48 N×QP, B×P; 49 N×P and Black can barely escape defeat.

42 N–R3   **N–Q5**
43 N–QB3   ....

43 ....   **N–B4**

Why not 43 ... N–B6? This move apparently wins the KNP by force. To my dismay, White had this surprising rejoinder: 44 N×BP!, P×N; 45 K–K4 winning back the piece. After the game, my opponent revealed to me that he had not seen this two-move combination. That was why he took almost an hour for his 43rd move, seeking an adequate reply to 43 ... N–B6. My opponent finally made his move in desperation.

44 N–R3   **N–K2**
45 N–N5   **N–B1**

46 N(N5)–B3?   ....

This is the crucial position. My opponent was in terrific time trouble at this point! Black is threatening to win the QBP by playing ... K–N5 and ... N–N3. For instance: 46 N–B7, K–N5; 47 N–R6ch, K–N6 followed by ... N–N3 winning the Pawn. If 46 K–B3, K–R5; 47 N–B7, B–K4ch; 48 K–Q3, K–N5; 49 N–N5, B–B5 followed by ... N–N3.

The only way to save the game was as follows: 46 P–R4, K–N5; 47 N–B7, N–N3; 48 N–K6!, P×N (if 48 ... B–K4; 49 N–Q8, N×BP; 50 N×KBP with an easy draw); 49 P×P, N–B1; 59 N–B6, threatening to regain the piece with 51 N–Q5ch followed by P–K7 with an easily drawn ending.

46	K–N5
47 N–R2ch	K–N6
48 N(R2)–B3	N–N3
49 N–K2	B–K4
50 N–B1ch	K–R6

(See top of next column.)

51 N–K2 ....

If 51 N–Q2, B–B5 wins. If 51 P–R4, N–R5; 52 N–Q2, B–B5; 53 N(B1)–N3, K–N5 and White is in "zugzwang."

51 .... **N–R5**

Threatening to win the QBP with ... N–N7ch. There is no defense for if 52 N–Q2, K–N5; 53 K–B2, N–N7 decides the issue.

Position after 50 ... K–R6

52 N(K2)–B3	N×N
53 N×N	B×N
54 K×B	K–R5
Resigns	

The final position. White cannot avoid the loss of his QBP.

A Risky Variation

One of the most popular openings is the Najdorf Variation of the Sicilian Defense. Exhaustive analysis has kept this variation alive for both sides. Among its leading exponents for Black are Tal and Fischer.

There are several lines that are playable for both sides. The most complicated is the one in which White plays 6 B–KN5 as in the following game. Numerous sacrificial possibilities are available to White, but whether they are sound is another matter. From past experience it can be safely stated that Black, with accurate defense, is able to repel all attacks. Whether this opinion will stick, only the future will tell.

Playing the black pieces in this game I decided to make a real battle of it and chose the Najdorf Variation. My opponent and I castled on the Queen-side. It became clear that the game was not going to end in a draw. I expected my opponent to attack but on his 16th turn he apparently changed his mind. He decided to turn the position into an end game by exchanging Queens. This exchange gave me the slightly superior chances. Inferior end-game play by White soon decided the issue.

SICILIAN DEFENSE

Rosenwald Tournament
New York, 1959–60

J. SHERWIN   S. RESHEVSKY

1 P–K4   . . . .

The present vogue seems to be the King-Pawn opening. The principal exponents of this trend are the Russian giants, Tal and Keres, and Bobby Fischer. The retreat from the Queen-Pawn opening is only temporary, in my opinion. The main reason for the constant change from one opening to another is the discovery of a new wrinkle to a popular variation. As soon as another wrinkle is found (and that invariably happens) the vogue changes.

1	P–QB4
2 N–KB3	P–Q3
3 P–Q4	P×P
4 N×P	N–KB3
5 N–QB3	P–QR3

The Najdorf Variation—extremely popular among experts and replete with possibilities. Tal had excellent results with it in the Candidates' Tournament of 1959 in Yugoslavia.

6 B–KN5   QN–Q2

More usual here is 6 . . . P–K3; 7 P–B4, P–R3 or B–K2, etc., leading to many complicated variations. I prefer the text-move because it limits the possible variations.

7 B–QB4   . . . .

Considered best

7 . . . .   Q–R4

Sharpest continuation. The other possibility is 7 . . . P–KN3.

| 8 Q–Q2 | P–K3 |
| 9 O–O–O | P–N4 |

The best way to develop the Queen-Bishop.

10 B–N3   . . . .

Tempting but unsound is 10 B×KP, P×B; 11 N×KP, K–B2!; 12 N×B, R×N; 13 Q×P, P–N5; 14 N–Q5, Q×P with equality at least.

The other sacrifice of 10 B–Q5 is also unsuccessful as follows: 10 ... P–N5! (not 10 ... P×B; 11 N–B6, Q–B2; 12 P×P, B–K2; 13 KR–K1, N–K4; 14 N×B followed by P–B4 regaining the piece with much the superior position); 11 B×R, P×N; 12 P×P (if 12 Q×P, Q×Bch), N–N3; 13 B–B6ch, B–Q2; 14 B×Bch, K×B and White cannot successfully parry the threat of 15 ... N–B5 followed by ... Q–R6ch and mate to follow.

| 10 .... | B–N2 |
| 11 KR–K1 | O–O–O |

Threatening to win White's KP with ... P–N5.

| 12 P–QR3 | B–K2 |
| 13 K–N1 | .... |

Threatening 14 N–Q5 winning material. If 13 ... N–B4; 14 B–R2 (threatening P–QN4), Q–B2 (if 14 ... N–R5; 15 N×N, Q×N; 16 B–N3 winning the Queen); 15 P–B3 followed perhaps by P–QN4 and P–QR4.

If 13 ... KR–K1 (to protect the KB) White has the sacrificial possibility of 14 B×P, P×B; 15 N×P in which White emerges with a Rook and two Pawns for two minor pieces.

| 13 .... | K–N1 |

| 14 P–B3 | .... |

14 P–B4 is met by 14 ... P–R3; 15 B–KR4? N×P winning a Pawn.

| 14 .... | P–R3 |
| 15 B–K3 | N–K4 |

With the possibility of ... N–QB5 followed by ... P–Q4 which would constrict the mobility of White's pieces.

| 16 N–R2 | .... |

Indicating a lack of courage. White should have continued with an attacking plan, such as 16 B–N1 followed by Q–B2. By exchanging Queens my opponent succeeds only in obtaining a slightly inferior end game.

| 16 .... | Q×Q |

Black gladly accepts the offer to exchange Queens.

| 17 B×Q | N(B3)–Q2 |

Black is attempting to rearrange the position of his Knights. Although Black has the better end-game chances, it is still very difficult to make visible progress.

18 B–N4   ....

The Bishop has no future on this square. Where it should be placed would depend on Black's strategy. Better was 18 N–B3 in order to play 19 P–QR4 with the idea of isolating Black's QRP. There might have followed: 18 ... N–B4; 19 P–QR4, P–N5; 20 N–R2, P–QR4; 21 N–B1 followed by P–B3 with better counter-play than after the text-move.

18 ....   **N–B4**

Blocking White's Queen-Bishop.

19 N–B1   **P–N4**

Although it is usually a good policy to exchange a Knight for a Bishop, I decided not to do so in this case because of the immobility of White's Bishop. My plan was to open the KN-file.

20 B–R2   ....

White is compelled to lose time in order to rearrange his pieces. This gives Black ample time to gain control of the KN-file.

20 ....   **P–N5**
21 N(B1)–N3   ....

21 P–KB4 is bad on account of 21 ... N–B5 confronting White with the problem of defending his KP.

21 ....   **P×P**
22 P×P   **N–B5**

Preparing to get my KB into action via KB3–K4.

23 N–R5   ....

After a long series of moves White is finally threatening something—N–B6ch winning the exchange.

23 ....   **N×N**
24 B×N   **QR–N1**

The purpose of Black's 19th move now becomes apparent—to gain control of the file.

25 R–N1   **B–KB3**
26 N–K2   ....

26 B–B3 is met by 26 ... B–K4 (not 26 ... N–R5?; 27 N–B6ch, B×N; 28 B×B with much the superior position); 27 P–R3, N–R5 with much the better of it.

26 ....   **B–K4**

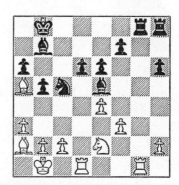

White's troubles are now starting. Black's threat of gaining control of the KN-file cannot be met successfully.

27 P–R3   ....

Not quite satisfactory is 27 B–B3 because of 27 ... B×RP; 28 B×R (28

R×R, R×R; 29 R–R1, R–N7),
B×R; 29 N×B, R×B; 30 R×P,
R–N1; 31 N–K2, R–N7 and Black is
on top.

If 27 P–KB4, B–KB3; 28 R×R,
R×R; 29 R×P, N×P; 30 R–Q1,
R–N7 with a clearly won position.

27	B–R7
28 R×R	R×R
29 P–N4	....

An awkward-looking move but there
is nothing better.

| 29 .... | N–R5 |
| 30 B–N3 | .... |

White is anxious to get rid of his
inactive Bishop.

| 30 .... | R–N7 |

31 B×N   ....

Forced, for if 31 R–Q2 or R–K1,
R×N; 32 R×R, N–B6ch.

| 31 .... | R×N |

White's Bishops are pathetically
immobilized.

| 32 B–N3 | R–B7 |
| 33 R–Q3 | B–K4 |

Threatening ... R–B8ch followed by
mate.

34 P–B3?   ....

A blunder which loses immediately.
Better was 34 K–B1 but after 34 ...
R–R7 White would have little chance
to survive.

34	R×P
35 R×R	B×Pch
36 K–N2	B×R
37 B–N6	P–KR4
38 P–KR4	B–N6
39 B–Q8	P–Q4
40 P–R4	K–N2
41 P–R5	P–B4
Resigns	

End-Game Technique

In this game my opponent chose an unusual variation against the
Sicilian Defense. Several pieces were exchanged early and we reached
an end game. My slight edge seemed insufficient for a win, but patience
paid off. The game is a good example of the technique of playing an
ending with a Bishop and Rook against a Knight and Rook, with Pawns
on the board. In the type of position reached in this game, the Bishop is
more valuable than the Knight.

SICILIAN DEFENSE

International Tournament
Buenos Aires, 1960

O. BAZAN	S. RESHEVSKY
1 P–K4	P–QB4
2 N–KB3	P–Q3
3 P–Q4	P×P
4 Q×P	....

This is very rarely seen nowadays. White has much better chances of getting an advantage with 4 N×P.

4	P–QR3

Important because it prevents the nasty pin B–QN5 after 4 ... N–QB3.

5 B–KN5	....

The purpose of this move is to make ... N–KB3 difficult.

5	N–QB3
6 Q–Q2	P–R3
7 B–R4	P–KN4

7 ... N–B3 was inadvisable on account of 8 B×N, NP×B with a poor Pawn position.

8 B–N3	B–N2
9 P–B3	N–B3

Black had to make some concession in order to develop this piece.

10 B–Q3	....

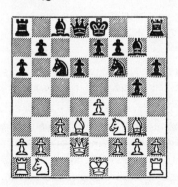

10	P–Q4

This enabled me to simplify the position. I discarded 10 ... B–N5 on account of 11 N–Q4–B5. However, 10 ... N–KR4 was a good alternative.

11 P×P	....

11 P–K5 is satisfactorily answered by 11 ... N–KR4 when White's KP is in danger.

11	Q×P
12 O–O	B–B4
13 B×B	Q×B
14 N–Q4	N×N
15 Q×N	N–R4
16 Q–N6	N×B
17 RP×N	Q–N4

I had this position in mind when I played 10 ... P–Q4.

18 Q×Q	P×Q

The double Pawn is no disadvantage in this position because Black can get rid of it by playing ... P–QN5.

19 R–K1	P–K3

To develop the King at K2, thereby enabling the KR to get into the game.

20 R–K4	....

Attempting to put pressure on the QNP by continuing with 21 R–QN4 followed by N–R3.

20	R–R5
21 R×R	P×R

The position looks approximately even but the Bishop is slightly more active than the Knight. This is due to the fact that White's Queen-side Pawns are on black squares.

22 N–R3   ....

22 N–Q2 is uncomfortable because of 22 ... P–R6.

22	K–K2
23 R–Q1	P–N5

To prevent P–KN4 which would enable White to put his Pawns on white squares.

24 K–B1	R–QB1
25 K–K2	R–B4

26 N–B2   ....

Not best. The Knight should have been kept at R3 to prevent ... R–QN4. Better was 26 R–Q2 followed by K–Q1–B2.

26	R–QN4
27 N–N4	P–R6
28 P×P	B×P

The double Pawn causes White trouble.

29 R–QN1	B–Q5
30 R–N3	R–QB4
31 N–Q3	R–B7ch
32 K–Q1	R×RP
33 R×Pch	K–B3
34 R–N4	P–K4
35 R–R4	P–R4

White is in trouble. The main threat is 36 ... B–B6 and ... R–Q7ch.

36 P–B4   ....

A desperate attempt to escape the bind, but there is nothing better.

36	R×NP
37 P×Pch	B×P
38 R–R6ch	K–B4
39 N×B	....

39 R–R5 is met by 39 ... P–B3, and 39 R–R6 is meaningless because of 39 ... K–N4.

39	K×N
40 R–R6	R×P
Resigns	

The two connected passed Pawns win easily.

INDEX OF OPENINGS

(Numbers refer to pages)

INDEX OF PLAYERS

(Numbers refer to pages)